THE
NEARLY MAN

FINANCIAL DEATH, SPIRITUAL LIFE

The True Story of a Living Christian and His Dying Business

JOHN CLOUGH

British Library Cataloguing in Publication Data
A record for this book is available from the British Library

Published for John Clough by Verité CM Ltd

ISBN: 978-1-910719-51-0

Cover design and typesetting by Verité CM Ltd
Print management by Verité CM Ltd
www.veritecm.com

Printed in England

Contents

Prologue: 25 January 2017 ....*5*

**'Do not conform yourself to the standards
of this world, but let God transform you inwardly
by a complete change of your mind'**...*7*

The Diary *17*

Chapter 1: Unsettled...*19*

Chapter 2: Worried...*37*

Chapter 3: Renewed – true or false? *57*

Chapter 4: Big God, big steps, big doubts, big prayers *85*

Chapter 5: A Scripture to hang on to...*103*

Chapter 6: Is the dream dying? *115*

Chapter 7: Is God in control? I'm losing it *129*

Chapter 8: Will somebody sack me? *143*

Chapter 9: Not prepared for answered prayer *157*

Chapter 10: Beside the self-destruct button...*183*

Chapter 11: Brilliant, yet disastrous...*197*

Chapter 12: The end of the chase *221*

Chapter 13: When you pass through the fire you will...*229*

Chapter 14: From the edge to the gentle slopes *237*

Chapter 15: 31 October 2007 – fifteen years later...*243*

Prologue: 25 January 2017

I'll be 70 on 9 April. We'll also have been married for forty years on that day. It's a big occasion, so we're having a celebration with about thirty others who we've come to know over the years. We're a happy couple.

I stopped working last July; an experimental retirement, I called it, because I wasn't sure if we'd manage financially or if I could cope with not working. But in September I rang my old boss and told him I wouldn't be coming back, and thanked him for leaving the option open for me to return. It's still a little strange, but I put that down to an adjustment period. The freedom is odd: no deadlines or targets, no getting up early and going to work in the dark freezing cold in winter, and returning in the dark. I can do the things I like doing, when I like. One can lose track of the time, even the days – so I keep a casual eye on the clock and the calendar.

We have three daughters – now in their thirties – all happily married, five grandchildren and one on the way. My wife is eight years younger than me, so she's still working. She likes her job.

A Georgian town house is where we live – a bit of English heritage, with character and original features. We have a nice garden, a summerhouse nestling at the top, and a shed built out of what was left over. The shops and cafes are close by, so we can walk to most places. We've been here over twenty years now.

I have the usual aches and pains one gets with age, but I just live with those.

It's quite an idyllic life, really.

But it hasn't always been like this. In 1988, after owning and running a successful transport business for sixteen years, things started to go wrong. Before that, I started a spiritual diary, so the events that unfolded were recorded. The following is what happened, but first, a testimony of how I became a Christian.

'Do not conform yourself to the standards of this world, but let God transform you inwardly by a complete change of your mind'

(Rom. 12: 2. The Good News Bible)

At age forty, I became a Christian.

Before that, I was an atheist, or agnostic. Like all my relatives and friends, I never even thought about a god. Religion and vicars were always ridiculed. Jesus was for 'Jesus freaks' like the man Bible-bashing at the top of his voice in the market square, with nobody listening and everyone taking a wide berth when passing. All the time, among all the other swear words, we used Jesus as a cursing word or an exclamation of shock or surprise, like 'Jesus wept!', 'Jesus Christ!' and so on.

To me, now, Jesus Christ is a friend, and the person who was sent to earth as a human being to reveal what the one true and living God is like. And when I say that, I still marvel at the transformation from what I was before to what I am now. Who would have thought such a change possible?

A few months after I became a Christian, the church I attended did a course on telling the good news of the Gospel to others. One of the first things I did was write down the events leading up to my complete change of mind, as described in the Bible, in the book of Romans, chapter 12, verse 2. Here it is. I have called our church 'Saints.'

My wife and I married in April, 1977. For seven years we lived in a two-up, twodown terraced house. The area had a good community spirit, with friendly neighbours to talk to over the garden wall and on the front doorstep, and there was always something going on when you looked out of the front window on to the street.

In 1985, the success of our business enabled us to move into a different area of larger houses and gardens. And although we were looking forward to this environment, we felt apprehensive as to how we would fit in with our new neighbours. With this in mind, it was with some reservations we accepted an offer from the couple next door to attend what was called a 'progressive supper', which was dinner at their house, then on to their church for dessert. As we had only met them in passing on the shared driveway to the house, or commented on the weather when seeing each other in the garden, we thought it would be a good opportunity to get to know them.

On the night at the church there was a speaker, an evangelist from Coventry, who talked about how 'there has never been a better time in this day and age of trouble and strife to turn to Jesus,' that 'Jesus was still alive and was waiting for me to ask Him into my life.' He was a good speaker, keeping everyone attentive and having a sense of humour; but the words, the so-called 'message' – I'd never heard such a load of drivel in all my life. One of the people there, Maureen Hooper, who at the end asked me what I thought, got quite a mouthful from me. I threw many reasons at her why I shouldn't become a Christian; I think she wished she'd never asked. I went home that night very satisfied that all my reasons for not being a Christian had been confirmed, and that it wasn't for me. The night was just a different experience, a good meal, and we'd got to know George and Cindy from next door a little better.

Nevertheless, some weeks later, I accepted an offer from them to do a six-week course called 'Down Your Street,' an introduction to Jesus. This would be done in what was called a 'house group.' I was a bit cynical about the whole thing, yet my curiosity was aroused; what was so important that made them want to share these things?

I went with George and Cindy to the first meeting, which was at Maureen Hooper's house. About eight people attended. The first thing that struck me was that they didn't say 'Hello' to each other – they hugged. I thought, 'How strange,' not being a hugging sort of person, assuming that they were all very good friends. The session started with two people saying how they had come to believe in Jesus and what they believed He had done for them.

My immediate thoughts were that the incidents they were describing would have happened anyway regardless of their faith, and when

I explained this was how I felt, they said they had the same thoughts before they believed. This reply touched a nerve, for it really said they were once non-believers, cynical, didn't feel the need for Jesus, and yet they were obviously curious at the time, just like me.

I thought about this quite deeply. They weren't Ministers drawing a salary to testify; yet they weren't like Jehovah's Witnesses or Mormons – who, to me, bordered on the fanatical. They weren't 'Bible Bashing', pressurising or trying to brainwash me. They were just ordinary people with ordinary jobs. At that meeting they were just answering my questions, reassuring my doubts, and above all, identifying with many of my cynical feelings. What's more, they were so calm about it. Here I was, ridiculing their faith left, right, and centre, yet an inner peace and charisma prevailed in these people throughout the whole evening. Come to think of it, all the Christians I'd met seemed to have this peaceful air about them. They weren't bothered about the material things of this world, no 'Keeping up with the Jones" for them. They talked quietly and calmly, and seemed to care about me as myself; they weren't interested in my status in life, how far up or down the ladder I was, or what possessions I had. I couldn't quite put my finger on it – what was it? It was one of those things you can't quite fathom. On similar occasions you would drop the matter in favour of more important things; but I wanted to know more.

It was for this reason, when they asked if the group could be transferred to our house so my wife could attend, without any hesitation I said, 'Yes.' (It would not have been possible for both of us to attend at someone else's house because of looking after our three young children.)

Over the next six weeks, my wife and I barraged them with questions and doubts about the Bible and Jesus. They all were very patient and shared their own feelings and early doubts with us, to the extent that there became a fellowship between us that we had never experienced before with other friends. It became clear to me that the 'something' that made our new friends different was this common bond they had – Jesus Christ. I felt myself being drawn towards it in an inexplicable way.

During Christmas 1986, the usual celebrations were taking place: the drink, the parties, the cards and gifts. I have to admit I have never particularly liked Christmas. Since we've had children it's been better, but I always thought it so hypocritical, for most people do not acknowledge the true meaning of Christmas and it's so commercialised. We know we're celebrating the birth of Christ, but that's about as far as it goes. I thought how very special Christmas must be for George and Cindy next door. How it really meant something special for them and they could enjoy it without having to drink themselves silly or stuff themselves with food. I thought what joy they would be filled with at this time. I was almost envious. I knew I could feel the same way if I wanted to, but there were still too many barriers and questions before I could start thinking about Christianity seriously.

The house group and 'Down Your Street' course had finished and we agreed to just let things lay and arrange another group in the future. My wife and I were now fairly well up on the basics of Jesus' life, but still not convinced enough to do anything about it. It was 'something to think about when we had nothing better to do.' After all, my wife was busy looking after three small children and a house, while I was busy looking after a business and fifteen employees. In fact, we both needed eight days in a week to get everything done.

A few weeks passed, with us carrying on with our lives as normal. We were a very happy couple, still very much in love after ten years of marriage, with three beautiful daughters, a nice big house, and financial and job security. We saw ourselves as good, kind people, helpful and concerned about others, and we loved our children dearly.

'So,' we said to ourselves, 'we don't really need to become Christians, do we?'

The end of February arrived, and it was time to go on holiday – two weeks on the island of Fuerteventura, in the Canary Islands. Cindy, from next door, gave us a book each, to read while we were away (the holidays are our only chance to read a book). Not long after we arrived, I glanced through my book, *Under Running Laughter*, by Dean Jones – an account of how he was converted to Christianity. It didn't look very exciting, so I went to the local supermarket and bought a thriller called The Red Fox, a best-seller that looked far more riveting reading. Within a week I'd finished it, so I started to read the other book.

Dean Jones, the author, was a film star appearing mostly in Walt Disney films such as *Herbie*. The book was an account of how the shallowness and non-fulfilment of his wealth and stardom made him turn to Jesus Christ for help. What struck me was that I could identify so much with his early doubts and feelings in coming to terms with believing in Jesus. How he held back on committing himself to this belief despite, like us, having knowledge of Jesus through learning and discussion. The main part of the book that stuck in my mind was how, in his lonely hotel room, he knelt by his bed and, not really believing anything would happen, cried out in sheer desperation for Jesus to come into his life and help him. Then how, seconds later, sobbing his heart out over the bed, a power entered into him and welled up inside him to the point where he felt he was burning like a fire. His tears were wiped away and a peace came over him like he'd never experienced before. The other memorable incident in his life was when, after he had been a Christian for some time, his entire (and very large) house was gutted by fire, and he wasn't a bit bothered – in fact he was almost praising the Lord for it. This, again, confirmed to me how overwhelming faith in Jesus must be, that despite losing everything materially, as long as you had hope in Jesus, everything would be all right. How wonderful, I thought, to have such a thing. Yet at the back of my mind I knew I only had to commit myself and I too would probably be on my way to receiving this gift from God. I thought, 'I must get *all* of my questions answered when I get back home.'

Many of my questions about the creation had really already been answered during the holiday. Surely the beautiful sight of mountains against the blue sky, rolling down to the golden sand and clear blue sea, with the warm sun and gentle cooling breeze didn't just happen by accident? It was all too organised; everything fitted into place. Maybe all this was created, but by whom? How can you even start to comprehend on such a huge supernatural scale? How difficult is it to believe Jesus is alive? You can't see Him, hear Him or feel Him. 'Can you feel Him?' I thought, 'Can you really feel His touch?' Dean Jones felt His touch by his bedside that night. That was Jesus' touch.

During our nightly little discussion we always had before going to sleep, we went through the things we *could* believe that you can feel or hear, but can't see. You can hear and feel wind, but you can't see it. Radio and television waves can't be seen, but the picture is there on the TV, and the sound comes out of the radio. Electricity can't be seen, but the power is always there. Sunrays can't be seen, but their warmth can be felt. You can't see air, but, without it, you can't live – and so it goes on. Take it one step further, into our bodies. Many emotions you can't see, but you feel them all the time: love, hatred, stress, jealousy, joy, etc. At overflowing point you can tell in a person's eyes, expression, or actions, but day-to-day they can only be picked up by someone who knows you well. Could all these thoughts I had be related to Jesus? In some way I was hoping so. But hoping is one thing; believing is another.

We returned from holiday on 12 March 1987. It was our second daughter's birthday, so we had a tea party at my sister's in Brighton; she had collected us from Gatwick Airport and we were stopping for the night. We went shopping in Brighton the following day before returning home by train.

Being back in the thick of things, there was so much going on... but my mind kept wandering in and out of thoughts about whether or not I believed in Jesus Christ. The questions and doubts I had weren't so important now, for when I really thought about what I wanted to know it seemed as if I already believed it anyway. We would often come out of the blue with something we'd obviously been mulling over in our minds for sometime, but it was only a comment just to confirm to each other that 'Yes, I suppose that is right!,' or 'Maybe we are wrong about that!' and, 'Well yes, that must be true, after all!' Little barriers coming down one by one to get at the truth. My wife had also read her book on holiday. Certain things had touched her, and I reckon she was a little in front of me on the road to wherever we were being led.

We were now back to our normal routine, having enjoyed a wonderful holiday – both head first into our respective jobs. Another invite to a progressive supper came from George and Cindy. This time we were going to hear John Delight, an Archdeacon from Stoke, and Ian Petit, a Benedictine Monk. Ian Petit got up to speak. He said so much we wanted to hear. We were both hanging on to his words from beginning to end. He interpreted into simple terms the truth we had doubted. This man explained them away in half an hour. My wife just had to speak to him. He held both our hands tightly and said a prayer. We went home that night feeling quite elated. So many questions had been answered; it was like a burden being lifted.

April came and the start of 'Mission '87 to Stafford'. John Delight and Ian Petit were speaking again, this time at Stychfields Hall, a venue in the town. We felt we both had to go, so we arranged a babysitter for the Wednesday and Saturday nights. Those two nights of worship, praise, prayer and teaching were like entering another world – a spiritual world where Jesus was king. Everyone was so happy. Friends hugged, kissed and held hands, and people we'd never met before went out of their way to say hello and ask how we were keeping. The feeling of love and peace was overwhelming, and the songs were wonderfully melodic, sending shivers down our spines. The prayers were deep and meaningful. The speakers told of wonderful things: miracles, promises, eternal life, answered prayers, the Holy Spirit, joy, laughter and happiness, and the good news that it all comes from Jesus Christ. He was, indeed, the key to all these things, the things this world so often cannot give. We felt, on those two nights, just for a few hours, that we were in the Kingdom of God. On the last night, anyone who felt they wanted to give their lives to Jesus was asked to go to the front to share their feelings with other Christians and speakers. My wife got up and went to the front, but I held back. I still had doubts. This was too big a commitment for me to enter without being sure I could follow it through. When I asked, she said she had not committed herself to Jesus. She just went up to be prayed for, but she was so excited I could tell she was nearly there.

All the family had been going to Saint's church since a few weeks before our holiday. The services never meant a lot to me. This was only to be expected, not being a committed Christian, but the fellowship and people were very nice. 'Nice' is an understatement. They were caring people who were concerned about us, and about how we were getting on, as regards coming to terms with believing in Jesus. In answer to many of my questions, there was really nothing I had to do at all. The answer was 'The Holy Spirit will do it for you.' 'It's a power that Jesus will give you and it will change you from within.' Again, something which is hard to comprehend, but a twinge of excitement was inside me. Could it be the Holy Spirit was already working in me, and changing me? Was this why I was far away from being so antiChrist, like the early days? My beliefs regarding the whole thing had almost done a Uturn. Could it really be this Holy Spirit, which I couldn't see or hear, was changing me?

There was a girl, who regularly came to church, who used to work for me: Sally. She had changed from when I used to know her three or four years previously; she now was confident and outgoing, instead of shy and timid. I got talking to her one Sunday after the service and, for about half an hour, I was amazed by what the Holy Spirit had done for her; and, seeing the difference, I knew it was true. She was a living testimony to what Jesus had done. I really believed what she was saying. I had heard people telling their story before, such as at Mission '87 a few weeks previously, but I had still been partly cynical enough to believe that incidents they put down to Jesus working in their lives were just coincidences and would have happened anyway. But here was someone I knew. After speaking to Sally, I felt maybe it was right – Jesus is alive and working. The words of one of those songs from Mission '87 came back to me, 'You're alive, You're alive, You have risen, alleluia, alleluia.' From then on, Sally and I talked and talked after the evening services.

By this time I believed the Holy Spirit was working in me. I wanted to go to Christ, but something was holding me back. Even at work on Sunday morning, with no intention to go to the 10:30 service, come 10:20 something inside was willing me to be there. Yet in church, on many occasions I would think, 'What am I doing here, there's nothing here for me'. I asked questions about this in church. In all cases, the answer I got about being pulled one way and pushed the other confused me even more. For the first time in my life, I was seriously told – by people I felt I must believe – that the devil really did exist and that it was Him trying to pull be back. Jesus and the devil were fighting for my soul. I was now totally confused and didn't know which way to go. George, from next door, said I mustn't get too caught up in my feelings, so I relaxed and just carried on with life.

By this time, my wife was doing daily Christian readings. On 21 April, out of the blue, she just came out with it, 'I've let the Lord into my life'. All I said was 'Oh!' It set me thinking again. Why *hadn't* I committed myself? I could not now think of one reason why I should not do it. Every possible avenue had been exhausted. I had come too far to go back.

It was like a door had been shut behind me and locked. There was now a locked door behind me and an open one in front. I was in the middle, in limbo – no man's land. The only way was through the open door. Why didn't I go? Was I frightened of what might be on the other side? No, I had been assured time after time there was no need to be fearful, that God would never make me do anything I didn't want to. I was afraid. I was afraid that I wouldn't be able to keep a commitment and would be a let down, that I would fail. Day after day I wrestled with this. I tried to liken it to marriage, but that didn't work because before you commit yourself to marriage, you're in love – and I wasn't in love with Jesus. However, I could liken it to a courtship. You have to go out with someone and get to know them before you fall in love.

The next day, at work, I opened an envelope addressed to me personally. It was a colourful printed card. At the bottom it just said, 'From a friend'. It read:

> I have seen you talking with your other friends.
>
> I watched in anticipation, trying to catch your eye,
>
> but you never looked my way.
>
> I have seen you walking on your own and passed by,
>
> but you did not recognise me.
>
> I have stood in front of you when you were walking towards me,
>
> But you turned and walked the other way.
>
> I wanted so much to get to know you, for I love you so much.
>
> But you just ignored me.
>
> To show my love for you I have given you the sky as your blanket,
>
> The earth as your bed, and the sun to keep you warm,
>
> But you still didn't want to know me.

I welled up inside. I knew that friend was Jesus. How blind I had been. The past nine months, since hearing that first speaker, had been a continuous succession of invitations from Him. Sally had noticed and sent me that card. My proud defensive attitude was in tatters. That was it; how could I refuse such an offer of friendship and love?

It was the following Thursday night, 27 May 1987. The three people who had been with me since the beginning of my search were the only ones at House group. It was on that night that I finally committed my life to Jesus. I had gone through that open door and shut it firmly behind me. I prayed to myself, 'Thank You Jesus, it's all over'. But how wrong can you be? It was just the beginning.

Rev. 3: 20

'Here I am! I stand at the door and knock. If anyone hears my voice and opens the door, I will come in and eat with him, and he with me.'

The Diary

9 November 1988 – 11 February 1993

Chapter 1: Unsettled.

9 November 1988
Wednesday night, 11.10pm

The business is not doing very well. Deirdre, who comes in monthly to check the figures, analysed a few things yesterday. It's not looking good. Only £1,400 profit from June to September inclusive, excluding the profit made on the sale of some land. We will have to reschedule runs, since we lost Masterpiece Mirrors, a major customer. The northern delivery runs are not paying some of the time. We must concentrate on southern runs, which make a profit. As of now, we are only going to Scotland once every two weeks and possibly the north-east also; we cannot shift goods quick enough for the south, but have not enough goods to go north. The £60,000 overdraft cannot be supported with our present level of profitability, and our outgoings are too high, particularly the wage bill, which we can't really do anything about. We can struggle for an unspecified time until the work picks up, which is a risk, or we can inject capital into the business fairly quickly through the sale of assets. The latter option has more or less been chosen. Thank the Lord He has shown us the way out. The answer is: sell our present property and buy the house we like next to the church; move down market and leave cash available to reduce the overdraft and pay off the Business Development loan, rough figures as follows:

Sell present house	£200,000
Buy the other house	£150,000
Left with	£50,000
Less	£20,000 (pay off Business Development Loan – BDL)
Less	£30,000 (reduce overdraft to £30,000)

We are left with a £150,000-house, less a £30,000 overdraft, a £30,000 mortgage, leaving equity of £90,000.

Position at present:

Present house	£200,000
Less BDL	£20,000
Less mortgage	£30,000
Less overdraft	£60,000
Equity	£90,000

Result: BDL and half the overdraft gets paid off, equity stays the same, but with a smaller house. No problem at all. Praise the Lord. That way everybody stays employed at Transportomatic.

My wife and I have been unsettled about this. Is the Lord telling us to move or not? Are these figures confirmation? Are we being divinely pushed – gently? Our desire to move is becoming more positive, an answered prayer. Some of our apprehension is even turning to excitement and anticipation. This is despite the survey we had done being a picture of doom and gloom. There were a lot of cracks and bowed walls mentioned, uneven floors and leaning chimney stacks; surely these are characteristics of a 17th century half-timbered house! Small suggestions, like pointing and flashings, could easily be done by builder friends. We went 'round again this morning, following the report through as we went. Looking at the defects, they're really not as bad as they sound! We were 'warming' to the house. My wife showed our youngest daughter around, and then she showed me around, it was lovely. However, someone else is now interested, so I pray, Lord, please, if this house is meant for us, keep it for us. 11.55pm

13 November 1988
Sunday night, 12.45am

I'm in and out of union with Christ again. Since we fetched that house brochure I've been like this. I can't get down to any serious work in the office and find it difficult to get stuck in. I definitely lack motivation, probably because our immediate future is not so defined. I suppose our uneasiness is partly due to lack of faith. We have been destabilised slightly, which is the time we should look to the Lord. It's making us spiritually slack. We aren't praying so often, when it's just the time we should be doing so. It's old 'smutty face' again prising the cracks open. Still, the more he does it, the more we'll get wise to it and cope better next time.

We went over to the proposed purchase again today to show all the children 'round. They like it. It's probably like Snow White's house to them – black and white timberframed. Lord, I pray we get on well and possibly sort a deal out when I go 'round to see the owner tonight. I'm dropping off to sleep so I'll close now.

14 November 1988
Monday night, 11.43pm

The meeting with the Bank Manager went well. There was no decision. He can't sanction that amount of borrowing, but the Lord was with me, so it was a good meeting. I went with the power of the Holy Spirit and I feel quietly confident, but cautious with it. Does that make sense? Think positively, the Lord is with us. (We only want to borrow £140,000 as a bridging loan to buy that house). I phoned the Vendor tonight to say it will be two or three days before we know. 'We'll keep our fingers crossed', he said. I said, 'You cross your fingers, we'll pray.' I've said that to my two employees in the office a few times. It works as a little witness with humour. The sort of remark people remember, only one sentence as it is.

A £140,000 bridging loan will cost £1,750 a month, £5,250 per quarter in interest at 3% over base rate. We'll see what my accountant's comment is tomorrow. A 'drastic move', I bet he'll say.

Praise the Lord that we are quite happy to move now. His desire is now our desire. My wife is overflowing with it; she can't stop talking about it. I suppose I'm slightly subdued as it falls to me to do all the working out and the rounds of the solicitors, accountants, estate agents and the bank manager; the secular law operators in all their glory, 'Money, money, money, it's a rich man's world', as Abba sang. The clock's just struck midnight; goodnight.

16 November 1988
Wednesday night, 12.30am

I got in from work at 11.30pm. A friend from Lincoln and I have been to the 'Christmas Make Way' at the NEC in Birmingham. This in itself would be lots to talk about, but today it's small fry compared to what the Lord is doing with other happenings.

In a fortnight, the Lord has more or less turned our lives upside down since looking at the house two weeks ago, when we had the impulse to look at it, but we didn't want to move. Well, today, fourteen days later, we heard from the bank that they will lend us the money to buy it. In fourteen days the Lord has given us the desire to move: that house is lovely now, after not feeling anything when we first went 'round. We made an offer £20,000 below the asking price and it was accepted, and now the bank will lend us the money, so we can go ahead. The Lord, praise Him, has saved that house for us. It had been up for sale for ages! We had been past it every time we went to church, but 'nothing' until two weeks ago. Our feelings must have been right, despite all that flak from the devil, putting doubt in our minds. We kept our mind – or tried to – on Jesus and prayed. And here we are, going to buy it. It's incredible! After the bank manager phoned the news through, I actually got excited and went home to tell my wife, when normally I like to be cool and unruffled. What a testimony to the Lord Jesus on how He moves in people's lives, Amen.

17 November 1988
Thursday night, 10.45pm

I'm back on a rock again. In the good times, we have the peace of mind to focus on the Lord Jesus and not be sidetracked by worries and mini crises. We'll then be equipped through good-time prayer to face the bad times when they come, which, inevitably, they do. To believe we go through life with no problems is not being honest with ourselves. Pray and obey during the good times to be equipped with God's armour to fight through the bad times and try and keep praying and obeying. Without regular praying and Bible reading during that time, we probably would never have known the will of God and would have missed that calling altogether; although Ron Dunn, the author and speaker, says, 'You never miss the will of God as He always sends something else in His own good time.'

We've been to Grange Lane Evangelical Church tonight to hear a Christian from Czechoslovakia. Christians over there do not have such a hard time as I thought. Russia isn't too bad either under Mr Gorbachev's more 'liberal' rule. He said for us not to feel sorry for them. God provides them with as much blessing over there as He does for us here and, in the same context, they do not envy our complete freedom to worship. He said the Lord provides the same blessings in relation to different circumstances wherever you are. Six of us went instead of House group.

Last night there were 12,000 people in the NEC main arena for the Christmas Make Way – quite a lot.

Please, Lord, send us someone to buy this house at the right time. Amen.

19 November 1988
Saturday night, 12.25am

A church member rang tonight to see if we had any special prayer requests, as he's leading this morning's service. We should have asked for prayers for someone to come along and buy this house. Not really. That's a bit much. A bit too selfish to pray in a service, when there's children starving in the world, wars and famines. We must be so thankful to the Lord for our comfortable lot here.

Lord, I'm anxious about the low level of business at work. October's sales were well down, even allowing for losing that large account. Please, Lord, give me motivation to go around canvassing for more work.

What a shame it will be if we have to rely on property deals to pay the overdraft partly off. It should be the profit from the business that does that. It will be a waste if we can't use the money more effectively, although I suppose paying the overdraft off is effective.

Some people say putting things about business in a spiritual diary is not on. I disagree, as it has a bearing on whether my spirits are up or down.

Having said that, worldly things shouldn't have a bearing on this. 'What human nature wants is opposed to what the spirit wants', it says in the Bible (Gal 5: 17). So long as you obey Christ and not worldly ways, Christ Himself will keep your spirits up. 'Leave all you worries with Him' (1 Pet. 5: 7 GNB). Again, as written in Scripture, 'Why worry about what food you are going to eat or what clothes you are going to wear, The birds of the air have plenty to eat and don't get cold.' 'If the Lord provides for the birds of the air, how much more will He provide for us, His dear children?' (Matt 6: 25-34). Thank You, Lord, for providing for me, and thank You for making me your child. Amen. 12.43am

20 November 1988
Sunday night, 11.52pm

I'm keeping up with my daily readings – Paul's second letter to the Corinthians at the moment.

It's difficult, once God has made a decision for you, to follow through right to the end without having doubts as to whether it's right or not. Of course it's right, if God has led you, but human feelings creep in. I'm referring to our house purchase, needless to say. Not so much the moving, that's all settled, but the finance side of it, like: Will we sell this house quickly for the price we want? Will we be able to afford to do improvements on the new house if any are suggested by the structural surveyor or Rentokil, as they will be best done before we move? As October was the business' lowest turnover for ages, can we pay our way, VAT, wages, bills, etc.? If we still aren't making a profit, is the overdraft going to go up and up? Is the bank going to make us stick to our limit?

I'm really pessimistic, aren't I? I'm putting all these financial problems before the joy of knowing the Lord, who has called us to do His will. I sound as if I'd be happier with the Lord 'sending me to Coventry' so I can be free to do what I want. As if the Lord has interfered with my life, poking His nose in when it's not wanted. I ought to be ashamed of myself. Receiving a message from the Lord and being able to act upon it is one of the greatest things that can happen to a Christian. So, John, have faith, trust that the Lord knows what He is doing and obey. From a secular viewpoint, it probably is a doubtful situation, but when the Lord's behind it, it becomes spiritually fulfilling, something this world cannot give. So rejoice and be glad, stop doubting and thinking about the pitfalls, the Lord is with you and will provide, trust in Him.

25 November 1988
Saturday night, 12.03am

We've had the structural survey report on the foundations and the roof. Foundations OK, roof not OK. The oldest part, about half of all of it, has extremely beetle-eaten horizontal purlins, which means we virtually need all new timbers in this section, plus new ceiling joists and ceilings in two bedrooms. Bad news, but good news at the same time, as the Lord has told us to move, which means that we will be able to get it fixed. A local roofing firm, who have a copy of the survey, are going to give us an estimate. The plan is to ask for a further reduction in the purchase price by the amount the estimate is, as they will foresee that anyone else buying it will have the same problem – we pray Lord the vendors will agree. Amen.

26 November 1988
Sunday night, 11.45pm

I'm decorating; just smartening the place up, really, as it's for sale. The Lord's been good to me; so far I've had no problems. I'm sailing through. Looking back, though, before I became a Christian, I would say there are things that would have annoyed me then, but not now; like going on to the skirting boards when painting the walls. As Jeff, in the office, says, since becoming a Christian I have less 'rough edges', less temper and more inner calm – someone's noticed, then.

Last night we went to see Dave Bilborough at Stychfields Hall; a good night of praise and worship. My wife bought his latest cassette, 'Part of a Mystery Tour'.

Diane's been 'round tonight. She looked quite bubbly and sparkly, like a Christian should look after receiving a bit of the Holy Spirit. At house group last Thursday night she really encouraged me with her praying, which included asking Jesus into her life. That may explain the sparkle.

A man who was visiting next door popped 'round to see us, Alan Godson (what a surname for a man of God). He's from Liverpool, a Church of England minister (he was the one who asked us to write to Brian Clough, a long time ago now). He flew in, had a few quick words and a prayer, and flew out again. A powerful man, not physically – spiritually. He had this air of 'spiritual authority' about him. I managed to slip in one or two gripes about the Church of England I felt I could say. He just laughed, although it seemed to be a laugh in agreement. As I said to my wife, there must be Church of England and 'Church of England' churches. He was obviously from an 'in-tune' one, all alive and bubbly. He said the Church of England's doctrine was very Bible-based. All I can say is it's got lost somewhere along the way, mixed up in man-invented customs, traditions and rules and regulations, no doubt; though I didn't get a chance to say that – it was such a fleeting visit. I'm dropping off reading tonight's entry. Goodnight, Lord. 12.12am

28 November 1988
Monday night, 11.40pm

I've just been reading, in Matthew, Jesus talking about anger. It really says to me,

'You are what you think'. For example: If I don't swear out of my mouth, but I swear in my mind or under my breath, then that is as bad. Although no one is *hearing* me swear, I have heard myself in my mind, so I am a swearer – you *are* what you *think*. Idealistic and puritan, one might say, but it gives a measure of how inadequate we are, how we fail miserably to meet God's standards. But praise the Lord, this is how God helps us, through His Spirit. The Holy Spirit pricks our conscience on such occasions and helps us to try better next time and, if we sincerely ask, He forgives us for that wrong. I must start reading more of the Gospels, as opposed to Paul's letters; more of what Jesus said and did.

I must also start the continuation of my testimony. It only goes up to May 1987, when I let the Lord Jesus into my life. It's getting further and further away, nearly 18 months now. Alan Godson said, 'Get it down on paper, because as you become more mature you forget the initial feelings of fresh conversion, a time you will never experience again'.

How can I ever forget that night's dream, when I slept after asking Jesus into my life the previous evening? The part I remember was around dawn, when the daylight starts shining through the curtains. I turn over and think, 'Only another hour or two before it's time to get up', and snuggle down expectantly, as if to really savour that last sleep before rising. I was flat on my back, semi-conscious, asleep enough to dream, awake enough to know reality. I've had this dream a few times. I was falling, just falling, in nowhere, but falling. I had a definite sensation I was falling at great speed, fast enough to know that, when you hit the bottom, you've had it. Before, when I hit the bottom, I always managed to wake up, so I never knew what my fate was after that 'thud'. I always woke up with a jump, relieved that it was only a dream; I was safe and sound in bed. This time, the falling just stopped; and there I was, flat on my back, feeling the bed underneath me through normal gravity. There was this tug of war inside me, but it was only up or down, not sideways or at an angle. I was completely horizontal, as if laid out in a coffin. Totally confused and anxious, I was pressed down, a heavy weight on me. I felt so heavy. The weight was pushing me into the mattress. Then, gradually, slowly, I was released: the weight was lifted. It was like things of weight and burden were leaving my body, floating out of me. I felt so light I could no longer feel the bed I was lying on. 'Snap out of it, John', I thought. 'Wake up!' But I was only dozing, anyway. I couldn't believe the bedcovers over my chest and torso were pulling against me! I could not feel the bed under me! I was being raised up! 'I must wake up, I *must* wake up!!' But I was awake, I was awake!

It wasn't for long, but I am convinced that the Lord Jesus raised me up. It was only for a few seconds, but I floated. Only enough to tighten the bed covers on top of my body. I am convinced it was Jesus lifting all my burdens off me. It was only of short duration, but it meant so much. It was like dying to myself and rising up again in Christ.

I thought it would take a pleasant toll on me and I would be different after that. I wasn't – I didn't feel any different at all. I had let the Lord Jesus into my life the evening before and had this 'dreamy experience' overnight, and nothing. No bells ringing or fanfares to mark this milestone in my life, this so called re-birth that was going to change the history of John Clough – nothing. My commitment seemed to be just something I said, more or less a passing comment. My 'sleepy' experience meant much more, as something had happened that I could actually feel. It was ecstatic, a feeling of triumph over an evil power. Something filled me with peace at that time, but now, the day after – nothing.

That day I went to work as normal. The weekend came, Sunday at church. 'Well, John, do you feel any different?' I just had to say 'No'. I did have a feeling of expectation, a feeling that something *was* going to happen, but nothing else. The days went by. 'What an anti-climax', I was beginning to think. Months of thinking about it, confusion, pulled this way and that, 'Down Your Street' course, house groups, talks with my friends at church... what a waste of time. I felt worse than before I committed myself. The curiosity I had previously had turned to complacency. The feelings I had at 'Mission to Stafford' were just a memory. 'I don't feel any different', I'd say to people at church. 'It'll come', they said. 'What, I thought, 'What'll come?'

Days turned into weeks. I was going into what I call a 'low phase', when there's no motivation and you can't muster any enthusiasm for anything. Everything gets very mundane and monotonous. I wouldn't call it depression, just feeling low, a phase, and a matter of time before you snap out of it. I'd had them before and they didn't last. I got back to my usual self sooner or later. 'Just ride it out and work it through', I said to myself. Still, more days went by and I was getting worried I hadn't snapped out of what was now becoming depression. I carried on with my life, but everything seemed to be tarnished with black and greyness that blotted out the light and colour.

It was one morning before going to work. A late start, because I had finished late the previous evening. The house was empty. My wife and three daughters were out and I was alone in the bedroom. I felt prompted to kneel by my bed and start praying – about what, I don't know. I wasn't very good at it. I just said to God, 'I'm sorry.' I started to shake and weep, tears dripping on to my bed, and while I just knelt there weeping, a feeling came over me that I had never in my life felt before. It ran through me like water – like a stream – from my head to my feet; it totally immersed me, followed by an all-over burning sensation that came from within like a fire. I was burning up. It was beautiful and I knew it was Jesus, and that He was real and alive.

Immediately afterwards, I felt completely renewed, washed, pure and blameless – a new creation. Later, I learned this was the Baptism of the Holy Spirit, the time when Jesus gives us His Spirit. Although I had already asked Jesus into my life, I hadn't repented. My 'I'm sorry' released the barrier of sin on to the cross and let in the Lord Jesus to dwell within me forever.

4 December 1988
Sunday night, midnight

I did the New Testament reading tonight in church, nervous as usual, but once I'm up there it's OK. Jesus is up there with me – praise Him. Isn't it good when the Lord helps us with the little things as well? Like nerves and shyness: human feelings, which are a part of our old character that restricts our freedom to be, and do, what God wants. He sets us free by helping us with the power of His Holy Spirit when we call upon Him.

I shared with three friends from church tonight my frustration at the apparent stagnation of the church. Church 'laws' getting in the way of the free movement of the Holy Spirit, putting people off who otherwise may have had an inclination to stay at church or call upon the Lord. If only the church proclaimed that Jesus is relevant today. We may proclaim the good news of Jesus, but it does not become effective if we do not tell people *how* to get in touch with God, or why. Do some of the congregation in churches not know Jesus as a personal friend, yet still proclaim to be Christians? Have they so far missed the point of Jesus' message? Are they filled with the Holy Spirit, for the spirit motivates and changes? Is this why the church isn't motivated and doesn't change? Is this why they stick with their traditions and bespoke denominational doctrines? I can't recall any of Jesus' or the Apostles' teaching instructing the church to be structured like it is. The established church seems to have made its own laws up, which in practice turn us away from Jesus, yet preaches to follow Him. This leads, naturally, to one of the most common comments about the church from the secular world: hypocritical. Preaching something but not carrying it out themselves and, worse still, lacking the zeal and drive to do anything about it. They have built their house on history, pomp, ceremony and tradition, and are firmly rooted in it. 12.50am

5 December 1988
Monday night, 11.25pm

I've been thinking, we must get some non-Christians into the house to share with, either through meals, or asking people we meet back. The problem is we don't really get out enough to meet anyone. Perhaps, Lord, you could open some doors for us. My wife and I have only led two people, that I can think of, to Christ. We must try a bit harder for Jesus. He's done a lot for us. We must not forget our main calling, to tell the good news to all people. Lord, motivate us with regards to this. Help us have the desire to go out, not wait for people to come to us. I know it's a little difficult with us having small children, but just now and again would be OK to start with. I wonder if we could be bold enough to, instead of going to our next Christian concert at Stychfields Hall, go down the pub and just get talking to people about Jesus. I'm sure we will have plenty of opportunities when we move as we'll have a lot more neighbours, and introductions to people, having just moved in to the area. Lord Jesus, make my desire so strong that I just won't be able to help myself, Amen. 12.02am

8 December 1988
Thursday night, 12.02 am

It's house group again tonight. We've just discussed our leading of the combined house group next Wednesday, plus a prayer and worship time. I feel quiet, peaceful, but not particularly at peace. There's a difference.

You can be peaceful, but not at peace about one or two things, which is what I am tonight. What am I not at peace about? Lift them to the Lord:

Jeff, from work, is on Holiday next week, and before I realised, I'd offered to lead the combined house group. So Lord, I need a short night at work, very short please, and time between now and then to prepare.

Although I'm really cracking on at work (we are well ahead, considering it's only the 8th), there are a few things, Lord, I pray You can sort out... like making a profit. It's essential, in view of me having to pay £11,000 in taxes on 1 January. I know I'm usually late, but what with the VAT looming and PAYE/NIC, *and* our biggest holiday payout at Christmas, there doesn't seem a lot of hope for my personal tax bill. We need more work, or we need to save money. More work is preferable, Lord, please. Thank You.

Selling the house. ASAP, please, Lord.

My attitude at church. Can we please be more Jesus-centred, and less CoE-centred? Can we please also get singing these new songs that Graham Kendrick writes, Lord? Thank You.

The obvious answer to the first part of number four is not to be in a traditional church, if you don't agree with what it does. But I believe someone has to be there to challenge it, like an opposition party in government, to present alternatives. 12.20am

13 December 1988
Tuesday night, 12.25am

I got home about 10.30pm, had dinner, read Christian Family Magazine, and now I feel OK. Coming home to a quiet house is nice after a busy day at the office. I can have a quiet time cooking my dinner and slowly wind down.

There's someone coming to view the house on Thursday at 1pm. Are you going to amaze us again, Lord, by these people being the ones who are going to buy it, so soon? I feel at peace. I'm going to sleep. Praise the Lord. 1.05am

22 December 1988
Thursday night, 11.50pm

We took possession of the new house today. It's now ours or, to be more accurate, the bank's. Our first impulse from the Lord to buy was 1 November 1988, and seven weeks later we're ready to move in. What a testimony to the Lord Jesus. I was only praying tonight at house group for me to be more appreciative of what the Lord does in our life.

I'm not reading the Bible or praying like I used to. My relationship with Jesus is shallow at the moment, but I'm OK now after my negative feelings last week. I'm back to my old self again, only the Lord doesn't figure too much in it at the moment. I'm quite happy about it though, and more enthusiastic about things. I look forward to the future. I just don't pray and read my Bible so much. 12.10am

3 January 1989
Tuesday night, 11.43pm

Last night, one of our drivers – Tom Brian – came 'round to talk about our faith. He's been searching for something for about five years. He's split up with his wife and feels guilty and depressed, in addition to the emptiness in his heart. How he felt came out at the Transportomatic Christmas party on 30 December, when he got talking to us. We told him the Gospel last night and testified to what the Lord had done for us. He was here for about three hours, from 8 to 11pm, and left with two tracts I gave him. We each prayed with him before he left and again before we went to sleep.

There is absolutely no telling by a person's character, or how well you know them, as to their reaction to the good news about Jesus. Tom is the last person I thought would respond to an invitation to come 'round so we could share our faith, but there you go – praise the Lord.

Barry came for dinner on New Year's Day (I met him in the Brunswick café, in town, a while ago). On that afternoon we appeared to be making some ground about Jesus. He's had his moments up to this time, but the reaction is usually, 'Change the subject' or 'In one ear, out the other'. This time he was listening *and* asking questions, getting quite interested. He came to church with me that evening and, out of the blue, on the way there, said, 'I think I'll make that commitment next week'. After the service I suggested he make it that night, but he said, 'No, I'll do it next week'. Nevertheless, I took him over to the vicarage to see the vicar, but he wasn't in, so it will have to be next week. I hope he doesn't get run over by a bus in the meantime as he'll go to hell, which is why one should make a commitment as soon as possible once your mind's made up.

Another good news story: On Christmas Day, Tony Daly and his son Nathan asked Jesus into their lives. In church on Sunday – New Year's Day – Tony went to the front, to testify, and my eyes filled with tears of joy. My wife and a friend were crying too – thank you, Lord, for an answered prayer.

The service on Christmas day was so in line with a commitment. It was a lovely theme: presents to you and me from Jesus on the tree, which the children opened, revealing sweets; then, a present at the bottom of the tree at the end of the service which had been 'forgotten', marked, 'From you and me to Jesus'. It was opened, but empty. 'What does Jesus want for Christmas?' 'He wants our hearts'. So, during the last song, anyone who wanted to give their heart to Jesus for Christmas was to write their name on a piece of paper and put it in the empty box. It was lovely. Lots of people did, including two of our daughters.

It's back to work tomorrow for the first day after the holidays. I want to go back to work. I'm not getting bored at home; more lazy and lethargic, getting up late and going to bed late. It's been nice though, plenty of time with the family. Today we've been to Telford, ice skating and shopping, and yesterday we went over to Graham and Justine's, my brother-in-law and his wife, to see John Christian, their new baby born on 28 December.

I've been ill with a 24-hour bug, which I've just got over, and now I've got a cold. This is not typical of me at all, which is another reason for going back to work – I don't get ill when I'm working.

We're putting the sale of this house with two estate agents. Now we have the house next to the church, we are doubly keen to get moved in and get cracking on the things that want doing. 12.29am

4 January 1989
Wednesday night, 11.37pm.

I must try and keep this a spiritual diary, as opposed to a diary of events and physical happenings. It's emotions and feelings I must try and concentrate on, feelings of the spirit and human nature, trying to draw on what God is saying to me. However, it must go hand in hand with the word of God through Bible reading and prayer. If I don't read the Bible and pray, how will God reach me? Lord, get me back to the state where it is not a chore to do this.

I have just watched the first part of 'The Nuclear Age' on TV, the sort of programme that used to frighten me to death, but since I've become a Christian and know God is in control, it doesn't worry me much. I believe that God will not allow us to blow each other up and destroy this world. We don't know, really. God will never give us the satisfaction of fully knowing the future. That's where faith comes in. If we knew every nook and cranny of the future, we wouldn't need faith. It's doubt and ignorance that fuel faith and bring hope for the future. Somehow, through the Holy Spirit, we have a peace about the future and, although getting there may be painful, at the end of the road it will be all worth it to be with our saviour, Jesus Christ. I only pray that my vision of this could be more powerful and realistic to increase my faith, hope, and conviction, to spread the news to others in a more urgent and powerful way. Amen 12.15am.

8 January 1989
Sunday night, 11.50pm

Praise the Lord. The entry on 3 January 1989 is an answered prayer. Barry did commit himself to the Lord, Jesus Christ. We went to the vicar's after the evening service. He read a few passages of Scripture appertaining to the subject of dying to the past and re-birthing into a new life. Further explanation came from the Journey of Life, a booklet by Norman Warren. Barry then said the prayer at the end of the book. We thanked the Lord and that was it – about 45 minutes, in all. The vicar went quite deeply into Barry's sincerity and true understanding of what it all meant. He didn't just ask him to make a commitment, full stop. 11.57pm

16 January 1989
Monday, 11.40pm

I am afraid to go canvassing for more work for the business, because I'm basically shy and too proud, or so used to the work coming to me. But just think: I have never gone out looking for work since becoming a Christian and having new beliefs. It will be a totally new experience through the eyes of a Christian. How, as a Christian, will I react to rejection or people not wanting to see me? Will I react differently to someone offering me work? Will the offer of lots of work fill my eyes with visions of pound notes, or will I thank the Lord and praise Him?

I will no longer canvas on my own. I can go with the Lord and His Power. Why all the fear and apprehension? How am I going to tell the good news of Jesus if I can't tell the good news of Transportomatic's service, of which I am the founder and boss? Think Jesus, not fear and apprehension. Think Holy Spirit power, not salesman power, and think honesty and integrity, not discounts and gimmicks.

Lord Jesus, help me through the power of Your Holy Spirit to have faith in myself and identify with you first, not this secular world in which we live, Amen.

Chapter 2: Worried.

31 January 1989
Tuesday night, 11pm

Today I went to the dentist, which I dread. I had a root that was causing me pain removed, had a filling and my teeth polished. I haven't got to go again.

My faith has been shaky these last two weeks. We've not had a lot of work at Transportomatic and the overdraft is £15,000 above our facility. We have had no one around to look at the house, despite an advert in the paper and two estate agents handling the sale. All these things have made me very uneasy and anxious, which is not Your fault, Jesus. But instead of turning to You for help and peace, I've looked at every problem from a human point of view and worried; worried to the extent of being withdrawn, subdued and unhappy. Oh, Lord, how I am sorry for my lack of faith in knowing that You will guide and look after me. Troubled times like these are Your speciality so I should turn to You, but I haven't. Crisis point has not been reached, so I haven't yet offered all to the Lord, Jesus. The wrong attitude – don't wait until crisis point. Treat every day as a crisis point and offer everything to God. You cannot do it all on your own.

I was at mini-crisis point just for a few minutes in the dentist's chair today. While waiting for my treatment, I thought, 'My fear of dentists is either going to be confirmed or dispelled.' I prayed and asked the Lord for the calming of my nerves and peace of mind – I got it. He didn't let me down. I had about fifteen minutes of treatment, which I didn't like, but it really wasn't worth getting so het up about. Lord, help me to know and realise that you are forever with me, more so in my times of anxiety. Help me to rise to my times of testing by turning straight to You, Amen.

28 February 1989
Tuesday night, 11.29pm

I note in a previous entry on 16 January 1989 that I lacked faith in myself and now had to approach my canvassing for work from a Christian point of view, taking Jesus' Holy Spirit with me when going into the battleground of winning work. Well, so far, it's worked. About four new customers are coming on stream. We look as though we are going to get a previous customer back, another one-time customer has come back after an unsuccessful diversion to another carrier, and new contacts have been made at the International Spring Fair at the NEC Birmingham, where I spent a day.

I am worried, however, that I have not yet paid my £11,000 plus personal tax bill, due on 1 January, and have no prospect of paying it unless I sell something or they wait another three or four weeks – which I can't see happening. The VAT payment is due at the end of March, though that won't be as high as usual because we aren't turning over as much as in previous VAT periods. So Lord, please lift this burden off me. I want to be able to pay my personal tax bill before it gets serious, Lord. I don't mind a distraint[1] notice, but when that runs out I really must have the money, and we would like to hold on to our car, as well. Thank You, Lord.

I thank you, Lord Jesus, that You have lifted me in recent weeks from my despondency and lack of motivation and enthusiasm – it's good to be talking to You again through this diary. Thank You that, despite secular things not going too well, we can stand firmly in the family of God and have You to consult and fall back on.

The house is not yet sold. We are running up a huge interest bill to the bank on the bridging loan, about £3,500 so far – £68 per day, to be exact. Bank charges will be high for this quarter, as we have constantly been around £15,000 over our agreed overdraft limit. So far we have a very understanding bank manager. I know, Lord, You won't try or test us beyond our limits, but don't cut it too fine, please. Help me to accept that

---

[1] A distraint notice is notification from the Tax Collector that unless you pay arrears due to them within – usually – 5 working days, anything that you own can be seized and sold to pay the debt. This is done by a visit from the taxman, who goes through your assets that are wholly owned by you to the value of what you owe, and lists them on a form. You then have to sign the form which states that the assets, in our case vehicles, although can be used, must be available to sell when the 5 days are up. The tax authorities (usually in this case, bailiffs) then return to either seize and take away your vehicles or receive the amount in full that you owe. Vehicles that are still under a finance agreement cannot be seized. It can also be described as a levy.

it is not for me to set the time of the sale of this house or the move into the new one. It would be good if we could stay here until the roof repairs at the new house are finished, as it's going to be a major job. The upstairs internal walls have to come down to floor level, so all we'll have in the old part of the house is a roofless shell with only the outside walls standing. So Lord, if we have sold and moved out of here when the work is to be done, find us a big static caravan to live in the garden – or can it be done in the student holidays, so we can go and live in the house we rent out?

Let's just summarise these requests:

That my personal tax bill of £11,268 be paid before the taxman has to force the sale of assets to pay it.

That we can pay our VAT bill, not too late.

That we find somewhere else to live when the new house roof repairs are being done.

If all these things be Your will Lord, Amen.

Dr. Cho, of the Full Gospel Church in South Korea, says, 'Be specific when putting your requests to God, and always ask in Jesus' name'. So there You are Lord. In Jesus' name I ask these, Amen. 12.06am

4 March 1989
Saturday night, 11.47pm

It's been a sunny spring day today, really warm for the time of year. God's creation is certainly beautiful when the sun is shining on the daffodils and crocuses.

These last two weeks I have been coming out of the shell I had withdrawn into. I'm really drumming up enthusiasm for work and life in general. I still have my moments of despondency, but generally I am spiritually quite high and motivated again. However, things still loom on the horizon, like paying my tax and VAT, and the high overdraft, also mounting interest on the loan to buy the other house because we haven't sold this one. Still, I say we have sold it, the buyers just haven't shown themselves yet. It's only money matters, anyway. 'Seek first the Kingdom of God, and the other things will come', says the Bible; so I must not be worrying about these things, knowing that the Lord will provide and lead me in the right direction. Give me the willingness to follow, Lord.

8 March 1989
Wednesday night, 11.37pm

Thank you, Lord, that we are getting figures together at work very quickly. As You know, God willing, I don't want to sell the car, and so I want to get as much money in as possible to enable me to pay my tax bill. The taxman will appear any time, but just hold him off a little longer.

I myself feel firm in faith, not bubbling, just firm, and I'm trusting in You to sort the consequences of our actions out. I took the sale off one of the estate agents today, as they have sent no one to look at the house, and generally are not as motivated and enthusiastic as the other, who has sent quite a few genuinely interested people 'round. Anyway, Lord, who cares? It's in Your hands. You set the times so we'll go for that. 'Who cares?', I said. Well, you care and we care, very much. It's funny how these everyday sayings like 'Who cares' take on a different meaning when you're a Christian. Thank You, Lord, that I can never again say 'Nobody cares', because I know if nobody else cares, You do. Amen. 12.01am

18 March 1989
Saturday night, 11.20am

It's my wife's birthday today. We've been to the Old Farmhouse Restaurant in Armitage, near Rugeley, for a meal. Friends babysat.

We had someone else to look at the house yesterday. Again, no comment, but he did ask before he left where the nearest Church of England church was – significant or not, Lord? I don't know, but it was not the most common of questions after looking 'round a house. Maybe this is it, Lord – Mr Gilman is going to buy it.

The bank interest mounts up, our overdraft mounts up. Our work at Transportomatic is moving slightly upwards, I reckon, but not enough to curb our gradual increase in bank borrowing.

We have had definite doubts, this last week, about whether we shall sell this house and whether we are doing the right thing by moving. We are putting alternative suggestions to ourselves, like put the new house up for sale as well as this one and whichever sells first, live in the other. If the new house sells first then we will have to keep a high overdraft, or sell our rental property.

It really is beautiful and secluded here, the daffodils and crocuses are out, and the blossom is coming on the trees. It seems a shame to move. We thought, Lord, maybe You just wanted to know if we *would* move from here for You and that's all. Now You know we would give this up, You are going to let us keep it. Of course this is assuming we heard You right in the first place, telling us to move, that is. Anyway, we have decided to stick to the original plan and not be sidetracked by doubts and despair. We *will* sell this house; we *will* move, we *will* get our overdraft down.

Thank You, Lord, that I have £6,000 towards my tax bill. I now need the other £5,268 fairly rapidly, like by Wednesday 23 March, or the taxman will issue distraint proceedings against me – not for the first time, but nevertheless, the vultures are closing in. I must chase some money Monday/Tuesday and get it in the bank. 12.10am.

29 March 1989
Wednesday night, 12.30am

We've sold this house, praise the Lord. Last Saturday the estate agent phoned: Mr Gilman had offered £190,000. We prayed and asked the Lord to give us a sign if we were *not* to accept; nothing had materialised by Wednesday, which is when we said we'd let them know, so we accepted yesterday. Things should start moving now fairly quickly – as Mr Gilman has the money – subject to a survey, which should be carried out next week while we're away at Spring Harvest. We'll be going with a lot to thank the Lord for in the past, and the prospect of an exciting future at the new house. I wonder what You've got in store for us, Lord?

We were just starting to think about the alternatives to selling this house as well, but decided we really should stick to our original plan, which has worked out, with slightly different figures:

Diary Entry 9 Nov 1988		Today
£200,000 Sell	Sell	£190,000
£150,000 Buy	Buy	£140,000 (inc. Stampt Duty, etc.)
£50,000	Left with	£50,000

The £50,000 left will go to reduce the overdraft. Originally the Business Development Loan was to be paid off also, but the bank penalty is too high. We now have got to go all out for more work from the Potteries after Spring Harvest, now we are over the house-selling hurdle.

At the moment, I feel equipped enough to do other things with enthusiasm and enjoyment. Not necessarily spiritual things, just everyday ordinary things like work, family life and working in the garden, etc. Despite being shaky financially, I feel elated and confident, and I know it's the Lord Jesus. I feel, for want of a better word, 'carefree'. I'm tackling things with a smile and a 'we can do it' attitude – thank You,

Lord. I know it's You living in me that makes me feel like this. Keep filling me with Your Holy Spirit and help me to remember to talk and have fellowship with You.

My wife and I are not praying enough together. We must get closer to You *together* before going to Spring Harvest on Sunday. We don't want to go in 'cold', we want to go worshipping and praising You, Lord. Amen.
1.09am

30 March 1989
Thursday night, 11.28pm

A tanker has been holed off the Alaskan coast spilling 11million gallons of oil into the sea, next door to one of the last uninhabited parts of the world, a part that is reserved for nature – man's greed spilling out all over God's creation and scarring it for years to come.

It's news, but not the main story; political and business intrigue is the big one. Tiny Rowland, boss of Lonrho, fights to gain control of the House of Fraser from the Al Fayed brothers. He's been battling for four years and some new twist has been found on the story in a leaked Department of Trade confidential report compiled nine months ago. An injunction from the government has stopped the Observer newspaper publishing part of it in a special midweek feature.

It's political and business intrigue, but of what consequence is it to us? The secular world treats it as so important. It won't affect most people's lives one way or the other; only those who are directly involved, and then only temporary. Millions of pounds spent to gain this or that, exhaustive efforts by countless people to effect an end that is not known to anyone. Yet the one thing that can change their lives – that has changed *our* lives – is absolutely free, requires comparatively little effort, is eternal, not temporary, is the most important thing in the world, it never makes the headlines, yet is staring everyone in the face. These people that claim to see all the best deals, these people that claim to hear all the best tips and inside information, are they blind and deaf? The one thing that *would* be of enormous consequence to them is of no consequence to them.

But whose fault is that? It's our fault. As the Ethiopian Official said to Philip in the Bible, (Acts 8: 26-40) 'How can I understand and read what I see if no one explains it to me'. So Philip got into the carriage and explained the good news to him, and so should we to others. But God's Spirit told Philip to go over to the carriage, so we should be asking to be filled with God's Holy Spirit – daily. Then one day we will be able to go over to someone and explain the good news of the Gospel to them, the good news that is of great consequence to all people. 11.57pm

31 March, 1989
Friday night. 12.40am

Mr and Mrs Gilman have been 'round today and everything is OK and going ahead with the move. We should be in the new house in a matter of weeks.

What a confirming twist God has given us to the end of our house-sale story; a confirmation to us that it was His word to move and, despite our doubts – particularly in the last few weeks – it is His will that has been done. There is nothing except God's hand that could have put this particular end on this part of our walk with Him: Mr Gilman, who is buying our house, has filled the job vacancy that Harry Richards left when he went to America; Harry Richards being the person we bought the new house from. God's solution to what we would think is a difficult problem is so simple. 1.30am

1 April 1989
Saturday night, 11.46pm

Tomorrow we go to Spring Harvest, our second time. I wonder if we'll come back all rearing to take off spiritually like last year, or were we like that last year because we went in cold? Was it the comparison between going into Spring Harvest and coming out that put us in that highly spiritually motivated euphoric state? I think this year we're going on quite a high. 12.12am

3 April 1989
Monday night, 10.55pm

Well, here I am, just got into bed in the end bedroom of a seven-berth caravan parked with others in a field adjacent to Butlins, a howling gale blowing outside – and into here through all the gaps in the window seals and doors which are typical of such structures – temperatures dipping to minus three degrees centigrade, tonight nothing but icy winds and today, hail. It's called Spring Harvest. It's our first night *here*, but not our first night in a caravan, and not our first night at Skegness. You may well ask, 'Why?'

Well, we arrived a day early, didn't we? We thought it started on Sunday 2 April, but no: Monday 3 April it is. Thank the Lord that one of my wife's sister's has a caravan at Skegness only about half a mile down the road. We managed to get in touch with her, get the key, and stop there last night, or else it would have been a hotel or B&B, short of going back home and coming back again today.

I think before becoming a Christian I would have gone 'spare' about a situation like that, but we all took it very calmly with nothing more strong in words than 'Oh, no!', and perplexity at how we had managed it, turning to laughter on seeing the funny side.

We haven't done a lot today, mainly because the weather is so bad. We managed a couple of hours at the fair, but after that we were frozen, so returned to the caravan to get warm. My wife's been to the Big Top tonight and our eldest daughter to a 7-8.30 session with her age group. The nitty gritty seminars, etc. start tomorrow. The children are at the ages when they all go to separate groups in the morning while we are at the main seminar.

You have to get together with other Christians, really, before anything starts to happen, which I haven't done yet since I've been here. I did talk to a man in reception while we were waiting to check in. He'd driven from Liphook, in Hants, and had a larger than normal crucifix 'round his neck displayed prominently in the 'V' of his clothes. I felt like telling him to wear just a cross, for Jesus was no longer on it and that He was risen and alive today, but of course I didn't. I'll be bold enough one day to do it, won't I, Lord? But there again, who am I to judge? He may have been a quite prominent and mature Christian who could run rings around me spiritually.

So Lord, Jesus, I pray that You will help me to get 'in the mood' for I don't feel too spiritual. This very moment I would rather be writing this in bed at home where it's warm and cosy and all my familiar things are near me. I thank You, Lord, that wherever I go You can come with me, which is all I should need.

5 April 1989

Wednesday night, 11.32pm

It's day three at Spring Harvest, still bitterly cold, with icy wind and rain. The wind has died down in the last few hours, but it's still cold, near freezing tonight. I pray Jeff and the drivers back home are coping OK, as there were pictures of quite heavy snowfalls on the TV news tonight.

I went to an optional seminar on rock music today – very interesting. Steve Chalke was the speaker. If you believe the earth and everything in it belongs to God and was created by Him – which, as a Christian, you should – then rock music is no exception.

A seminar my wife went to on sharing your faith said that to catch people we have to have the right bait, as when you want to catch fish (ref. Jesus' words, 'I will make you fishers of men'). Well, the right bait in the case of many young people would be rock music in church.

An interesting word also from the main seminar this morning: when praying, don't just ask Jesus to forgive our sins, be specific and elaborate. Tell Him what sin or sins you are referring to; be honest. The Scripture referred to was, 'If we say we have no sin we deceive ourselves, but if we confess our sins, God is faithful and just'. A passage we read at just about every service at church, one of those we say so often it becomes automatic and the deeper meaning can be lost. We say it without having to think about it, just a general blasé confession, which is not honest enough.

Our three daughters are doing very well, considering they've been split up for their activities, as each of their age falls into different groups this year. We've been swimming in the quiet pool today. I always remember when I go swimming that it is one of the first things I did as a Christian with the help of the Lord, Jesus – learn to swim, that is. Thank You, Lord. 12.17am

9 April 1989

Sunday night, 12.15am

The last day of Spring Harvest and also my birthday. That makes me 42 in the flesh, not yet 2 in the Spirit, and our 12th wedding anniversary. We'll call at the Little Chef on the way back and 'live it up'.

At a seminar today on growth, some things picked up: 'Your church won't grow until the Christians in it grow. If the Christians in your church grow then the church will grow automatically, not the other way round'.

It has been a good week, though not quite over yet. We are not going back home 'fired up' as we were last year, probably because we were praising the Lord when we arrived. However, at one of the main seminars we were warned about being 'Thermometer Christians', our spiritual life going up and down according to how we feel, according to whether it was a 'good service' or a 'bad service' at church, etc. We should be 'Thermostat Christians'. When we are getting cold, our thermostat should cut in and we should plug into God to warm us up by praying and reading the Bible. In testing times, plug in and draw on God's power. As one of the speakers said, 'We all have shares in God's "Power and Light Company"'. Thermostat Christians, when getting too hot, ie. doing too much, too many committees and church activities, should switch off, sit back, think and listen. God has more desire to tell us things than we have the desire to listen to what He has to say; so always make time to listen to God. A good example: at the seminar, we were told to be quiet for one minute and write down the things we could hear, like chairs creaking, someone coughing, the wind, the tent flapping, singing outside... all the things that, if we were talking or listening to someone or something else, or doing something else, we would not have heard. That's how we are: so busy doing other things that we can't hear what God is saying. If we'd only stop, have a quiet time, and listen to Him. 12.50am

11 April 1989
Tuesday night, 11.50pm

Back to work yesterday. I didn't enjoy it, and I'm pretty sure it wasn't just because I'd been away for a week.

I was somewhat demoralised by the letter waiting for me from the bank when I got in, the gist of which was: 'Your account is now overdrawn £91,000, well in excess of the facility granted to you. Can we therefore have debtor's and creditor's lists as soon as possible, in particular, details of monies immediately due to you', signed the 'Senior Manager'. The only bright note was that he wrote, 'Pleased to see a firm offer has been made on your house, this should be the first step to removing considerable weight off your shoulders', meaning the bridging loan for the purchase of the new house, and my large overdraft. In fact, thinking about it, I am in considerable debt to the bank at the moment. I'll write it down:

Liabilities

£91,000	Overdraft
£140,000	Bridging Loan
£30,000	Mortgage
£28,000 (approx.)	Business Development Loan
£5,000	Personal Tax
£7,000	VAT
£9,000 (approx.)	PAYE/NIC
£310,000	TOTAL LIABILITIES

Assets/Estimated Realisations

£190,000	Sale of present house
£40,000	Sale of rental house
£140,000	Value of new house
£8,000	Value of Mercedes car
£50,000	Estimated value of vehicle fleet
£3,000	Estimated value of pensions/insurance
£431,000	TOTAL ASSETS
£310,000	Less liabilities
£121,000	NET EQUITY after everything sold/ paid off

Calculation after moving in to the new house and present house sold:

Liabilities	
£50,000	Overdraft
£30,000	Mortgage
£28,000 (approx.)	Business Development Loan
£5,000	Personal Tax
£7,000	VAT
£9,000 (approx.)	PAYE/NIC
£129,000	TOTAL LIABILITIES

Assets	
£140,000	Value of new house
£40,000	Value of rental house
£8,000	Value of Mercedes car
£50,000	Estimated value of vehicle fleet
£3,000	Estimated value of pensions/insurance
£241,000	TOTAL ASSETS
£129,000	Less liabilities
£112,000	TOTAL EQUITY

I've been saying to my wife that my prime reason for not enjoying the business as much is that the thought of making money no longer motivates me. I have no big ambition anymore to be a *big* transport company. I *am* worried about the large overdraft, but at the same time I'm not motivated enough to rush out and do something about it. Any other businessman would probably be rushing around trying to pull as much extra business in as he could, but all I do is make the odd phone call to a prospective customer in a matter-of-fact way, and continue to hope and pray that the work will find *us,* and, in the meantime, the overdraft creeps up. Probably at the back of my mind God is saying to me that the work will gradually build up on its own, and to just hang on in there.

I'm really quite an inadequate person as regards business. I have no strategy whatsoever for situations like this, I just drift along and hope for the best. I don't know whether to call it faith, complacency, or couldn't-care-less.

All the signs are there: not enough work, losing money, overdraft going up, unable to pay the taxman until money comes in. Yes, all the signs are there – for what? For bankruptcy, for the bank not co-operating, to sell? I don't know. Is God's peace and security making me complacent? Am I thinking, 'It doesn't matter, God will look after me, whatever happens?' Is God trying to tell me something like, 'Sell the business', or 'Do something you can really put your heart into'? Maybe He's yelling at me to get off my backside and go out and get as much work as we can cope with and build the business back up again. Is He saying do the latter, and then when we're back to being very, very busy and making good profits, sell? At the moment, Transportomatic will not go for much, probably assets only after I've paid all the debts. Is God saying to me it doesn't matter what you get for the business, just sell it and get what you can, if anything? Dear Lord Jesus, please look after me and my wife and family, whatever happens, Amen. 11.59pm

15 April 1989
Saturday night, 10.50pm

I'm not filling this in enough; it should be more often – fewer words every day instead of lots of words once a week.

I made an effort tonight not to watch any TV, which I didn't, on the principle that if you take rubbish in, you'll put rubbish out. At teatime we sang some songs that we all knew, then I went through a few that I like out of the new Spring Harvest song book, went to see Charles Metcalf, at Bednall Head Farm, to get some empty fertiliser bags, came back, had a go on the computer, made a cup of tea and came to bed. 11.02pm.

23 April 1989

Sunday night, 11.02pm

I'm in the computer room at home to prove everything comes from God. Do we believe that everything on this earth and in it comes from God as he created it? Yes. Right, write down everything you see in this room and trace it back to its origins, from what it is originally made:

Plastic	Oil from the earth
Carpet	Wool from sheep or nylon from oil
Paint	Oil from the earth
Glass	Sand from the earth
Curtain material	Cotton from bushes or poly material from oil
Wood	From trees
Wallpaper	From wood from trees
Plaster	Gypsum from the earth
Varnish	From oil
Brass	From iron ore/copper etc. out of the earth
Foam in the chair	From oil (I think)
Metal radiator	From iron ore out of the earth
Printed material	Ink made from oil or chemicals or animal/ plant dyes from creation
Pottery	From clay out of the earth

And so it goes on...

It can all be traced back to God's creation. Without the creation I would have nothing material, and yet it is these very things that often distract me from thinking about God and divert me from His path.

7 June 1989
Wednesday night, 12.06am

It's been a long time since the last entry; such a lot has happened.

The entries in this journal for 30 March 1989 and 1 April 1989 regarding the sale of our house to Mr and Mrs Gilman did not come to pass – they had to pull out. We had this bad news on arriving back from Spring Harvest. Mr Gilman suddenly lost his new job. However, God new what He was doing, because I am writing this in the new house. We have lived here for a few weeks now. Despite the bad news from Mr and Mrs Gilman, we thought the Lord was telling us to leave the old house and trust Him. We felt we had only done part of His will by not moving – so we moved without selling. A week after moving, we sold for £200,000, £10,000 more and the original figure we wanted. Completion is on 19 June. How good the Lord is when you trust Him and do all His will. The good thing is we have sold to Christians. They were living in a caravan in Rugeley after being let down on a house in Stone, so the Lord has worked in their lives too. We always wanted to sell to a Christian family. They have three children, the same as us, and the school they go to is literally across the road – isn't the Lord good? Doesn't it go to show, if everything seemingly fits together, like it appeared to with Mr and Mrs Gilman, it is not a sign that it is the Lord's will. That's a lesson He has taught us and we must be on guard next time. The Lord has the last say, wait on Him to act in *His* time. 12.33am

8 June 1989
Thursday evening, 7.24pm

At 7.45pm there is a PCC meeting. Help me to do Your will in the meeting in a loving way. Help the meeting be as spiritual as it is normally, fabric of the church. Help our church members face the challenge of encompassing *all* You have to offer, Lord. We have largely ignored areas such as spiritual gifts, freedom and space for Your Spirit to move, evangelism, counselling, nurturing, and young people. We need young people with leadership and specialist qualities to do Your work; in Your name I ask this, Amen. 7.30pm

8 June 1989
Thursday night, 11.26pm

The PCC meeting tonight did not take on the form of anything too different than usual, but there was, much more than previous ones, a spirit of openness and friendliness towards one another. No one had any gripes or bad feelings about anything.

21 June 1989
Wednesday night, 11.58pm

The men's fellowship was tonight organised by me, with the help of Len and Reggie, from church. We showed the Glen Hoddle video, followed by a fish and chip supper. A disappointing turn-out, which flattened me somewhat at the beginning – we were hoping for 25, 11 came – but as the night went on we became a close fellowship with four people's testimony drawing the peace of God to us. Two non-Christians were there, one from across the road, and a friend of Len's called Frank, who has the swap shop in town. I pray for them, Lord, particularly Rob from across the road, that he is nearer to You tonight, that You have become more real to him, in Jesus' name I pray, Amen.

I have felt deeply unmotivated today. I have had the day off and virtually wasted it through complete lack of drive and purpose. No plans have been fulfilled; I've felt lethargic and fed up, fallen asleep twice despite ample sleep last night. I got really low before the preparation for the men's meeting. The devil really knows when you're going to glorify the Lord. He digs his talons in if you don't resist him with the power of Jesus Christ, which I wasn't motivated enough to do. But, as the night went on, You lifted me, Lord, and I thank You once again that You didn't let me down. Help me to resist attack more vigorously and use Your powers available to me; the power, the cross, the blood, and the name of Jesus. At these the devil flees, we bring him to his knees; he has to acknowledge that Jesus is Lord. Oh Lord Jesus, help me to resist attack and attack back. Indeed, not even wait for attack, but attack first in Your name, by the power of the blood of Jesus, for ever and ever, Amen. 12.20am

26 June 1989
Monday night, 11.39pm

My wife and I have been to see Billy Graham tonight at Wolverhampton, a satellite link from Earls Court in London. We took Frank, the swap-shop man who came to the men's fellowship fish-and-chip supper last week. He enjoyed it, praise the Lord. I asked Steve Dimmock, a driver from work, to come along, left him a ticket and phoned him at teatime, but he declined to come; he said he didn't fancy the 'American way' and mentioned tele-evangelists, but, Lord, help me to keep asking as I believe deep down he wants to know You.

It's the first time I've seen Billy Graham. It was a very basic Gospel message with an appeal for people to come and accept Jesus quite quickly. The response at Earls Court and Wolverhampton was very good – in fact, tremendous. His message was 50% Scripture, 50% modern day reality, and tying the two in, with parallels drawn all the time between New Testament Scripture and today's problems and happenings. It was almost too simple and easy to believe for the non-Christian, I would have thought, but in reality, accepting Jesus into your life is very simple and easy. It's the bit after that's hard, trying to *live* in this world as a Christian. No wonder we need constant nurture and encouragement when we're new Christians. It's easy to give up, but hard carrying on if we're not careful about how we start off. The numbers at the big meetings are a lot to do with the awe and wonder of it all – the fact that about 70,000 people come together to hear about Jesus. It just would not be the same if there were only 70. 12.05am

27 June 1989
Tuesday night, 11.01pm

I will shortly be in a position to reduce considerably my overdraft from the sale of our last house. This would be the optimum time to sell the business, if we are to continue making a loss. If I don't, the overdraft may creep up again and I'll have nothing to sell as I have now, to get it down again. Or I can go all out to increase rates, get more work and try and get back into profit. But that's the risk. Will we get back into profit thereby having no need to worry about the overdraft going up again? That's my worry. The other problem is that, to get back into profit, we will have to get busier, which means longer hours, more organisation and personnel, and of course, more hassle. Is it all worth it, just to make money and live a 'comfortable life'? I'd have less spare time and see my family less. But as a friend at church suggests, why not get someone in to run the business for me, leaving me free to do something else? Another problem; what do I do instead of transport? What openings are there in Stafford?

But all these thoughts, Lord, are through my human strength alone. You know the answer and I know I should pray hard about it. I have thought about retreating for a week on my own and just sorting it all out with You, as it seems so vital to my future as a Christian – just get away from it all and pray until I get an answer. But I hardly pray about it anyway without doing that, so I should pray in my present situation first. There is a negative side to my work as regards the odd hours, hassle, pressure and responsibility, but there is also a positive side to it; freedom to come home when I want to, have holidays when I want to, not having to be in every morning at 8am, etc. On the one hand I'm tied; on the other I have a lot of freedom. I suppose every job has hassles and frustrations, but Transportomatic problems really get me down. Sometimes I cope really well; sometimes I'm at my wits' end. I reckon the real answer again is 'seek first the Kingdom of God' and everything else will take its course. Maybe the answer is to spend more time with You, Lord. Maybe I don't share these burdens with You enough. Maybe I try and sort it out in my own strength and shouldn't. Without You I can't cope, with You I can. All in all, Lord, I have a problem – or should I say, *we* have a problem. You live in me and I live in You, so if I have a problem, then so do You. I always give in to worldly desires and let the secular world get me down. The answer here is to let my trust in You *overwhelm* my worldly desires and secular hassles; I have my priorities wrong. Again we're back to 'seek first the Kingdom of God', spend more time with You. In this area, my discipline lets me down; when you're your own boss you can get lax about it. You're very good at disciplining employees to the neglect of disciplining yourself. So Lord, spend more time with You, but to do this pray for discipline – exactly what I've known for a long time but never got down to.

Now I'm on the subject of 'Better use of my time'. I don't make the most of the time available to me. I lack discipline in this area and therefore waste a lot of time: putting things off till tomorrow that could have been done today, staying up at night when I should be going to bed, taking my time over breakfast when I should be rushing off to work.

I can remember when every morning I was up very early to go on a delivery run and back late every night – continuously. I only had the weekends to catch up on sleep. All the paperwork had to be done at weekends also. I don't think I could do that now. I'd never see my wife and the children. I'd be bad tempered and irritable, run down and uptight. Yet I did that for years. I could never do that again; I'm just not motivated and dedicated enough. Oh, for something interesting enough to bring back that dedication, but not such long and awkward hours. I really should count my blessings in my present circumstances when I look back at the so-called 'good old days'.

Thank You, Lord Jesus, for what I *have* got. It is sometimes difficult to look on my present situation as being really fortunate and blessed. Compared to my early days in business, I have a wife, children and a home now. In those days I was on my own and my long hours didn't affect anyone else. Even when I was courting my wife, she had a job as well, and work colleagues who shared a house with her to take her time up when I wasn't around. Times change, and thank You, Lord, for having a job now where I can be around whenever I'm needed and have more time to see the family. Oh, praise the Lord for everything!! Our bad times are ecstatic compared to some people's, so I thank You, Lord. Amen. 12.21am

Chapter 3: Renewed – true or false?

7 July 1989
Friday night, 11.35pm

Looking back at the last entry regarding not being able to cope with all the problems of the business and, 'is it worth the hassle', it does not seem the obstacle it was when I wrote it. Giving up is silly now I have that extra something – the Spirit of the Lord – to help me. If I built Transportomatic up to a net profit of 23% of turnover in my own strength in the past, think how much more the business could be built in the strength of the Lord as well. I am somewhat renewed today.

I also see the Lord weeding out the people in the business that are not good for it. In the last two weeks, one of the loaders has resigned and on Wednesday afternoon a driver resigned, enabling us to advertise today for their replacements: new, fresh people into the business, who are not set in their ways. The two people who have left, although good workers, were not quite right – with the loader, you were never sure if he was going to turn up, and the driver had bad habits, a chip on his shoulder, a peculiar attitude, and was rather set in his methods. We have interviewed two people today. One we have set on, starting Monday, and the other will start if he agrees to be a driver/loader. Someone else whom we have previously interviewed has phoned. He should be OK, if we need a third person. It's no coincidence when the first three people who reply to an advert are suitable, when normally we are hard pushed or cannot find anyone out of *all* the people we interview. God is working in the situation. I am becoming confident in the business' future.

So Lord, please guide me through the future, blocking me when needed and pushing me when needed, diverting me back to the right path when I go off the straight and narrow, and please, Lord, I ask You to keep my eye on the vision of a rebuilt business. I ask that I can incubate this vision into reality through faith and the work of Your Holy Spirit. Please spur me on, but slow me down when I start going too fast. Keep my spirits up and the devil away from putting any doubts and fears in me. In Jesus' name I ask. Amen. 12.16am

8 July 1989

Saturday night, 11.38pm

I believe, Lord, You have given me a vision of Transportomatic in a new warehouse with lots of work, better conditions and facilities, and earning more income than it ever did. I believe, Lord, that You are going to give Transportomatic a rebirth through Your Holy Spirit and it's already starting. Help me to hang on in. I'm sure I shall have doubts and fears and be under attack from negative thoughts and desires. I claim now Your protection and immunity to such attacks. I pray for the humbleness to call on Your name in such circumstances and ask for Your grace and mercy in listening to me. In Jesus' name I ask this. Amen. 11.52pm

12 July 1989

Wednesday night, 8.50pm

I'm babysitting for one and a half hours while my wife is at a meeting to discuss the summer holiday Sunday School Project; I'm going back to work after.

Lord, I pray for our two new employees. What is on my mind is that we have to 'mould' them into our way of thinking and doing things. The new driver seems he might be set in his ways, a bit slap-happy about driving hours and precision, though I may be judging him too soon. Help them to get into it and ease my mind of the burden of worrying about them. The new loader/driver seems unsure of himself, and a bit disoriented. He definitely wants a leader, someone to show him the way. I want to spend some time with him, Lord, doing roping up, general stacking and weight distribution. Please help me to be keen to do this to increase my confidence in his ability. Also, I'm slightly concerned that one of the other loader/drivers isn't very happy about me taking on a driver 'over his head' so to speak, although I did explain the situation to him. I don't want him to leave as well. This feeling has prompted me to start paying night money when loading, which will give them an extra 73p an hour after 8pm, although I know it's not *all* money motivated, Lord. I must try and get alongside my employees more, get to know them better, break a few barriers down so I'm more at ease with them and they with me; give them a sense of purpose, thereby increasing their dedication and sense of belonging.

Lord Jesus, I pray for the breaking down of these barriers. It will not only make it more enjoyable for me at work, but also for them. In Jesus' name I ask. Amen. 9.20pm

30 July 1989
Sunday night, 11.32pm

Next Sunday night we are doing the service, so we had a little meeting tonight to start planning it. I really must fill this in more often; it's so bitty when it's once every few weeks. I forget what previous entries were all about, it doesn't flow, and it's not encouraging or helpful in my relationship with the Lord when it's not a regular entry. I do remember, however, spending a lot of time writing and praying for boldness to go out and canvass for work for Transportomatic. That boldness is coming, but the Lord isn't working by giving me this. He's working by not making it such a big deal to go out. He's making it so it's more natural. Not to get myself all hyped up and over prepared, but to just get all the right information together and call in a few places when I've got some time to do it.

I'm still concerned about our new driver. He's far too blasé about his job: such duties as phoning in, getting all his deliveries done and not bringing any back, etc. These are being undertaken with far too lax an attitude. I must speak to him. He doesn't organise himself very well and is not taking it seriously enough for our standards. Be with me, Lord, when I speak to him. As you know, I don't like criticising people, but when it's for the good of the business and peace of mind, I must. 11.52pm

31 July 1989
Monday night, 10.55pm

I'm spiritually up and down at work today, and other days too. Up and down like a yo-yo – or spinners, as they're called now.

The problem is I get easily discouraged. It doesn't take much to knock me down, to demoralise me. An employee making a stupid mistake is enough, or the bank phoning and asking if I've got any large cheques to pay in because I'm way over my overdraft limit. Lord, help me to keep on an even keel, emotionally.

I try not to be a 'thermometer Christian', so I must try not to be a 'thermometer businessman' either. I should be a Christian at work – or anywhere else, for that matter – so if I'm not a thermometer Christian then I'm not a thermometer businessman; Christian and Businessman should be inseparable. If I'm a thermometer businessman, then I'm still a thermometer Christian. No, what it is, is I tend to forget I'm a Christian. No – I don't put my Christianity into practice at work. I tend to lose sight of You there. I still push You out of my thoughts too much, and because I don't involve You – I don't let You in – I find it difficult. Two heads are better than one, as the saying goes, especially when one of those heads is Yours, Jesus. So I believe that's it, Lord! I get demoralised when I push You out, then I try to do things without You, on my own. Without You the devil gets in with negative, doubtful, fearful thoughts; he steps in: 'When the cat's away....'

Help me to bring You in as my partner in the day-to-day running of the business. Lift my spirits, Lord, when I get low and help me to make decisions with the help of Your strength, and not on my own. 11.35pm

3 August 1989
Thursday night, 11.45pm

Our house group is taking the evening service this Sunday, so we've been planning it tonight. We've also started a course on redemption, which should be good.

I don't feel like writing this tonight. My mind's wandering to other thoughts, Lord, I'm sorry. Be with me when I do the sermon on Sunday evening. Calm my nerves and give me the words, please. I plan to hold up a £1 coin and ask who would like it, absolutely free, no strings attached. All you have to do is come and take it. Hoping that no adults will, so I can illustrate that a child has taken it because children take things as they see them, they don't complicate things. Adults would be thinking there is a catch, or that they'd have to do or give something in return. It should illustrate that, by taking a £1 coin, you should take God's word for what it is and act upon it, no questions or analysis before doing so. Hence Jesus' words in Matthew 18: 3, 'I tell you the truth, unless you change and become like little children, you will never enter the Kingdom of Heaven'. I'm dropping off, goodnight. 11.58pm

27 August 1989
Sunday afternoon, 4.45pm

A chance to fill this in! It's Sunday, the Lord's day, but I'm not that close to Him at the moment. I say to myself, 'It's because I've been too busy at work, not enough time for the Lord', but it's a poor excuse considering that He is with me all the time. It's learning the art of bringing Him in to every aspect of my life, not just when I'm not too busy.

Very frustrating times at work: often totally demoralised and fed up. Enough to yearn to be set free, for that's what the business is to me at times, a prison where I can't break free. I'm a slave to it and the business is my master. It rules my world. It sets the early mornings I have to get up for and the late nights I go to bed. It sets many times for me to be frustrated and worried – but not often, if at all now, rejoicing or happy. It appears, at times – most of the time, recently – to be a millstone 'round my neck. I'm in the water, trying to keep afloat, but the weight keeps dragging me under and I don't often get the chance to come up for air. How nice it would be to be pulled on to the warm sunny riverbank by the side of the fast-moving waters of life and watch it all rush by from a position of peace and security. It's the uncertainty of life at the moment that keeps me bobbing up and down in those cold waters, not knowing whether I'm going to sink or swim. One can just keep fighting the current that seems to flow against me most of the time.

Is this the aftermath of a holiday, when we do get the chance to just sit and let the rat race go by? Is the relative serenity and slow pace of life on holiday just something I can taste once or twice a year, or can I opt out and break away from all this rush and bother? It seems not. We are busy at work, but not yet making any money, so the sale of the business would not realise a great deal, if anything, after all the debts are paid off. We would probably have to sell the house to settle everything.

Where we stayed in the Yorkshire Dales is an attractive style of living and working for me, where the hosts are a Christian community who live and work there. It would suit me to do that, but of course I have a business, wife and family and they want single people aged between 18 and 30. The concept of being involved in, or running a Christian guest house or hotel in a picturesque area does attract me, but it's a bit 'pie in the sky' at the moment, unless, Lord, You know otherwise.

So what happened to the vision of rebuilding the business again with the Lord's help? (see entry on 8th July 1989). Well, it's still there and I'm trying to pursue it. We are gaining new customers and increased rates will be implemented, but we are still not making money, still not paying debts, still struggling to pay VAT and my personal tax. This is the dilemma I'm in: if we carry on getting more work and taking on more people, we still make a loss. If our debts get bigger, then as time goes on it will be harder to pay them off and we will eventually reach a point where our debts exceed our saleable assets – insolvency.

The hope is that more work – and a better rate for doing it – eventually turns a loss into a profit: a huge risk to take, one that is literally make-or-break. Without Christ I don't think I would be taking this risk. My salvation is in Jesus Christ, both from a personal and a business point of view. I have that extra chunk of confidence in Jesus Christ that drives me – though somewhat anxiously – to step out and take a big risk. I know that, whatever happens, Jesus will look after me. It's so hard to say this in faith, at the moment. I am that uncertain and frightened about the present and future I feel that a statement like this, at this time, is almost *blind* faith. My being nearly reduced to tears when things go wrong at work is really a near loss of nerve. With such odds stacked against me, when frustration gripped me when delivering in South Wales last Friday, on two occasions I cried out to the Lord in a loud voice to help me.

This is that extra help in full manifestation against all odds. When what seems like the burden of the whole world is pressing down on me, I can reach out and grasp a piece of God's hope. This is the true surge of God's power that keeps me going. Without that I would be weeping by the roadside on the verge of a nervous breakdown.

2 September 1989
Saturday evening, 6.45pm

I've just got half an hour before I go to the preparation at Trinity church for the March for Jesus, on 16 September.

We've had a nice family day today. We had lunch in the Soup Kitchen after everyone, except me, rehearsed at the church for tomorrow's service, which is being taken by the Sunday School. We then did a bit of shopping in town.

This afternoon, the owners of this house – prior to the people we bought it from – came to see us: they became Christians here. They say their church is 'bursting at the seams'. Pentecostal churches definitely have more attraction to the non-Christians than churches such as we attend, because they reflect the joy and happiness of the Lord more. Their church activities are livelier, the services are not so structured and they are more in tune with spiritual gifts and the Holy Spirit. However, to me it does not follow that you worship in a church that you personally enjoy most. We are called to bring the joy, happiness, spiritual fulfilment and gifts to all mankind, which includes the churches themselves. A lot of churches do not have this joyful, meaningful relationship with Jesus. Individuals might, but not everyone. Unfortunately, many of the leaders and decision makers in our churches have no personal relationship with God through the Spirit of Jesus, so therefore it is difficult to make, or they do not make, spiritual decisions. Spiritual things take second place behind material matters such as the physical running of churches, structure and tradition, ceremonies and rituals. Unbeknown to many, church services are structured in such a way that movement and working of the Holy Spirit is ignored or restricted in a serious way, putting Jesus and His Spirit into second place behind traditions, customs and procedures. It's been going on for so long that nobody seems to question or challenge these 'regulations' as to whether they are biblical or not. Sadly, it's a case of 'We do it this way because we've always done it this way'. However, I can see that if the Holy Spirit is not living in you, you will not be convinced to do anything different. You have no Spirit to 'grieve' at what you are doing, so you will not be challenged from within yourself. It's the Holy Spirit that convinces, converts, and motivates change.

One of the joys of knowing the Lord personally is this inbuilt yardstick He gives me as to what pleases Him and what doesn't. He challenges me constantly about the Anglican structure, services, set readings, the lectionary year, set prayers, collects, creeds, etc. Yet I know I should not judge, for God will do that at the end of the age – I will be judged for judging. Also, during the time I am getting uptight about these things, I could have peace and be praying or worshipping the Lord. Is this one of the ways the devil comes as a so-called 'Angel of light'.

My wife is upset about her stepfather's death earlier today, but as the day went on, her spirits lifted. The visit from our Christian friends we didn't previously know was a boost, especially because they were born-again Christians like ourselves (in my opinion, there isn't another sort of true Christian: it's impossible to have been a Christian all your life).

I think it's worth expanding that last opinion. In John 3, Jesus said to Nicodemus, after he asked, 'How do you enter the Kingdom of God?': you have to be 'born again'. In Paul's letters, he states that you have to take off the old self and put on the new – death to the old and birth to the new. So you cannot possibly have been a Christian all your life; there has to be some stage when you make the decision to ask Jesus into your life and do it, and that decision cannot be made until you are old enough to decide for yourself, which is certainly not when you are born into this world; so no one is a Christian all their life.

7 September 1989
Thursday night, 11.22pm

I must speak about my work at present and all this week.

I think a manic-depressive is a person who is on top of the world one minute and ready to 'throw the towel in' – so to speak – the next. If I'm wrong, then it's the wrong word, but that's how I am at work.

Last night I had to load overnight. I don't think it was the fact that I was tired and run down, but the burden of the business, the responsibility of the whole thing, was just about reducing me to tears. Every thought that came into my head was confused and negative. It was seriously 'I've had enough of this' and 'I'm going to get out once and for all, sell up; nothing's going right; I don't enjoy it; it's just one big hassle'. All week I've had a very short fuse, and it's getting shorter. Please. Lord Jesus, don't let me run out of fuse and explode. Today I've been irritable with the children. Normally I warm greatly to the children after a hard day. I usually find them a shining light when I come home; bringing me back to the basics of family life, love and concern, and the security and foundation that comes with it. But today it was a sharp 'No' to every request. My youngest – who's only four – said, 'Are you in a mood about your work, Daddy?' How perceptive children are. I think to myself, 'John, when you start taking your frustrations out on your children, it's time to pack in'. I've never done that before – today I did.

I wonder if I'm under attack from the evil one, or are these signs from God that the time has come for a change of direction. I'm a big believer in constant spiritual battles in the heavenly realms, as Ephesians 6 says. I don't believe my feelings about the business are 'flesh and blood' feelings – in other words, just human nature, a bad patch I'm going through. I believe such extreme thoughts recently are the result of spiritual battles, the devil telling me one thing, Jesus telling me another. Who is winning? I know who wins in the end, but can my futile mind cope with a spiritual battle? In order to hold out, do I have to pray more and read more Scripture? At these times, I don't feel like Bible reading or praying. I don't feel very near to God, but deep down I know He's carrying me. Deep down I know there is a reason for all this hassle. If only He'd reveal the purpose of it. It's the same old story; if He was to reveal everything, we wouldn't need any faith, would we? It's through faith that we go on, it's through faith that we put up with it. I ask, 'If I was not a Christian how would I cope?' My answer is, 'If I was not a Christian, I would probably not have all this hassle in the first place'. If I didn't know Jesus at all, the devil would not attack me, for he'd have nothing to fight for. I suppose this is what 'carrying the cross' is. 'Take up your cross and follow me', Jesus said. Also, the way of the devil is an easy way, a six-lane motorway. The way of Jesus is through a narrow gate with lots of obstacles to get over.

Oh, Lord Jesus, please get me over this obstacle as quickly as You can, so I can again have a trouble-free walk on my journey with You. Amen. 11.57pm

23 September 1989
Saturday night, 10.40pm

I have started to read *Pilgrims Progress*. The friend who has lent it to me says I will enjoy it, and he's right. 'Get the modern English version first', his wife said, 'and then read the original' – it was written 300 years ago. It has been evident to me from reading this book that the Christian journey, as it was then, is still the same today – proving once more that the story of salvation stays the same, and God is still as faithful and loving as He was then. He never dates – He is eternal.

I see myself in what I have read so far. The road to eternal life and the 'Celestial City' is a difficult one, full of obstacles, temptations and danger. I begin to see that the difficulties I am having at work are all part of the Christian journey. I *can* take the easy road and pack it all in. When 'Christian' meets two false Christians in *Pilgrims Progress* called 'Formality' and 'Hypocrisy', they take one easy road each, 'Danger' and 'Destruction'. Christian chooses to take the correct way up the 'Difficult Hill' – difficult, but nevertheless the right way for a Christian to go. He is spurred on in the knowledge that the Lord's strength is with him, and that the right way eventually leads to eternal life and the 'Celestial City'.

Knowing that this hope will come to fruition if he follows the right road, no matter how difficult the way is, he battles on in faith with the eternal promise from God in his mind.

This makes me feel better about how to cope with the hassle mentioned in the last entry. That week was probably the worst week I have ever had in business (see 7 September 1989). However, at the end of that week I was shaken into action by the Lord to do something about it. As well as myself, I think He also must have said 'Never Again!'. That week, on about three occasions, being so exasperated and frustrated, I shouted out loud, 'Oh, Lord, please help me!'. At the time, nothing happened. I don't know what I expected to happen, but I was looking for instant relief, a bolt from the blue, an instant sense of peace – anything to relieve the pressure and frustration of that awful moment. Through this non-instant reaction and silence from the Lord, He is teaching me to be patient; He is teaching me to be more faithful and trusting, because, in time, the answer to those pleas came.

Looking back, it did not make sense for God to answer immediately, for in my exasperation, I was thinking irrationally and was far from calm. I therefore would have most likely interpreted an instant answer from God irrationally – and I was not calm enough to hear or detect one, anyway. So God waits until I am ready, calm and composed.

It happened at the end of that awful week. Come Saturday, I had caught up on my previous lack of sleep from earlier in the week, was fairly refreshed and, being my weekend off, relaxed and in a good mood – my usual weekend self. Praying and reading the Bible came more easily. Unknown to me, my wife and children had been praying for me. She and I also prayed. During the course of the day, something I thought of a few days previously struck me as a distinct possibility to put into practice. God had already put the opportunity there for the asking. Paul Johnson, one of our previous employees – one of the best also – had asked to come back and work for us. At the time – a few weeks ago – there was no vacancy. However, since then a loader had left and I had offered Paul a loading job, half expecting him not to take me up on it, as he is a driver and likes driving. But he accepted and agreed to start as soon as he'd worked a week's notice at his present job. It struck me to ask him to be our Yard/

Warehouse Manager and do some route-planning. This would ease my burden considerably. A new job created while still retaining the present system, and a chance for me to eventually be home early at night, as route planning was my evening duty. I really believe the Lord laid this idea on my heart in answer to my pleas a few days previously. It did enter my mind a few days ago, but I was in no fit state to think it through rationally or even detect that it was an answered prayer; but that weekend I was really prompted by the idea.

I rang Paul and he came down at teatime. He agreed to give it a go. Today at work, a week later, I started to introduce the system of route-planning to him.

24 September 1989
Sunday night, 11.13pm

The meeting with the bank manager next Wednesday haunts me. Our annual accounts are awful – the worst ever – showing a loss, the first ever in 17 years' trading. Liabilities are £50,000 more than assets, which is why we've sold the rental house. Our turnover is down, our wage bill astronomically high as a percentage of sales, but the stupid thing is we're quite busy, which points to two main problems: our rates are not high enough and our wage bill is too high. Wages we cannot do anything about, so our rates have to go up. Many of our rates did go up by 7.5% last Monday 18 – which will make a bit of a difference, but not enough, so we have to get more work. The warehouse is already stretched to take all the goods, so if we have more work, we'll need more space, which is more expense. Lord Jesus, we need a miracle.

26 October 1989
Thursday night, 11.40pm

Well, Lord, this time last year, the bedroom and house I'm writing this in weren't even thought of. The first mention of the house next to the church is on 3 November 1988 – not recorded in this book – and is only mentioned as an 'impulse' from You. You edged us forward and we have now, on this day, been the new owners of this property for ten months.

I was out on my calculations though, as to how the overdraft would end up. I estimated £30,000; the Business Development Loan repaid, and keep the rental property. In fact we have a £70,000 overdraft, have not repaid the B.D.L. and the rental property has had to be sold, so all in all I was £100,000 too optimistic.

It just shows the two contrasts: how badly we've done in the last twelve months and yet how good the Lord has been to us in giving us this house. Obviously, a thriving business and a healthy bank balance are not Your will at the moment, Lord Jesus.

There is also such a lot going on in our lives, spiritually, much of which has not been recorded because of not filling this in on a regular basis. As one of the Ministers at the NEC Pray for Revival said last week, 'We all too often forget what we've prayed about and therefore never know if our prayers are answered, and as a consequence miss out on God's demonstration to us of his love, and that prayer has power, and does work'.

Looking back at the beginning of the journal, I see the prayers for the purchase of our present house answered. I see on 27 October 1988 – not recorded in this book – a prayer for Tony Daly to come to know the Lord. On Christmas day he did, praise God. If I had never entered such prayer requests at the time in this journal, I probably would have forgotten I'd prayed about them and therefore would not have seen God's answers at work.

27 October 1989
Friday night, 10.05pm

I still have moments of panic that the business is not going to turn round, particularly when I see the end-of-month figures still not showing a profit. 'Don't worry', I say to myself. 'The Lord is with me and He'll look after me.' Oh, Lord Jesus, I do pray You will. Sometimes I get so fearful of the future. It's got to be through faith that things will turn out right. As the Scripture says, 'Will anyone live a day longer through worrying about what the future holds?'. The answer is no. God sets the times, (Ecclesiastes 3), not me. I shouldn't get anxious. I should have more faith. I should be sure through faith that God will look after me.

Just a few things worth mentioning that are, or have, been going on recently:

1. We have sold our rental property through financial necessity.

2. We should have sold the car to pay part of my 1 July personal tax instalment, but we couldn't – although we didn't try that hard. My dad offered to lend us the money, the equivalent of what the car was up for sale at, so in the end we took him up on it: £8,000. His cheque went straight to the tax collector.

3. The house group continues on a Thursday night, a study on redemption.

4. Lots of employees have left Transportomatic, about six in all – half the workforce. All have been replaced; two have come back. Some of our new ones are good; some, not so good.

5. Our youngest daughter started school in September, leaving my wife on her own all day. She did a bit in the office to start with, but we decided not to carry on with that. She's joined a Christian drama group, mostly from the Elim Pentecostal Church. They are called 'Question Mark', taking drama with a Christian message into schools.

28 October 1989
Saturday night, 11.24pm

We've put the clocks forward one hour tonight, so it's really 12.24am.

I've been demoralised again today by Transportomatic's end-of-month figures. We are still losing money – over £6,000 in September. £5,500 of that were bank charges.

Oh, Lord, when are we going to start showing a profit? We are busy at the moment, in fact we need a bigger warehouse now, but the rate of return is still not good and the wage bill is too high. Lord Jesus, get us a bigger warehouse, please. If we get a lot more work we'll have nowhere to store the goods. We need about 6,000 square feet with a vehicle inspection pit, more than one loading door, parking for the wagons on level ground, offices, and somewhere to put the diesel tanks, and not out of town. There's nowhere suitable at the moment, so please get something to come up.

Lord, teach me not to depend too much on the financial state of the business to rule my spiritual state. Give me the joy of salvation and knowing You, and security in the Lord Jesus as a Christian should have. Amen. 11.40pm

31 October 1989
Tuesday night, 11.30pm

It's Halloween tonight. On my way home from work I saw three young children, no bigger than our youngest, knocking on doors asking for 'trick or treat'. One child was dressed quite elaborately as a witch. Harmless fun, they say, but is it? I have no doubt that while those children were having their pretend fun, elsewhere adults were preparing or practicing more serious witchcraft with a deadly evil meaning, as close as Cannock Chase, where it is on record witches' covens exist. So Lord, I pray for You to bind with the blood of Jesus all evil spirits that have been brought out this night through witchcraft and occult practices. Amen.

We had a committee meeting tonight at church to approve the 1990 church budget. I know nothing about budgets. Anyway, we discussed things that we have to discuss.

3 November 1989
Friday

Wednesday was the praying meeting at church. When we pray in a group with all church members, people are very reluctant to speak out anything other than the usual. The spirit of freedom to speak is not there. There is a barrier between us and God, and between ourselves, not dealt with. I think confession and repentance before God and among ourselves is essential for more meaningful prayer and for things to start happening. We still have the barrier of sin in the way of God hearing us and us hearing Him. It is like trying to talk to someone in the next room with the door closed. The barrier is the door. We need God to come and take the barrier away and the door will be opened so we can go in and talk face to face. As others say, we must get ourselves right with God before we can start putting other people right with Him.

7 November 1989
Tuesday night, 10.50pm

My wife's gone to a meeting of the 'Question Mark' drama group of which she became a member some weeks ago. They go 'round the schools doing short sketches with a Christian message or take an R.E. lesson. She's also taken on the job of organising the school pantomime, which is for the children, acted by parents and teachers. The first meeting for that was tonight at our house. She said she was determined to say a prayer before starting and, praise the Lord, she did.

10 November 1989
Friday night, 10.25pm

I've either stepped out in faith today, or done a really stupid thing. I've committed the business to buying an extra second-hand truck for £9,500 – through finance, of course – and I have to put £2,000 plus VAT down as a deposit.

This is at a time when the business is losing money. I still owe my VAT for period ending 31 August 1989, the PAYE tax people came in today to levy for £7,800 owed (they had to levy as I didn't have the money), and the other week I borrowed £8,000 off my Dad because I couldn't sell the car to pay part of my personal tax liability. I am not sure, at times like this, whether I am a totally irrational businessman or totally convinced of paying work in the future. I just felt it was right to buy it. Maybe God is prompting me. An accountant would probably tell me I was bent on ruining myself, putting myself yet further into debt, but somehow, in the long run, I don't think I am. I'm my own worst enemy. By such actions I plunge myself into doubt and fear for the future of the business. Visions of going bankrupt and having to sell the house constantly pass through my mind. Half the problem is I know I have to stick it out because I can't imagine myself seriously doing anything other than what I'm doing now, even though I am making a mess of it. So Lord, show me the way; I can't wait forever for Transportomatic to make a profit, because in the meantime we may go bust. We have only our house left to sell to pump yet more money in – which would only keep us afloat temporarily if we keep losing money – and, at the end of the day, we would lose all our assets. I can hear You saying, Lord, 'What's wrong with that? It's better for a person to lose all his possessions but be saved than a person to gain the whole world and not be saved'. Well, Lord, just You give me the *desire* to lose all my possessions if that's how You want it to be. Amen.

13 November 1989
Monday night, 12.14am

I ask You to help me over the coming week at work, Lord Jesus, to get all the October invoices completed tomorrow and start getting some figures out and some money in. I need the money to pay the taxman and the deposit on this new motor we are buying. The PAYE people came for some money last Friday and I didn't have it, so they had to levy. I've got two weeks to get it. HELP! 12.41am

14 November 1989
Tuesday night, 12.28am

Thank You, Lord for our answered prayer today. I got all my job sheets done for October.

Thank You for today, Father; thank You for my wife, family and home; thank You for all our material possessions, they don't really belong to us and they don't belong to the bank – they belong to You. Help us to use them wisely and to their full potential, and give us the humble responsibility to get rid of the things we can do without, In Jesus' name I ask. Amen.

15 November 1989

Wednesday night, 11.50pm

Well, Lord, we have signed the Hire Purchase agreement to buy the truck. I've paid the deposit, so it's just a matter of tying the loose ends up. A bit of a hiccup today, though. I gave the finance company the cheque for the deposit yesterday, knowing I'd have to get some money in to cover it. The bank rang this morning to say they had the cheque there and if I didn't pay funds in today they'd bounce it. I wasn't expecting the HP Company to send my cheque *direct* for clearing, so I had to phone round and arrange to collect at least £3,500 worth of cheques from customers and get back to the bank before they shut at 3.30pm. Three customers obliged and I ended up with over £5,700. The first cheque I went to collect at Stoke-on-Trent hadn't been signed, so our mechanic had to go and get that later while I shot off to Hixon and Wolverhampton for the others. I made the bank with seconds to spare. I also had to call Jeff in from his day off to man the phones and keep the business going while I was out. Anyhow, Lord, everything turned out OK. We are now assured of our truck, praise You.

I thank You that October's turnover was the highest for a long time. Whether we made any profit or not is yet to be known.

I ask for a good idea in house group tomorrow, Lord, instead of doing the usual study on redemption. It was heavy going last week, so I feel this week we should have a change, something fresh.

It's our youngest daughter's birthday tomorrow. Give her a good day and a nice birthday party. In Jesus' name I ask. Amen. 12.15am

16 November 1989
Thursday night, 11.19pm

I went to see the vicar to see what our house group should do next, as we are on our last study on redemption tonight. He said, 'Don't do anything, have a break, get as many of the group to attend the Tuesday night prayer meeting instead. It is essential that as many members of the church as possible get together to pray as one body. We need to pray together. We need to confess past sins to God and old hurts and grievances to each other. The Holy Spirit will not work in the church while unconfessed sin is present; it is a barrier to God working. We need to get ourselves right before we can get equipped to do God's work. We need to start praying in the Spirit and walking in the Spirit.'

Lord Jesus, make me aware of my unconfessed sin. My deep-rooted unconfessed sin that I probably do not realise is there. Break down my barriers that stand in the way of Your Holy Spirit's anointing on me. What are my deep-rooted sins that need to be confessed to You and to other people? Amen. 12.02am

19 November 1989
Sunday night, 12.25am

I'm late to bed tonight because I've been sorting out my sheets of church music. Many I've had in plastic folders for a long time, waiting to be put into a file; but I have accumulated so many others since then, I need loads more folders and possibly another file. This is a measure of how little we repeat songs in church. Never getting to know a particular song well enough not to have to look at the words and think about how the tune goes, and therefore being able to sing from the heart, not a piece of paper.

I shouldn't get annoyed about this, should I, Lord? I confess to You there are things that go on in church I don't think are in tune with what I believe. Is this frustration because of a grieved Holy Spirit within me, or is it my human emotions responding? If it's my human emotions, then it will be a barrier, because the Scripture says, 'What the human nature wants the

Spirit is opposed to' (Gal. 5: 17), but if it's the other way 'round, then help me to say something. In Your name I ask. Amen. 1.00am

21 November 1989
Tuesday night, 10.05pm

I'm just reading back on 23 September 1989 about Paul. This has made me conscious that I have not fully implemented the plan described then, an answered prayer not fully acted upon because Paul is not route-planning yet. I've done a weekend with him, but that was it. Lord Jesus, help me to carry the plan through. Amen.

My wife is doing pantomime rehearsal every Tuesday night, so I babysit and none of us get to the prayer meeting in church. When our eldest had gone to bed I prayed for about twenty minutes until 9pm for the church and our brothers and sisters in it. That's the beauty of knowing the Lord Jesus; one can join at home in prayers going on elsewhere. We're all in union with Christ Jesus. He's everywhere, so through Him we can transcend distance and material barriers and join in.

We had that second hand 16-tonne truck delivered today. Now, Lord Jesus, all we want is some work for it. We need lots more work, anyway. It's not abundant this week and we need it for after Christmas, when we slack off. This task of getting more work still seems quite daunting to me sometimes, and this is one of those times. So build my confidence and faith up, Lord, to meet the challenge. in Jesus' name I ask. Amen. 10.25pm

9 December 1989
Sunday night, 11.20pm

The number of times I've forgotten to get a new blank book from the stationer's for this journal must be nearly every day for two weeks. The Lord came to the rescue. This book was found in the filing cabinet at work – it's ages old. I can remember sketching in it when I was at Art College, which would be 1963 (those pages have been ripped out now).

A lot has gone on since 21 November 1989, the last entry:

1. 'Christmas Cracker' restaurant opened in town. All Christians are helping voluntarily. I've been down three times. It's great, going extremely well, lots of money raised and a Tearcraft section as well.

2. The vicar says barriers are coming down at the Tuesday night prayer meeting, praise God.

3. My wife's organisation of the school pantomime is going well. The most important thing about that, from a Christian point of view, is the prayer she says with all the non-Christians prior to each rehearsal.

4. The 7.30am Wednesday prayer meeting is still going, although only two attended last week.

5. There are regular new faces at church (since the new vicar started) and still keep coming, praise God.

6. My wife is involved in Sunday school and now does regular teaching. Good new material has arrived. The children seem to like it better, with lots of new interesting literature to bring home from church. 11.43pm

20 January 1990
Monday night, 11.26pm

At last I have been moved to write. I feel that the Lord is about to do something in my life that is worth recording on paper. It's going to be quite tough, but the Lord will 'clear the road, make wide the way'. I've written to Christian friends requesting prayer cover. I felt it necessary in this instance. I am preparing for battle and the more troops called up, the better. This thing has to be prayed through. We are working with the bastions of the secular world here: the bank, solicitor, estate agent, and a multinational company based in California, USA, and comparatively big money; things I myself am not very good at. We therefore need the Lord to 'boldly go with us where I've never been before'.

We are on the verge of securing a three-year warehousing and distribution contract worth approx. £100,000 per year with Jacuzzi UK Ltd, which is just what we urgently need to make the business viable again. We will need 7,000 sq. ft. of storage space to carry out the operation and, by the grace of God, we have found it. A warehouse of 5,300 sq. ft., which itself is not big enough; but the tenants next door – another 5,300 sq. ft. – say they want to let their unit go, making 10,600 sq. ft. Too much for the contract, but ideal for the contract plus the rest of our work – we could move.

Oh Lord, please make this plan come together. Please make the bank back us on this. They seem so twitchy at the moment, about to stop supporting us, or at least very near the end of the line. Lord Jesus, make them hang on until the contract with Jacuzzi starts seeing its fruits. It really makes it a daunting task when you don't know what the bank is thinking or you get the impression they're losing confidence. Just guide me, Lord. I know You and I can do this and pull it off. Thank You, in Jesus' name. Amen. 11.51pm

2 February 1990
Friday night, 10.57pm

Things look very grim at work. I went to see the bank manager yesterday, who was very enthusiastic about the prospective new contract – but also said that if things do not improve dramatically in a very short time, the bank would no longer support the overdraft. I suppose that's a subtle way of saying they'll call the money in. Two months' PAYE/NI which are due were supposed to be paid last Monday after the distraint notice had run out, but I still haven't got the money – it's £8,000. I went to see them today to ask for a few more days to pay, and they have given me until Wednesday morning. If no payment is made then, they will take steps to remove and sell the two vehicles in the fleet that the bailiff listed as saleable assets. I asked if the car could be listed instead but they said no, it was too late to do that. I still owe the VAT due at the end of last December, which now has a 20% surcharge added to it. The first £8,000 of my personal tax bill this year, due on 1 January, is still not paid. I have to pay £16,000 altogether in personal tax for the year 1990, out of what I do not know, as we are still making heavy losses. In October we made a profit, but it has only been followed by heavy losses since. Lord Jesus, some people say as a joke, 'We'll pray for a miracle'. I'm serious, Lord; I really do need a miracle. The car is up for sale, which should fetch £7,000 or more, so I pray I can sell it and get the money by Wednesday morning. If that doesn't happen, then I will attempt to get enough money in from customers to pay the tax bill in the meantime, or at least most of it. I have about £4,600 that could be borrowed in the Building Society, but once it's out I doubt whether it will be put back, and we need that money for the roof repairs on the house. 'Trust in the Lord' – how difficult it is in this sort of situation to really confidently and wholeheartedly trust in the Lord. I pray, Lord, for increased faith in You. Fill me with Your Holy Spirit to give me strength and wisdom during these testing times. In Jesus' name I ask. Amen.

4 February 1990
Sunday night, 10.37pm

It was prayer and worship last night at George and Cindy's, prayer and worship at Covenant Hall yesterday, two services today with a praise service tonight, so a lot of rehearsal – I'm quite drained with playing my guitar.

There are quite a few people praying for us at church for Transportomatic to get this contract to distribute the Jacuzzi products. I hope we will hear about it this week. In a way I feel selfish for asking people to pray for us, as it's something that will only benefit the business. That's why I must witness about it, testify what the Lord does. The main thing is that if I know lots of people are praying, then whatever the outcome will be God's will. If only my wife and I were praying, then in a situation with as many complications and implications as this, I do not feel just the two of us would be adequate prayer cover. Prayer cover in situations where evil or secular forces can infiltrate is essential, and the more, the better.

Paul, our employee who has come off the road to help in the warehouse and route planning has got himself a flat, so we have given him a cooker, furniture and pots and pans. I notice something about us when situations like this arise. We give things away to friends: we don't sell them. It's either since we've become Christians or we're lazy now – can't be bothered with the advertising or taking them down to the auction. I think it's the first reason. Jesus said, 'Give to those in need and expect nothing back'.

5 February 1990

Monday night, 11.25pm

We have been reading Isa. 43: 1-3, which a couple at church showed us after they prayed for me while I was visiting the bank manager. It says the Lord is with me during these times of trial and testing – words of comfort, giving security no matter what happens.

Friday last, 2 February, I was praying in this journal for a miracle – how do I get £8,000 for Wednesday morning? Thank You, Lord, for a miracle! We've sold the car tonight for £7,000. Don't forget, Lord, that's only half the request. The other half is to have the money by Wednesday morning. So far I only have a deposit of £100 from the purchaser. Lord, I pray for the other half of the miracle to be fulfilled. Amen.

Thank You as well, Lord, for half an answered prayer prayed on 20th January for Transportomatic to get this contract we've quoted for. The UK manager of Jacuzzi phoned today to say that things were looking extremely well and positive. He just wanted about four more things requested by his boss in the USA ironed out. These I will confirm in writing tomorrow.

Oh Lord, we're nearly there! I pray that Your will be fulfilled, not mine, however attractive to me personally this is. There is a lot of fighting to do yet. We need premises, if we get the contract, and the only hope I can see are those units mentioned on 20th January 1990. Lord, I pray Your victory will be won in this and we get them. This involves praying that another company who have first refusal don't sign a contract to assign the two leases to them. In Jesus' name I ask. Amen.

6 February 1990
Tuesday night, 12.06am

What's on my mind most, Lord, is that Mr Fitzpatrick, the man buying the car, hasn't been to collect it yet. He rang to say it would have to be tomorrow or Thursday. This, Lord Jesus, leaves me with no money to give the tax office. They want £8,000 tomorrow morning – or rather later this morning, as its past midnight – or two of our trucks will be towed away to auction to raise the money. Lord Jesus, please help me! I myself have one or two plans that are what I would call 'botched'. Maybe I should go in and tell the tax office that I have sold the car but won't have the money until Thursday or Friday. Oh Lord, I pray You can help me sort this out. in Jesus' name I ask. Amen.

7 February 1990
Wednesday morning, 10.59am

Thank You, Lord; the money was provided for the taxman this morning. I had £4,500 approx. in cheques in the post, so I used £3,500 of that and drew £4,500 out of the Building Society, which I can put back tomorrow when we have the money from the sale of the car.

I was reading in Isa. 55: 1-2 about people with no money. It says that God will provide food and wine and quench our thirst at no cost at all – which He does – but we only find that out for ourselves when we completely and utterly trust Him. We have to trust You, Lord, a lot more during these hard times. We are still OK spiritually, which I suppose is what matters.

The equity on the business' balance sheet at the end of December showed a deficit of £32,000, which means that if I paid all my bills and got all the money owed to me in, I'd still owe £32,000 – the business is hopelessly insolvent.

However, as I am self-employed, there are private assets that can be taken into account – such as our house and cars – so it's not completely hopeless. Thankfully, we are spiritually not down, we are healthy and happy, have enough to eat and clothe ourselves, still have two cars – albeit old ones – a nice house and garden, lots of friends in Christ and other friends, so thank You, Lord, for our blessings. We really are extremely well off.

Today I went into the estate agents that are handling these two warehouse units, to see if that other company had signed for them yet. They haven't, thank God. Keep them stalled a bit longer, Lord, so we can have the units. I also continue to ask You that we get the Jacuzzi contract we've quoted for. In Your name Jesus. Amen.

9 February 1990
Friday night, 11.05pm

I do wish, Lord, that members of our church would participate in open prayer more freely. There seems to be a barrier to this openness and feeling relaxed in Your presence. I almost feel I should pray sometimes only because no one else does. It's like no one wants to talk to You, Lord. Maybe they're all listening instead, and I'm the one who can't hear You. I remember Your words, Jesus, that we are not to 'babble on' in prayer like pagans who think their flowery words will impress (Mat 6: 7), but to keep it simple and clear, and be precise in what we are asking. For example: it's no good me just praying for Transportomatic. He wants to know *what about* Transportomatic, so I get precise and ask for the Jacuzzi contract, and the warehouses. But everything is 'if it be God's will', not ours. As it says in the Lord's Prayer, 'Thy will be done on earth as it is in Heaven'. So, Lord, I pray that You bless my requests with Your will. Amen.

11 February 1990
Sunday night, 10.35pm

I broke a string on my guitar in worship this morning, which put it all out of tune. That's never happened before in church.

It was my Mum's seventieth birthday dinner today. We all met at Amerton Farm restaurant, 1pm sit-down. I still feel a barrier between me and the rest of the family (not my wife and the children); we're not close at all. We only talk about 'surface' things and are never open enough to express feelings, worries and 'deep' things. Thank You, Lord, that I can talk to You about deep feelings. I think it's partly because I can't see You, or don't have to worry about what You think, but having said that, it's mainly because Your love, grace and mercy is so abundant. Part of Your grace is me not having to worry about what you will say. Your love is so much, Lord, that nothing we do or say can turn You off us, which is one of our great fears when dealing with our fellow human beings. We just keep quiet to save the hassle and embarrassment of 'What will people think or say of me'. Thank You, Lord, we can say those secret things to You. Rom. 2: 16, 'God will judge men's secrets' means he already knows the things we keep to ourselves so, in a way, to me, Lord, it's an invitation to tell You things I don't want to tell other people. It's a gift, the gift of Your listening ear to everything and anything without fear of reprisals, embarrassment or ridicule – You love us so much. Thank You, Jesus. Amen. 10.56pm

12 February 1990
Monday night, 10.41pm

My wife is ill – aching, sore throat, blocked up nose – so I filled in by taking the children to school, collecting them, cooking the tea, washing up, putting them to bed, etc.

Jacuzzi rang today to say they were drawing a draft contract up for us to look over, and they want copies of the leases on the proposed warehouse units and the last rates' bill. The last two we cannot supply until we are offered the units, which will only be if the other company doesn't sign the contract to take them by this Thursday, 15 February. We are praying they don't. We pray now, Lord, that You stall them by the wonderful means known only to You. Oh, Lord, receive this prayer and thank You for all our friends who are praying for this, in Jesus' name. Amen.

Chapter 4: Big God, big steps, big doubts, big prayers.

14 February 1990
Wednesday night, 12.20am

It's after midnight, so this is also the deadline day for the other company to sign the contract on the warehouses we want. If they don't, then the option comes to us. Forgive me, Lord, but all along – regarding this business – I have not had complete faith that it is Your will for us to go this way. This seems such a big step into the unknown that it is difficult for me to comprehend what the future will bring. From the outset of this so far, I seem to have never been convinced, never really known if this is the way we should go. Not convinced like in previous situations, such as moving house, praying for Les and Linda's baby, the conviction You gave us to go to Austria despite two of our daughters being ill, and the conviction that our eldest daughter was healed by You after being rushed into hospital – all pre-journal happenings. With all those there was never any doubt once we had prayed, and You had given us the peace of Your Holy Spirit. I don't feel, Lord, on this Jacuzzi contract, that You have ever convinced me that it was right or that the outcome was 'yes'. I believe, Lord, that in this particular instance it's either that the answer will be 'no' – so I have not built my hopes up too high – or that it's *after* we get the contract and warehouses that my faith will be most needed. That it will not be until then You will convince me and guide me, because I will not actually springboard into the unknown until *after* the go-ahead is given on the contract and units. Just getting the verbal go-ahead is a fairly simple thing. It's putting into effect the contract and whole operation, which will be difficult and need Your guidance. Maybe it's me relying far too much on my human feelings and not just relaxing and letting You do the work, Lord. We humans are too impatient, aren't we? We want to know right away, when everything should be in Your good time. You know the future, we don't; which is where our faith in You should come in, shouldn't it? So Lord Jesus, one of the *last* prayers on this subject: I pray, if it be Your will, that the other company has not signed by the end of today and the lease is passed on to Transportomatic, and I pray that we are awarded the Jacuzzi contract. Thank You, Jesus. Amen.

15 February 1990
Thursday night, 12.07am

Thank You, Jesus, for an answered prayer. The estate agents handling the warehouse units rang this morning. The other company has not signed the lease contract, so it's now passed to us. Just think, Lord, a warehouse that doesn't leak, a tarmac yard, heating in the warehouse... what have I done to deserve it? I and my fellow Christians have prayed and trusted You, Lord, and we thank You, the glory goes to You. Help me, Lord, in all the slow, confusing, complicated arrangements and planning over the next few weeks to trust You; to have patience and humility and not to be too daunted by the task ahead. I know, Lord, You and I can do it. Thank You, Jesus. Amen.

16 February 1990
Friday night, 11.08pm

What an about-turn! How situations can change in such a short space of time! Today has been one of those days that has left its mark clearly on me; one which I will remember for a long time. The thankfulness to the Lord still stands. We still praise Your name despite what has happened, because we know it's Your will.

This morning I phoned the estate agents to discuss the next stage regarding the warehouses. They were 'mystified' at my call, as they had an appointment with the owners' solicitors to sign a contract with the company who yesterday were supposed to have not signed. I immediately phoned our solicitor, who promised to look into it right away. She came back to me about 12.15pm to say that the other company had done an about-turn and had promised to sign by 2pm today. My heart sank. I was very moved to go home and pray against the other company signing; I was convinced the deal was still for us, that this was the devil's last-ditch attempt against us. I felt we had to fight it out so I went home to my wife.

We arranged to meet at the vicar's at about 12.30pm. He and his wife immediately downed tools in the garden and marched into the house. We took our positions in the lounge and started to pray. For one and a half hours we prayed for victory. We prayed for God's will, we claimed the warehouse units in His name, We prayed that Transportomatic's name would be on the lease agreements, we prayed for the solicitor's involved, we prayed every which way and more. We glorified God and the gift of business. We fought the battle, all four of us, with Jesus at the head and a company of angels surrounding us. We had to win! The Holy Spirit came among us; the vicar's wife was in tears about three times.

Towards the end I felt the finger of God on me, pointing out that I had been putting business and material things before Him. I felt that this was the time He'd picked to 'hit' me, and I confessed. I confessed in tears that the Lord had so many times in my Christian life taken second place. I confessed that we had clung on to material possessions instead of clinging to God – how hard it was to sell the car was an example.

But at the same time I praised the Lord for chasing me and not leaving me alone. He finally got me on this one, as He inevitable does. The Lord kept pointing the finger, kept showing me the sticking points, even when I didn't listen to Him or turned the other cheek. He got me in the end – yes, He did – he got me in the end. Error correction, because He loves me so much and, of course, it didn't hurt one bit. Because the Lord loves us, He cushions the blows to His children, and when this happened to me, it almost overruled what we originally intended to pray about. For a time this seemed more fundamental and important, deeper rooted. Something had been sorted out that would be with me for the rest of my life.

We finished praying at exactly 2pm. It's the longest I've ever prayed. The vicar showed me how to fight a spiritual battle; not a major one, for it was not a life or death situation. He seemed convinced that it had done the trick, for during that time he prayed so many times that we had won so that the Lord may be glorified. I promised God I would testify to the employees what He had done in my life. And what a testimony to God's power and the power of prayer to my solicitor and Jeff, in the office, who both knew I'd gone home to pray.

The testimony was not to be. At about 3.15pm I arrived back in the office. Jeff had left a message on my desk, '2.56pm: your solicitor rang'. This was it, they hadn't signed! She came on the phone and said the opposite: they *had* signed.

My reaction was only, 'Well, it's obviously not meant to be, it's not God's will', which of course it wasn't, after all that praying. I was disappointed, but slightly excited at the same time, as this meant that God has something else in mind for us, something better, more suitable.

I rang Jacuzzi to tell them what happened, and that as of Monday I would be looking for somewhere else.

Writing this, I'm feeling more disappointed than earlier, especially when I think back over the last two years at the things that have fallen through, business-wise. I've lost two big customers, the property deal at Castle Street in the town collapsed – a prejournal happening – visits to another haulier proposing a merger didn't bear fruit. Our ability to make a profit has collapsed and we've had to pump £70,000 into the business from the sale of our last house to keep it afloat. Even that has now been eaten away and was only of temporary benefit. The whole business side of my life over the last two years is as if it was never meant to be, as if I should not be doing it, as if I'm just no good at it anymore; it's always last minute disappointments. Just when we think we've made it, everything collapses around us. I always nearly make it, inches from a breakthrough – I'm just a nearly man. The balance sheet and accounts testify to that. In fact, over the last two years as a businessman I have failed miserably. I have managed to turn a net profit in 1987 of £77,000 to what at the end of the twelve months to March 1990 will possibly be a net loss of £50,000. Yet, we're still trading!

If an accountant came to assess the business right now he'd more than likely advise Voluntary Liquidation. At the moment, we're trading on hope and potential.

Oh Lord, here's one plea on what to do. We've carried on in hope and faith that it will eventually turn back to profit, but how long do we have to wait? Time has already run out. We exist only by Your grace – or is it the bank's grace? Oh, Lord, do something quickly. Amen.

18 February 1990
Sunday morning, 3.30am

I've come downstairs, as I couldn't sleep. Normally I sleep very well and comfortably, but on odd occasions I wake up to what I can only describe as a serious attack of doubt. Not doubt in the Lord Jesus, but doubt in the business, almost to the point of panic. Could it be that, when we are asleep or just woken up, our minds are that clear of the usual day-to-day clouding that the stark realities of what's truly going on present themselves crystal clear? Money; yes, money again. I'm lying in bed with all the problems of the finances of the business going through my head. Figures shoot out at me. £5,000 plus owed to the VAT since the end of November, with a 25% surcharge added and still no way to pay it; £8,000 plus to the taxman for PAYE/NIC; £8,600 owed and on final demand for personal tax; bank charges of £3,000-£4,000 soon to come out of the account again; £8,000 still not repaid to my Dad. I cringe at these figures flashing through my mind to the point of covering my head in my hands and cowering under the bed quilt. I'm on the verge of panic! I toss and turn. I know it's an 'attack' and the devil will take full advantage, so I keep saying, 'Jesus, protect me' or I start singing a chorus in my mind, or blurt out a hurried prayer in my confused head.

Now I'm downstairs it's not so bad, but up there it was hell. It was like the devil prodding me and saying, 'Look – it's a hopeless situation, pack it in. You haven't got the money to pay all these debts and you never will. Liquidate the business now, as every day that goes by you lose even more money. If you hang on waiting for a so called miracle, which won't come, it'll be even worse. Cut your losses and pack it in'. So I picture in my mind going to see my accountant, and he says, 'Yes, it would be better to wind the business up'. Then I picture how I tell my good friend Jeff, in the office, and the other employees. I picture going 'round other hauliers in the area trying to sell them a business that isn't worth anything. The picture doesn't end there. I imagine telling my wife and trying to explain to the children why Daddy doesn't go to work anymore, and why we have to sell the home we've come to love so much.

How do I reconcile God's word of telling us to move here when nine months later it's up for sale and we've got to go? I think to myself, 'God wouldn't allow that!', but then the doubt comes back and I think again, 'Would He?'. And so it goes on. A multiplication of complications goes on and on.

Yet thank God I've got this journal to lift things up to Jesus. I feel better for coming downstairs and doing this. I am comforted in knowing that Jesus is in this somewhere and that He is working on it. I'm comforted that He doesn't sleep and is always active in our lives when we are not, but I am saddened with myself that I am so often blind to His will and really am at a loss as to what to do. This is our weakness, 'He turns our weaknesses into His opportunities, let's give the glory to the Lord... all things impossible by faith will be made possible', the words from the song *Rejoice, Rejoice, Christ is in You* echo in my mind.

My problem at the moment is knowing *who's* talking to me. Is it the devil saying 'Liquidate the business, pack it in', or is it Jesus? That is my weakness: I lack the wisdom of discernment; I don't know whom it is who speaks to me. If I was sure it was God, I would obey, or would I? If I was sure it was the devil, I would reject it, or would I? The battle goes on; the intriguing network of spy and counterspy, espionage and sabotage in the heavenly realms with God's children as players in the drama. The bullets fly, accusations and admissions – but from which side?

Throughout all this confusion, is it enough to say, 'I believe in God, the father almighty, maker of heaven and earth, of all things seen and unseen. I believe in the Lord Jesus Christ, the giver of life. I believe in the Holy Spirit'? Is it enough to say, 'I know I'm saved'? I thought today, Lord Jesus, how I could title this spiritual journal. An apt title at present would be 'My Life in Hell Since Becoming a Christian'. Do I really mean that?

It's now 4.40am. I've had a cup of tea, the washing machine struck up at 3.55am and it's now very noisily going into a spin; I'm cold, and I must have unknowingly been scratching my little finger, because it's bleeding – hence the stains on the paper. I'm going back to bed. Thank You, Lord, I feel much better. Amen.

18 February 1990
Sunday night, 11.55pm

The Lord's day is over and a renewal of my spirits with it. There is no doubt that being with other Christian people is an encouragement in itself. I have, in the last few weeks, through this work trauma, got to know more about the proper workings of a church family as God intended it – the Body of Christ, and the meaning of prayer support when my wife and I often feel we would not be very effective on our own. So we thank the Lord for providing this route to God when we are having difficulty getting there ourselves – we have had such a lot of other things on our minds. It's comforting to know that members of the church family can pray with a rational mind on our behalf. Thank You, Lord, that when we are so open to attack, we have prayer cover from our Christian brothers and sisters to stop the devil from dragging us down. Yes, we have doubts and fears in times like this. Doubts, like 'Is it because we are lacking in faith it is so difficult?' and 'If the Lord is with us, then we have nothing to worry about, so why are we worried? The Lord will look after us, why be even worried about losing the house?'. We think that, because we are creaking under pressure, our faith is not strong enough and we are spiritually lacking in a big way. Well, that's quite right, that *is* our weakness, we *are* lacking, and we *aren't* worthy, but if we brush our pride to one side and admit to God this is the case, then He will turn our weaknesses into His opportunities, He will strengthen and encourage us – all is not lost. The situation sounds bad, but we are still healthy and have a smile. We are still fed, well clothed and have a comfortable home, praise the Lord for that. Amen.

I was saying to my wife tonight that us not getting the warehouse units is a similar situation to when Mr and Mrs Gilman pulled out of our previous house. It was an unexpected let down, a time when we were angry with God, when it seemed so right that they buy it. But look what God did! Someone came along within a week, offered us more money, and completed the sale very quickly. God had something better for us then, maybe that's the case now. God did not allow us to get those units we thought were ideal, because He has something better for us. He knows something we don't, and we have to trust Him on that. He is, after all, the all-knowing, all-seeing, almighty God, creator of things seen and *unseen*. We have to trust that He knows best, no matter how big the disappointment or how illogical it seems. In these times He is saying, 'Trust Me, I know what I'm doing'. This is guidance. With so many people praying, particularly that final 'last push' of prayer for one and a half hours, it *has* to be God's will, 'Thy will be done'. This is God guiding us away from what we thought was the right path. We were going the wrong way, down the wrong road. This is how God changes our direction, how He corrects our course – guidance through prayer.

20 February 1990
Tuesday night, 11.38pm

I've had half a day off work today and put some damp sealant on that wall that won't dry out in the study. It appears to have worked. Praise God that at last I have found something that has done the trick. I've bought some lights and shades as well, that look really nice.

My wife is fully recovered from her flu, over a week after she went down with it. The children are coughing a bit, and our eldest aches today from a roller skating party yesterday.

23 February 1990
Friday night, 11.47pm

What a week for the weather. In February we are having beautiful spring days, warm and sunny. Last Tuesday night was the warmest February night ever recorded. It's so warm that even though the heating is switched on in the evening, the thermostat, which is set at sixty-five degrees, is not cutting in. The daffodils, crocuses and snowdrops are all out at the same time, and when the grass is dry I'll have to cut the lawn. I remember last year cutting the lawn in January.

My wife organised an evening out bowling at the new Superbowl today; eleven adults and five children. It was a good night with people from the church. Everyone came back to our house for supper. It's a further chance to get to know one another and do things together, other than go to church.

There is a warehouse and land up for rent at Weston, near Stafford: 6,360 sq. ft. including offices – plus the land, which, after going to see it, would suit us. It's not big enough to warehouse Jacuzzi and ourselves, but nevertheless the landlord, according to the estate agents, is going to extend it.

As usual I am impatient and already excited about it, which I shouldn't be as there is always more to do than you think; it takes time, and there are always snags. This time we are the first to register our interest, and we are dealing through someone we know at the estate agents, someone I believe will act just as much in our interests as in his client's. The landlord of the premises is a person whom I had a little tiff with a very long time ago. He has a van-hire company and once, when I hired a van, I didn't collect my mini car until about a week after I returned the van. He wanted to charge me a parking fee and I didn't want to pay. I hope he doesn't remember it or, if he does, won't hold it against me.

Lord Jesus, I very much pray, if it be Your will, for this unit. If this is the right one, then help and guide us to make the right moves. Help me not to be impatient (or is it impetuous?). Thank You that someone has already expressed the desire to take over most of our present yard if, or when, we move. I pray, Lord, that the Jacuzzi issue does not lose momentum because of us not getting the last units, which is inevitably causing delay. In Jesus' name I ask. Amen.

25 February 1990
Sunday morning, 1.40am

I'm very late-to-bed tonight. I would have been in bed by about 11.45pm, but I made the mistake of switching the TV on and getting interested in a science-fiction film that lasted until 1.15am. Although it held my attention, it has not benefited me at all – just a waste of time, really. Now I'll be tired tomorrow.

Lord Jesus, give me a good night's sleep (what's left of it). Protect our house and family and give us a really good day tomorrow. In Your name I ask. Amen.

27 February 1990

Tuesday night, 12.02am

Today I committed Transportomatic to having the unit at Weston to execute the Jacuzzi contract – which Chris, at Jacuzzi, informed me today we have got. Our quote has been accepted and a draft contract for us to look over will follow shortly.

The doubt comes in. I think to myself, 'Is this going to be another episode like the last units we tried to rent?' But no, we are first in line this time and the feeling is more positive because of this. The doubt is that this unit may not be big enough to house us and the Jacuzzi contract, meaning we would have to operate out of two separate sites, which would be inconvenient and costly.

But trust the Lord. Don't trust in the warehouse units, don't trust in solicitors, estate agents and landlords. Trust in the Lord – put Him first. I confessed, when we prayed with the vicar and his wife, that I had not put Jesus first. Now I must start putting Him first and the rest will come. 'Seek first the Kingdom of God... and all these things will be added to you' (Mat 6: 33). Lord, help me to put You first. I'll try not to worry too much over this contract and the workings of it – I'm not entirely convinced *how* it's going to work – but I know You, and can therefore do it somehow. Thank You, Jesus. Amen.

28 February 1990

Wednesday night, 12.30am

Problems! Problems! I knew we would hit snags with this unit at Weston. Our solicitor rang today, the estate agents won't give her the name of the landlord's solicitor and they're intimating that another interested party, who came into the picture after us, is now, for some reason, in front of us. So I've written to them asking for an explanation and dropped the letter in personally on the way home from work.

Oh Lord, I hate it when things like this happen. It's almost like being persecuted or someone has a grudge against me. It gets terribly personal. Shall I go and see the landlord and have a word with him directly or do I just leave it to You, Lord? When things like this happen, everything else seems to take second place. My wife invited lots of people 'round at teatime for a pancake, but this was on my mind so I couldn't get into it fully and it's still weighing heavily. I'm easily swayed, Lord, and my mind runs wild. I think now that we've lost the unit, that we're not good enough, that the landlord wants a 'better tenant'. Well, I haven't even had a chance yet; the landlord knows nothing about me. Oh, Lord Jesus, give me a chance on this or find something better quickly. in Your name I ask. Amen.

2 March 1990

Friday evening

Well, praise the Lord. What was I worrying about in the last entry?

Thursday morning, our man at the estate agents rang to say we could go ahead on the unit at Weston and the landlord had accepted us as prospective tenants. What a U-turn, praise the Lord, an answered prayer: all doom and gloom on Wednesday afternoon, all sweetness and light on Thursday morning – with a 7.30am church prayer meeting in between, when we prayed about it. Today I had a letter from the agents with a brief confirmation in writing.

Oh, Lord, I pray the bank reference to the landlord will be OK. They bounced a cheque today and stated in the letter that they will not tell me in future prior to them returning a cheque. I hope that doesn't mean they're going to be bouncing cheques willy-nilly; if there's anything that demoralises me at work, it's hassle from the bank. They have so much power when one is heavily in debt, like Transportomatic is. They could break the business just by calling the money in, which they are entitled to do at anytime.

I can remember in the past, in this journal, Transportomatic – business, in general – was rarely mentioned, but it weighs so heavily on my mind at the moment that it's nothing but; it's dominating my thoughts.

Oh, Lord Jesus, come into the foreground, take first place. Fill me with Your Holy Spirit, cleanse me and forgive me, and really, thank You again for what I've got. Thank You for a nice house, a family and wife, a business and friends. Help me to appreciate all these things. Amen.

3 March 1990
Saturday evening

Although I feel better now, the letter I got in the post at work this morning from the bank manager was yet another blow to add to previous ones.

What he said was in reply to a letter I had written, asking for continued support, especially during the start up of the Jacuzzi contract. He said without cash flow/profit forecasts and a host of other things, which are 'fundamental' – a word he used more than once – they could not offer their support. Indeed, he said they may be obliged to go the other way, which, to me, means they may be ready to pull the plug. What a thing to do when we are at last on the verge of a definite possibility of making a continuous profit. It wasn't only what he said, it was the 'tone' of the letter that was worrying: so negative and I'd say even malicious. It was as if the writer was taking it personally and fast losing patience with Transportomatic. It deflated me for the rest of the day. I was 'in a mood', as my youngest daughter says. I haven't been able to get it off my mind all day; one of those heavy burdens weighing me down, but as the day went on, it lightened. The Lord does not lift these off me instantly when I pray, but I'm sure He knows how much I can carry.

Nevertheless, at this moment, Lord, I am worried. I am worried the bank will give up on us and call the money in at the worst possible moment with the impending new contract. The thing that also worries me, regarding that letter from the bank, is that judging by the tone, it appears highly unlikely they will supply a good reference for our prospective landlord at Weston. This will really put the cat among the pigeons.

So Lord, I pray You have read all I have written. I know You probably cannot change the situation, but at least You can take the burden of worry off me. I lift it to You. Oh, Lord, fill me with Your Holy Spirit. Make me bold for Transportomatic against these setbacks. Help me to step out in faith and win. Fill me with expectation and renewed enthusiasm. In Jesus' name I ask. Amen.

4 March 1990
Sunday evening

Thank God for Sundays. Friendship with other Christians eases the anxiety and tension in our current business position at Transportomatic. Therapeutic, I suppose a psychiatrist would say. As a friend said to me at church today, 'Fellowship with other Christians is essential along the often difficult path with Christ'. When He seems so far away, it's often a word from another Christian that says, 'I *am* with you, trust Me, do not be afraid'.

I stood in at Sunday school today. Psalm 23 was central to the teaching. I feel as though I am walking through 'the valley of the shadow of death' at work, especially when the bank communicates with me such as yesterday morning. But when these things weight heavyly on my mind, then the Christian life on a Sunday helps me to put it all in perspective.

9 March 1990
Friday evening

What beautiful spring days we are having – sunny and fresh. Praise the Lord for the goodness of His creation and how we enjoy it.

Jill, in the office, left last Friday. Jeff and I have been managing on our own so far. Leena, whom I know from a firm that used to be one of our clients, came to see us on Tuesday about coming to work for us. She's going to let us know. Bob, a driver, gave his notice on Monday, so I'm interviewing tomorrow for his replacement. A female friend from church is popping in to help out with job sheets now and again until we get a replacement for Jill. I pray, Lord Jesus, that during this time of interviewing you give me wisdom and discernment to decide on the right person.

It so happens that – although we have not finalised the figures for February – it is going to be the best month we have had for a long time, which is most unusual for this time of year, being traditionally slack. Praise You, Lord, for this and thank You. How the feeling of optimism comes over me when the sales figures increase. I pray, Father, that by the power of Your Holy Spirit we start to be consistently higher in our sales.

Last week – week ending 3 March –, I made an appointment with my accountant for 2.30pm on Monday. His office rang on the morning of the appointment to say he was ill, so I asked to see one of his senior partners, which was OK. I was pleased about this, because this particular senior partner is a Christian. It was good to tell him we had been praying about the business and the Lord was working, something my usual unbelieving accountant would probably not have appreciated – for when the figures run out for bank managers and accountants, there's nothing left. But for Christians there is something else. There is faith in the Lord Jesus to put the business right. Transportomatic's viable figures ran out a long time ago. Thereafter faith took over, which has sustained us throughout this period, and now we are beginning to see that faith being honoured by God. Unfortunately, the bank manager's faith in figures ran out recently, and now I believe his patience has run out – judging by that letter, which still weighs heavily on my mind.

This is why it's good to see a Christian accountant – I believe You fixed that meeting for me, Lord. I showed the bank's letter to him. Thank You, Lord, that he knows our bank manager personally and that he is going to phone him up and make sure we get a good reference from him for the unit at Weston. Thank You that he is going to prepare cash flow and profit forecasts and supply the bank with accounts once we have cleared February's figures. I felt much better when I left him, that he had seen things from a Christian point of view. Praise the Lord he knew about that faith in Christ that can instil the conviction of business confidence in the future.

I think when it comes to confidence in the future, Lord, I may go over the top. A sales rep from our local Mercedes Truck Dealer came to see me this week – only a social call. His car was a Mercedes 190D, like the one we've just sold to pay a tax bill, but it was black and an 'E' registration – really nice. He said it was coming up for sale shortly. Oh, Lord Jesus, how I am tempted to buy it. I asked him to find out how much it was and let me know when it was available. Was that a bit daft, Lord, considering I still haven't paid my VAT for the end of November, I owe about three months' PAYE/NIC, have a personal tax bill of £8,000 – though my accountant now tells me not to pay this, pending an appeal – and still owe my Dad the £8,000 I borrowed off him last year to pay another tax bill? Temptation has been put in my way in the form of a black hunk of metal with Mercedes written on it. I thought to have it on a three-year lease, thereby not paying much down and meaning we would have to keep it three years – the longest ever we would have kept a car. Well, Lord, if it be Your will, I'll pursue the matter. If it's a daft thing to do, then give me a sign. From a financial point of view it seems extravagant, but You know the future, so block it if it's not meant to be. Balaam's donkey comes to mind on this one, Lord (Num. 22: 21-35). I'm tired now – it's 11.46pm. Goodnight.

10 March 1990

Saturday evening

I've been interviewing today, Lord. There has been no one who I would say is wholly suitable for the job, although I have only seen four people and weeded some out on the phone. I'm dreading taking someone on who isn't going to be very good and therefore going to have to leave after a while, resulting in me going through the whole process again. But such are the things that go with being an employer. No call from Jeff Dimmock yet about the driving job I've offered him, but Leena has called – who is a prospective replacement for Jill. She wants details of the pension scheme before making a decision.

I'm tired. Goodnight, Lord.

13 March 1990

Tuesday evening, 10.09pm

Thank You, Lord, for showing me You are with me today:

1. I prayed on the way to the bank that they would let me have a bankers' draft for the VAT. It was important. If I didn't pay today, they would come with the bailiff tomorrow. You didn't let me down Lord – they gave me the money.

2. In today's post we received the draft contract from Jacuzzi, an answered prayer confirmed. Thank You, Jesus, and forgive me for not having more faith.

3. Leena rang me this evening to accept the job in the office. She'll start on 23 April, after we come back from Spring Harvest. Thank You, Jesus. I pray for her to come to know the business, and You also.

Thank You, Jesus, for showing You are with me after my doubtful times that come over me quite often. Continue to show You are with me, Lord. Help me to recognise the signs, open my eyes and ears to Your will and teach me to trust. Help me to count my blessings: our middle daughter's birthday party today; Lucy, from church, helping us out in the office; my wife doing Christian drama in schools; a beautiful spring day yesterday; and house groups. Thank You, Lord, that I was invited to play my guitar at Ken's house group tonight and thank You for giving my guitar playing back to me after fifteen years of not even picking one up before I knew You.

Please stay with me, in Jesus' name. Amen.

15 March 1990

Thursday night,midnight

With all the early mornings this week, I'm getting tired and run down. There's a lot to do at work, so a lot of hours are needed. I'm doing Jill's job as well, plus the extra work created by interviews, wage-rate changes and getting the end of February figures out, so accounts can be prepared for the bank. Despite this, I am quite enjoying the business and thanking the Lord for the gift of work. He is starting to do a wonderful thing here, praise Him.

As mentioned in the last entry we have the draft contract from Jacuzzi, an answered prayer, but most amazingly, the sales figures for February, traditionally a slack month, are way up on previous months – in fact, £4,000 better than any other month in the current trading year. On seeing this, I must admit, my immediate thought was maybe Jill had entered a figure into the computer of say, £4,000 instead of £400 on the sales invoice ledger postings. I have not checked yet, but it is only a slight chance, so more than likely the figures are correct.

I feel like the priest in the film *The Miracle*. He preached the age of miracles was not dead, that miracles were still happening nowadays. Yet when God saw fit to use him as an instrument for a miracle, he refused to believe it. I've been praying for a miracle at Transportomatic – that God would turn the business around – with lots of other people; but now it's starting to happen, I'm having trouble believing it. I'm looking for earthly explanations; the same as that priest was convinced there would be a medical explanation after he healed a blind man. And I still think that it is probably only a 'flash in the pan' – a fluke month as regards the sales figures, that we'll be back to the normal low £20,000s in March instead of the low £30,000s, which is February's figure. I'm still thinking in terms of we might not finalise the Jacuzzi contract, that we won't actually sign and implement it. Who am I to talk about faith in the Lord Jesus Christ when I am so lacking in it myself? Lord, forgive me. Talk about living the victory life!

Lord, Jacuzzi are coming to see me tomorrow, so please be with me. Help me to be myself and not get anxious or nervous. I pray the key to the premises at Weston will be at the estate agents for me to collect; I have to show Jacuzzi round. There I go again – I haven't even enough faith to believe the key will be there. I put it down to all the let downs I've had in the past, when not a lot worked out as regards property and work. But the Lord won't let me down.

Chapter 5: A Scripture to hang on to.

21 March 1990
Wednesday evening, 7.45pm

I'm annoyed with the bank, Lord. They're bouncing cheques left, right and centre – and direct debits a few days ago – but today it was the rent cheque to our current landlord. Oh, Lord, bring the money in. Thank You that I was able to deposit £7,000 today from only three phone calls, but the PAYE/NIC taxman wants £8,000 by Friday and the self employed Schedule D tax is also due then; however, only the PAYE is on a distraint notice. These distraint notices and levies are getting to be every time now. We know the procedure off by heart, but the worry and anxiety never goes away. We are walking a tightrope. If we can just hang on until the Jacuzzi money starts flowing and get out and secure additional work on top of that, we'll be OK. I know you're looking after me, Lord, but just to tell myself that and trust in Your word is so difficult.

After being shown this Scripture by a church member on 5 February, the vicar today has given me the exact same one, and I know it's You speaking, Lord:

> Israel, the Lord who created you says,
> 'Do not be afraid – I will save you.
> I have called you by name, you are mine.
> When you pass through deep waters, I will be with you.
> Your troubles will not overwhelm you.
> When you pass through the fire, you will not be burnt.
> The hard trials that come will not hurt you.'
> Isa. 43: 1-2 (Good News Bible)

The vicar was talking to me at this morning's prayer meeting. I said I was finding it difficult to pray and be an active Christian with all this business pressure on me. He said, 'As long as I can hang on to a piece of Scripture'.

Well, Lord, I hang on to this one, particularly verse two: 'When you pass through deep waters I will be with you, your troubles will not overwhelm you. When you pass through the fire you will not be burnt, the hard trials that come will not hurt you'.

When you don't feel like praying, and can't get into your Bible; when you think God is far away and you can't see Him through all the confusion, worry and anxiety; when everything except God takes priority in your mind – keep fellowship with other Christians and ask *them* to pray for you. This is what I'm doing. This is part of the meaning of the 'body of the church' (1 Cor. 12: 12). When part of the body hangs limp and is inactive (me), the rest of the body compensates and works that little bit harder until the limp part is restored. Through the rest of the body, Jesus will heal that part. This is done through prayer, encouragement and friendship support. If the Bible isn't speaking to you any more, as long as you have fellowship with other Christians, He will speak through them. God spoke to me through a church member on 5 February – who first showed me this Scripture – which today has been confirmed by the vicar.

If you've stopped attending church because you're going through a bad patch, you feel God's not with you anymore or for a hundred other different reasons, you will not come back to God by staying away. If you want to meet with someone, you turn up – you don't stay away. Get an appointment with God and keep it! If you don't keep an appointment with the doctor, you don't get healed.

Nor is your medication instant. We may get instant relief, but usually not – it can take a while. So it is with God. We have to be ministered to over a period of time; quite often we have to be healed in stages – slowly. Powerful remedies are available, but usually our bodies cannot take it all at once, so it's only metered out according to how much we can cope with. So it is with God's remedies for us. When we have a cold or tummy bug, it may be quite normal to do nothing. Just ride it out and the body will fight it with its own natural resources. So it is sometimes in the church body. If we're spiritually not well, we just ride the storm while the church's body of natural and supernatural resources fights it with prayer, encouragement, fellowship and practical help. But whatever you do, *don't stay away!*

I've just 'been there' lately; not taken in a lot at services or prayer meetings, even had a few short dozes in prayer times – who knows whether you're asleep or praying? – needed matchsticks for my eyes in some sermons... but at least I'm there. If you're faithful, He'll act in His time. He already may well be acting, but you're too far away from Him to notice. Often it's only on reflection and hindsight you realise He was acting all the time, when you look back on that barren, desolate time. Only then do you see what He did, when at the time it was as if He wasn't there, that nothing was happening.

I read *Footprints*; the man, when looking back over his life, says to God, 'You were walking by my side for most of my life, Lord, but in those times of anxiety, worry and confusion, when I needed You most, there was only one set of footprints, You were not there'. God replies, 'You are right my son, in those troubled times I was not by your side. There is only one set of footprints in those times because I was carrying you'.

I pray, Lord, this is so with me. No – I *know*, Lord, this is so with me, praise You.

24 March 1990

Saturday evening

Despite the debt problems at work I praise on – not 'plod on', as our previous vicar said. I get panicked and frightened after things have just happened. Today I had an awful twinge of it when the tax collector rang me asking for £8,266, the personal tax I've owed since 1 January. But as the day goes on, it fades a bit and doesn't *totally* occupy my mind. I haven't paid the PAYE/NIC yet because I'm still way over my overdraft limit, despite banking quite a lot of money in the last week. I'll try again on Monday, Lord, after banking some more.

My wife and I are in a drama at the Mother's Day service tomorrow, my acting debut. Please, Lord Jesus, whatever You do, don't let me forget my lines and don't let the other three forget theirs. I just claim that drama for You, for Your glory. In Jesus' name. Amen.

29 March 1990
Thursday evening, 11.55pm

Thank You, Lord, that I didn't forget my lines on Sunday. All went according to plan and I pray it spoke to people. Because it went OK, I'm all keen on drama now.

Thank You for another answered prayer. I went to the bank on Monday to ask for a draft for all the tax due to PAYE/NIC knowing full well I was over my overdraft limit and, after a tense wait while the cashier consulted the manager, I got all £8,046 – another hurdle down.

Also, Lord, I still pray for those warehouse units at Weston to be ours. It's not moving very quickly due to a few snags on their part, such as the fact that no one can supply any plans to draw the boundaries on and another snag which may become a major obstacle: the prospective landlord's solicitors have asked for up-to-date accounts – no more than six months old – to prove our financial stability. Well, Lord, You know how shaky our present finances are; our last two sets of accounts are awful. On paper we are insolvent to the amount of about £35,000. I pray, despite this, we get those units soon, although I know everything is in *Your* time. Please give me a sign that everything is OK.

You've just shown me that Scripture that came up tonight in house group – John 16: 33, 'I have told you this so that you will have peace by being united to Me. The world will make you suffer, but be brave, I have defeated the world' (GNB).

1 April 1990
Sunday evening, 11.18pm

Thank You, Lord, for what I believe will prove to be a fruitful weekend on an Evangelising course. Courses are only theory, the fruit is in the practice which is yet to come, but with Your help and Holy Spirit to guide me, I am confident and convinced enough on a long-term basis to say it is not a case of 'I've just come back from the course so I'm all fired up'. I pray I will feel the same next month or next year.

At one point, on the course, it was quite amusing. You mix with about twenty-eight other people – all dressed fairly casually – not realising there are quite a few vicars and their wives, and, unless you ask, you don't know who is who. I couldn't help smiling when someone came up to me and asked if I was a vicar. Me! Very funny.

Back to work tomorrow, Lord, after my 'escape' weekend. Thank You that Jeff looked after the business, I pray everything went according to plan. I pray I can get up early in the morning and get stuck into work, taking all the knocks and bombshells with grace and calm. Please send some money in the post or help me to phone people to send us cheques. In Jesus' name I ask. Amen.

8 April 1990
Sunday night, 11.25pm

It's my birthday tomorrow – 43 – and our thirteenth wedding anniversary. I've got the day off, more because I've got some turf I want to lay, not because it's my birthday. I'm thinking I will probably have to go to work at odd hours this week, in addition to normal hours, to get all business duties wrapped up before we go to Spring Harvest next Saturday. I pray, Lord, you will give me enough time to get everything done; thank You, Lord, that I did plenty last week.

13 April 1990
Friday evening

We're off to Spring Harvest at Skegness tomorrow. Praise You, Lord, that it hasn't been too much of a last-minute rush to get everything done at work. There are still things to do before Monday 23 April, but I have next Saturday and Sunday to do those as we're back from Spring Harvest on Friday. I pray, Lord, that Jeff will cope with the business while I'm away. I ask in particular that the bank will let him have the wages and that he is not embarrassed in any way if they decide to start bouncing cheques.

I ask, Lord, that money comes in to pay the outgoing cheques that are in the system. Amen.

I have to lean on Jesus more at the moment. We are still in grave financial trouble at work but, like before, we now have nothing left to sell to pay overheads. The last thing that went was the car, to pay a tax bill. All that is left is the house... but that's wrong, isn't it? – we have Jesus. Thank God I'm a Christian! When all the figures run out, I have faith. That's all we have left, faith in Jesus Christ to supply our next payments, faith the income from work will increase enough to pay the PAYE/NIC and the next VAT bill (due now).

Is it stupidity that we are moving forward at work, wanting another wagon and more staff, refurbishing and painting an existing wagon? Or is it faith in the future? We carry on spending money we haven't got, assuming we will have it in the future, when the bills are due. I've just been looking for the passage of Scripture that says, 'When You ask in Jesus' name, believe you have received it and it shall be yours'. I couldn't find it. Is that what I'm doing? I believe so much that Jesus is not going to let the business go down, and that when I ask in my prayers for more work, I believe that we will get it, so I spend accordingly and trust in the Lord that we'll have the money to pay. Or am I being stupid?

15 April 1990
Easter Sunday afternoon, 12.30pm

We're at Spring Harvest and I'm sitting in chalet Number BF26, feet freezing; yet another icy wind for the third year running.

As soon as I arrived here, particularly last night, I wanted to go straight back home. This unexpected feeling can be put down to a few things:

1. The drab, sparse, tatty, cold chalet we're in. A far cry from the centrally heated comfortable home I live in (how well the children adapt, not a single moan from them).

2. I dread facing seminars and crowds of other Christians milling around. I want peace and quiet, a proper holiday doing nothing. I'm not ready

for all the input, sharing and praising the Lord. I don't want to mix. Last night I was quite determined not to go to any seminars at all.

3. The transition from working late Friday night straight to Spring Harvest Saturday morning is too quick; I haven't had a period to 'wind down'.

I think it is a combination of all three. However, I am attending things and made up my mind to go to the main seminar for 'Daily Mail readers' (middle of the road). I am not going with enthusiasm, more an attitude of 'Well, I'm here so I might as well go!' Lord, I ask as the hours go by, You will slot me in to the proceedings. Ease me in to become an integral part of this event. Amen.

15 April 1990
Sunday night, 10.42pm

I went to the main seminar today, from 2.15pm to 3.45pm, and enjoyed it. I went to the 'Alternative Celebration', from 7.15pm to 9.45pm, and enjoyed it. The Lord filled me with His Holy Spirit. I asked in worship for Him to put the business burdens out of my mind, so I off-loaded the lot on to Jesus and He filled the space. I went all hot and tingly. It was a very business-like filling to take the place of a business-like gap. He has started to work on me. I'm now glad I'm here despite the cold winds, primitive chalet and strange bed. Thanks be to God, Who is giving me the victory over my troubled mind. Amen.

20 April 1990
Friday night, 11.40pm

I'm back home; just slipped into my own cosy bed, enthused at the thought of my first decent night's sleep for a week.

After Spring Harvest I do not feel a lot different than when I went, but to me that is not a particular disappointment. The word I am looking for is sustenance – I've had sustenance, not a feast after a long period without food. I thank God that Spring Harvest has not been an injection into my spirit to keep me burning until it goes out. It's been more like a visit to the doctor's to check the long-term treatment is correct, a confirmation that no U-turn, deviation or drastic action is necessary. God has said, 'Keep taking the tablets, but do not doubt that what I am giving you is right. Remember, you will feel ill if you do not read my word and pray'. Over this last week, He has said praying and reading the Bible is not enough, *doing* is His will. Doing. Action. So tonight we prayed – downstairs this time, not in the lazy bed position – for forgiveness for not *doing*. We prayed for forgiveness for not praying. Not once did we pray together at Spring Harvest – not once, out of all that receiving of the word, worship and Holy Spirit, did we give anything back. We talked *about* God, we read His word, we sang about God, we listened about God, but not once in our chalet did we *talk* to God. But His grace is so abundant, He loves us so much, He still wants to pour out His Spirit on us.

22 April 1990
Monday night, 11.25pm

We prayed with our eldest daughter at teatime, as she's a bit ill: she's tired and has a headache. I failed, at first, by going up to my bedroom and praying on my own. My wife suggested we pray *with* her. Our new motto is 'don't think or talk, *do*'.

We were told by our solicitor today that the landlord of the unit at Weston we were supposed to be leasing wants to pull out. It wasn't the blow to my expectations I thought it would be, having solely relied on that to execute the upcoming Jacuzzi contract. Jacuzzi are not happy, although they had a sense of humour about it. I pray, Lord, they will hang on. On hearing this bad news I went straight out to see Morgan James, the owner of new warehouses at Ladfordfields Industrial Estate, and hey, *presto*, he has 7,200 sq. ft. to rent – not ready till the end of June, though.

The irony is these are the first units we looked at months ago, and they hadn't even started building them. There was nothing to look at except a pile of steel girders on the ground, so we didn't bother – and this was as far back as last October. The incident never even got a mention in this journal, it was seemingly so insignificant. Probably this is the Lord's way of saying, 'This is what happens when you don't keep hold of what I first give you. You deviate and go off the path and end up where you first started, so why bother straying in the first place – keep faithful and hang on'.

That's all I'm doing with the business, hanging on and having faith that we will eventually start making a consistent profit. If we had not had bank charges deducted in March, we *would* have made a profit. As it was, we lost about £3,500. But praise the Lord, everything is a gift from God, including business losses. There's a purpose behind it all somewhere. The devil would say, 'Yes, the purpose is to go bust', but the Lord would say, 'It's to test your faith, deepen your faith in my promise that no matter what happens, I will be with you, do not worry'. How difficult that is when cheques are bouncing everywhere. We cannot obtain our spare vehicle parts on credit anymore. We are on a 30% surcharge with the VAT now. We only write cheques to silence suppliers who are screaming for their money in the *hope* money will come in to pay them. Direct debits are not being paid, and I'm wondering when the bank will refuse to allow us to draw the wages. To keep going under the banner of hope and expectation is very difficult.

As of 31 March 1990, our equity was minus £35,000 – which means I would have to pay someone to take the business off my hands. Can God really reverse this situation in time, before the bank pulls out or I lose my nerve? What a mess it all is. Is God *really* going to get in there and sort it out?

The bank manager wants to see me on Friday – what does *he* want? Is he going to call the money in or is he going to get right behind us and support us? To be sure, the present situation is not satisfactory, with cheques being bounced indiscriminately, a total inconsistency of actions. They always take their interest and charges out without fail – more than £4,000 this quarter in interest alone. The overdraft now stands at £82,000.

14 June 1990

Thursday night, 10.20pm

A lot's happened during the time I haven't filled in this journal. To name three things:

1. The meeting with the bank manager mentioned in the last entry was good news and bad news, but either way not what I expected. He wants to send financial planners into the business to give a report on our 'position'. I suppose that's good news. The bad news is we've got to pay for it. When they're lending money to you to the tune of £82,000 you have to agree to that.

2. The vicar has designated me to spearhead evangelism in our church – *me* – using the 'Down Your Street' course as a basis.

We've had a team in James and Linda's house in Baxter Green doing the course with them. Tonight was the last one. We have been in once a week for seven weeks.

No commitment has been forthcoming off either of them, but it's been well worthwhile, a good experience for both us and them. You really have to trust in the Holy Spirit, as the response sometimes is almost nil, and some of the course is very heavy going. On the occasions when there is no response, you would think that dismay would set in, but it doesn't: the Lord blesses just for obeying. Maybe my disagreement with a comment someone made once that 'We are not called to be successful, we are called to obey', is changing. We are called to tell the good news, the Holy Spirit convinces and converts, and if a conversion does not happen, then it means the time is not right for them. As long as they know a little bit more than they did before, then they are a little closer to Jesus. And that's something to rejoice about – thank You, Lord, for the opportunity to go and visit. We need another house now, please, to keep the ball rolling; we don't want the evangelistic effort to fizzle out. Please, Lord Jesus, find another house for us to visit and, incidentally, find us another bank to bank with (that's a story for another day). Amen.

16 June 1990
Saturday night, 10.45pm

We have a new car; well, a second-hand new car. A 'Y' registration Fiat Uno, and the story of how we got it is worth telling – it's a tale of the Lord's doing.

For some time I have thought about selling the Morris Minor, as it uses a lot of oil, the exhaust fumes smell awful, no seat belts are fitted, and it's nearly thirty years old. Sooner or later, something major is going to go wrong, so let's sell it. Since buying the Mini off my old secretary, I have come to like it so much I thought another Mini would be nice. Ben, our mechanic, and I went to look at two: one in Burntwood for £725 ('V' reg.), and one at Strongford Garage for £950 ('Y' or 'A' reg.). For some reason, £850 was on my mind as a figure to pay. These cars were OK, but not really a good buy as regards bodywork, and both had high mileages. I said to Ben I'd look in the Newsletter, the local paper, early Friday morning (8 June, that would be), get up early and start phoning, which is the only way to catch the good buys. But I didn't get up early; I got up at the normal time. As I was pulling into the yard, at work, parked on the street right in front of me waiting for the garage next door to open, was a Fiat Uno with a sign in the window 'FOR SALE £850 TEL. 44414'. I couldn't believe it! I knew straight away this was it. I asked the owner to drive it over our inspection pit for Ben to look at. He said it was in good condition for the year. The owner brought the documents 'round later that day. I offered him £800, which he accepted.

Later on I went home for lunch, and on opening the post there was a cheque from the taxman payable to *me,* not the business, for £547; for what, I do not know – must have been my accountant, working behind the scenes. That went most of the way to buying the Fiat. Now, I thought, all we have to do is sell the Morris Minor. The handbook for the Fiat was in a plastic-covered wallet with the name of the original garage in Hereford where it was bought. On the front cover, in large letters, it read 'GODSELLS', which must have been the name of the garage. Yesterday we advertised the Morris in the Newsletter. Last night we sold it for £800 – the man brought the money 'round this morning. That's God working!

Chapter 6: Is the dream dying?

2 September 1990
Sunday night

Again, how often it has slipped my mind to purchase a new blank book to write this Journal. The last entry 16 June – two and a half months without a page filled in.

Things have gone from bad to worse or, more precisely, worse to disastrous. The business financial position is possibly at the point of no return. £60,000 in the red if everything was sold and all money owed paid out, and all money I personally owe paid out, which means this house would have to be sold to pay off the balance. But, praise God, we have resigned ourselves to this reality. If it's God's will it will happen, if it isn't, it won't. What a stressful time in the meantime!

I dare not write a cheque against the current bank account, they are *all* bounced. We pay our bills cash, banker's draft or postal order. All credit worthiness has gone with our suppliers. It's cash or banker's draft when the goods are bought or we get no goods. We've been threatened with various court actions. The biggest threat is potentially from the taxman – VAT, PAYE and NIC. I have asked for an arrangement with the VAT, but no response yet. £500 per week has been arranged with the tax collector to pay arrears off, which puts us further behind as the current wage bill runs up £1,000 a week due to them. I have a summons threatened for personal tax and capital gains tax if not paid by 5 September, in three days' time. Needless to say, I haven't got the money. We have written to various leasing companies to release us from mobile phone leasing agreements, as we cannot afford to pay them. The phones are already out of the trucks because we can't afford the calls.

Jeff, my good friend and right-hand man, has had to go; we could no longer justify paying him. Redundancy was the only course of action, costing me more in the short term. This means most of his work falls on to me, though Leena will handle some and Paul is doing route-planning in the week.

We have had two engines blow up in as many weeks, which couldn't have come at a worse time. We struggled to pay for one replacement, but cannot afford the other yet; so we have a wagon sitting doing nothing.

In the meantime, the bills mount up, the overdraft goes up, my stress and anxiety goes up and up and up.

Jeff left in June, and by August I'd had enough. I just had to get away. So last week we all went off, spontaneously, to North Wales in one of the wagons (one of the drivers said he'd have a holiday, so there was one available for us to take). It's amazing how a small truck can be converted into a motor caravan just by putting a few mattresses, an old carpet, a cupboard and a camping cooker in. We had a great time and the children loved it, but it wasn't long enough. And I'm now back at work. It starts all over again, only worse, as we get more and more into debt.

So I still ask myself, 'Why do I carry on? Why not say enough is enough?' A few months ago I would have answered, 'Because the Lord is going to turn the business around', but now I'm not so sure. Again, 'Is all this hassle the Lord telling me to pack it in?' The reading in church this morning was Matthew 11, which included verses 28–30: 'Come to Me all who labour and are heavy laden and I will give you rest'. I thought, 'That's a promise from God I could use'. So why don't I? Why don't I just throw it all away? Reasons are as follows:

1. Fear of the future. What will I do? I've done this for 18 years – I don't know anything else. I'm not trained in anything else. So I think, 'Go to Bible College, go on the dole', but that sort of income would not sustain the mortgage and the family. So these thoughts and counter-thoughts go 'round in my mind all the time.

2. It would be such a hassle on top of all the other hassle (which often brings me near to breaking point, without adding any extra).

3. The potential of the business has never been greater. OK, the Jacuzzi contract is still not signed – albeit imminent – and mirror work is starting soon (October/November) to B&Q; a lot more work, which I am confident will produce profits. Then again, is it going to be more hours worked and more hassle, or will going back to profit change my outlook and attitude to the business?

4. I'm sure pride comes into it, and we don't want to lose our material things. Jesus said to the rich man, 'Sell all your possessions and give them to the poor and then you will have treasures in heaven, then come and follow me', and the rich man went away sad. Maybe that's why I'm sad, because I won't give things up.

I'm also wallowing in a lot of self-pity. 'Woe is me, life is useless, it's all useless, chasing the wind', to quote Ecclesiastes. 'But it's a gift from God.' 'Some gift', I think – more like a millstone 'round my neck.

3 September 1990
Monday night

I've just said on the phone to Paul, at work, that one of our drivers will go to hell because he has built his own little world around him, which suits him, and he doesn't care about anyone except himself. SORRY, LORD, I SHOULDN'T HAVE SAID THAT. I picked up the Bible later on, and in Jas. 2: 1, the first bit I read was, 'My brethren, show no partiality as you hold the faith of our Lord Jesus Christ'. A slap across the face for me! And there is always, 'Do not judge others', and 'Take the log out of your own eye before you take the speck out of your brother's eye' (Mat. 7: 1-5)

Considering I wasn't looking forward to going back to work today, it hasn't been bad at all. I had to go to work yesterday afternoon also, which ran into the evening, so I missed the evening praise service. Working on Sunday? Personally, I don't have any sympathy with the Lord's Day Observance people, but I do nevertheless, feel a little guilty. God doesn't mind, really – I don't think – if it's a necessity.

4 September 1990
Tuesday evening

The pattern develops in one's mind. Sometimes it's a neat orderly one, with all the different pieces fitting together; but most of the time it's a jumbled mess. Sometimes I get visions of exactly how it could be, but most of the time it's lots of pieces I just can't fit together. My biggest problem, Lord, is discerning who makes the pattern. One way of looking at it is that You are Lord and Master of everything, so whoever makes it only does so with Your permission. So Father, if the evil one does get at me, it's only with Your permission, so I praise the Lord for everything. But do I?

Help me to think positive – to count my glass half full, not half empty, my mind as half intelligent, not half stupid, to be half expectant, not half apprehensive, to be half positive, not half negative. I seem to see the black side of everything these days, Lord. It's always doom and gloom, not the glimmer of hope I crave. Change my heart, Lord, change my attitude. Help me to give the benefit of the doubt; the encouragement, not the criticism. In Jesus' name I ask. Amen.

17 September 1990
Monday night

We made a crashing loss in August, a most depressing sight when viewed on the profit and loss sheet.

The bank would not let me draw cash to pay for fuel being delivered today. The fuel company came with 2,200 litres of diesel at 9.15am (fancy expecting me to have nearly £900 in my back pocket at that time on a Monday, when the bank doesn't open till 9.30am). They came again at 2.00pm. I still hadn't been to the bank, because of the busyness of the office. I went to the bank; they wouldn't give me the money in spite of me paying £2,000 in. The fuel man came back at 4.30pm, but I had to send him away – no money. No money for the phone bill – another £900 – and I told them I'd be sending it after I received a disconnection notice a few days ago. However, I did pay our domestic gas bill – after they came last Friday to cut us off but that was only £76.34.

Still, none of the aforementioned are comparable to what we owe other people, like £19,000 (PAYE/NIC), £15,000 (VAT – it'll only take *them* to pounce and that'll be it), £5,000 (capital gains), £1,200 personal tax

– still not paid with summons on their way for the last two because I didn't pay by 6 September so there will be court costs now as well. We cannot pay most of our suppliers. The ones we owe fairly large amounts to we are 'drip feeding': £500 there, £1,000 here, but usually not until they phone up asking for it. Our £85,000 overdraft – with a facility of £70,000 – is £15,000 over my limit. Creditors are more than my debtors. We're showing a loss of £7,600 in August, which makes a £17,000 total loss so far, only five months into the trading year. I can't pay the vehicle fleet insurance. The brokers are buying us time, but that can't be in place indefinitely. The mental pressure on me is enormous. People phone up everyday wanting money – most of them quite understanding – which piles the guilt on me. I owe many people as far back as March, a few from February, one as far back as January. Direct debits are constantly being dishonoured by the bank. I can't write cheques anymore, as they'll all bounce. My personal mortgage's direct debit has been dishonoured twice. My self-employed stamp hasn't been paid by the bank since June, according to a letter from the Social Security yesterday... and so it goes on.

In the meantime, more bills keep coming in; the wages have to be drawn every week (thank God the bank are still letting us draw the wages); and through all this I have to believe God is in control. Well, I surprise myself, because I really do believe He is! Actually, the bank is in control, but God is controlling the bank, *they* are there by the grace of God.

Sometimes I think, 'Where's your sense of humour, John?' But then I think, 'This is really not funny. But if God is in control, why are you worrying, why are you not at peace?' Well, because I'm human, with human feelings, and I don't yet know God enough to be 100% trusting in Him, and there's still a lot of the old self in me, which is why I feel very fearful quite often in these circumstances. Why not shake it all off, throw the towel in? Because if God has convinced me He is in control, to throw the towel in will be an act of defeat, of not trusting Him. To give up will be to give in to Satan's subtle taunts of taking the easy way out. Anyway, who will want to buy a business that has been losing money for two years? If I pay everything off and get all the money in now, according to the latest balance sheet I will still owe £68,000.

I reflect on the past and wonder where the future is going:

1970

I moved from Lincoln where, with my first wife, we lived for one year in a caravan, having previously come from Stafford. Lincoln was my base to tour the country playing in a soul band. We backed artists coming over from the USA – Mary Wells, The Ronettes and Sam the Sham, to name a few – but when that ceased and we were offered a summer residency in Rimini, Italy, I didn't fancy it and left. We towed our 18ft long caravan home (bought for £250) and all our possessions to Stafford behind a Landrover (not ours) and parked it on a 'caravan site' – basically a field with an electric cable and water pipe poking out of the grass.

I got a job as a sales engineer at a local diesel engine manufacturing plant – English Electric Diesels Ltd. During the time I was there I bought a red transit van to run a local band about in the evenings. A friend in the office knew someone who had just started a business. He wanted to get his goods delivered to various places throughout the country; I had a van that could do that. Initially I had days off 'sick' to do the work, but when the 'sickness' became too frequent to be credible I gave in my notice. The work built up and eventually I had enough money to put down a deposit on a brand new four-and-a-half-tonne Mercedes truck costing £2,700. I invented a name, 'Transportomatic', and had it sign-written on the truck, which I had painted orange and black – I wanted to be noticed. I was in my mid-twenties, rearing to go, and hooked.

To start with, I was happy with equalling the £28-a-week income I had in my previous job, and any I had left over was ploughed straight back into the business. We sold the caravan for £350, having now got enough income between us to buy a brand new three-bedroom detached house in Stafford for £6,500.

The problem was I was so engrossed in my ego and ambition to succeed that we never had any spare money – it all went back into the business. I slept, ate, and breathed Transportomatic. The garage, front room and hallway of our new house became the warehouse; the third bedroom, the office; the kitchen, the canteen; and the dining room, the staffroom where the only conversation was transport. We had little furniture, and many of the rooms were not decorated and had no carpets – I had no time to do this, and the money that would have been available for our home was being ploughed into the 'future'. I complained bitterly to my wife at any resistance to this lifestyle, accusing her of 'rebellion against the cause'. My selfishness soon infiltrated the romance and freshness of our marriage; sex became a relief from tension, not an act of love. We stopped our romantic evenings out for meals and down the pub. My wife now visited our friends alone and had to find female friends who would give her a social life – *I* was too busy building a business. Our arguments got more heated. I yelled a lot and, on odd occasions, lashed out in anger. We were going in opposite directions.

Eventually, I asked my wife to leave – my broken-down marriage was restricting my march forward into success and, in the game I was playing, she was on the wrong side. As far as I was concerned she had the wrong ideas, the wrong attitude, and I couldn't understand why she couldn't think like me and share my excitement and ambition. The house was sold for £11,250 and the equity split between us. After two years' separation we were divorced on the grounds of 'mutual agreement'. We had been married about five years, I think, but who was counting? The only thing I counted was money.

I was accused many times of being ruthless. This 'ruthless' image only served to inflate my ego; after all, wasn't being ruthless a necessary quality in the business world? I decided this was a part of my image I liked, and over the following years I proved it to myself many times by 'bulldozing' my way to where I wanted to be, treading over anyone who got in the way.

With my part of the equity left from the sale of the house I bought a flash car, a Marcos 3 litre – a sleek streak of red fibreglass that was fast. It hugged the road so close that the underneath grounded on the slightest ramp. I was fulfilling my image even more now. A successful businessman is not only ruthless; he has a fast car as well, doesn't he? If you want to be sleek, flash and fast, you need a car to match, don't you?

I thought the excitement and thrill I got out of having my own truck, business and fast car that *I* was attracted to would correspondingly attract other people – particularly the female kind. It did, but not my kind of people. I found out that cosmetic, false relationships founded on ego and materialism were not for me. Instead of being just plain John Clough, I was trying to fulfil and model a stereotype; in my image-building endeavour I was basically trying to fit a square peg into a round hole. I became disillusioned and went into a period of feeling down, searching for my identity.

I still enjoyed and fitted well into my business, but now I approached it from a different point of view. I started to get serious when I realised I had more than likely found my vocation in life. All I wanted to do now was give a good service that no other transport company could offer. I found a need that no one else seemed to be fulfilling and decided to exploit it as best I could. Fragile goods – no other transport service I knew could handle fragile goods without damaging them. *This* was my marketplace and I decided to target it.

As the other things I did were not 'the real me', I slipped into a period of about 12 months in which all I did was work. The rest of the time I just moped around, feeling unwanted and rejected, refusing to go any further than the bedroom when I was tired, the toilet when nature called, the bathroom when I smelled, the kitchen when I was hungry, and the lounge settee any other time.

At that time I was renting a house with my friend Rick Broker, and it was him who eventually persuaded me that I couldn't waste my spare time wallowing in self-pity (guess what he did for a living? Yes, he was a truck driver). He got me out of the house and into a social life once again, which I approached from a different angle this time, seeking relationships with *genuine* people.

1975

I met my wife. She was genuine. It was the last dance at a local Country Club. I was the only one without a partner, just sitting on my own waiting for my mate John White, who was on the floor (not literally) with a girl called Marissa. Then suddenly this voice said, 'Do you want to dance?' I looked up and there was this girl with long, straight hair and a smile. That was good enough for me (I liked girls with long, straight hair). We smooched through the last dance trying to talk over the voice of Rod

Stewart singing *I Am Sailing*, and eventually I got the message she wanted a lift home. What she didn't say was that the two girls she lived with also wanted a lift. So there I was with my friend John and three girls, and only a two-seater sports car outside. My powerful, flash 3 litre had, for the first time, become an embarrassment. I was driving, John was in the passenger seat with one girl sitting on his knee, and the other two girls sat on the gearbox cover with their heads out of the sunroof. To compound my embarrassment, every time I wanted to drive over one of the numerous speed ramps on the long driveway from the club, all the girls had to get out of the car – remember? 'The car hugged the road so well that the underneath got caught on the slightest ramp' – as the extra weight of three girls, slim as they were, made it impossible. It took us about fifteen minutes to drive 500 yds. Fortunately it was all a big laugh, and this humour was to typify our relationship in the future – which, at that time, we had no knowledge of. It wasn't long after that I sold the car. My girlfriend, as she was then, had a Morris Minor, which was much more fun. I shed the false for the genuine in my choice of cars, too.

After that first meeting, it was a long time before I saw her again, and that was only because she left her jacket in the boot of my car that night. Rick, whom I shared the house with, found it, thinking it was a rag of some sort – it didn't look *that* scruffy. He started to use it to check his car oil level before we both realised it was a jacket. I sheepishly took it back expecting a good telling-off and further embarrassment. But no, her sense of humour prevailed and she asked me to come to her house for Christmas dinner (she obviously subscribed to 'the way to a man's heart is through his stomach'). From then on we started seeing each other, and eventually rented a bed-sit. From the moment we started to fall in love, I began to change. The ruthlessness, ambition and ego didn't go away, but it mellowed and was strictly confined to business matters, not spilling over into our relationship. Unknowingly, she was beginning to 'tame' me, and I was quite willing to *be* tamed.

There is no substitute to falling in love. All the fulfilled ego trips, realised ambitions and material success in the world cannot compare with the surpassing beauty of falling in love. That's why kings and queens, captains of industry, politicians, pop stars, prime ministers and presidents – those who seemingly have achieved everything – have all, in many cases, given it up because they've fallen in love. They have all realised that their hearts' desire cannot be found in fulfilling ego, prestige and materially motivated ambitions. On a much smaller scale, I also, was beginning to realise this.

1977
We married.

1977
We bought a terraced house for £4,900 – a two-up two-down.

1980
Our first daughter was born. My wife gave up work as a nurse.

1983
Our second daughter was born.

1984
Our third daughter was born.

1985
We sold our terraced house for £14,900.

1985
We bought a four-bedroom detached house for £90,000. We put £30,000 cash down and borrowed £60,000 against very healthy business accounts. It was the most expensive house up for sale in Stafford at the time; I know because I went round all the estate agents – I was still a bit hooked by the status, prestige and money monster.

1985-1988
Extra land adjoining the house was bought for £5,000. We converted the house to five bedrooms, spending large sums on improvements, including extra car parking and landscaping, and we bought a white Mercedes car. All these were purchased in cash – the money from the business was rolling in.

Yes, the money was rolling in and it seemed to be just falling into our lap. Sometimes I couldn't believe it. The first twelve months in that house was like having a whole hotel set in its own grounds to ourselves – to us, it was huge. Not only had I achieved material success, I also had a lovely wife and three beautiful daughters. The goals I had set myself had been achieved and my ambitions fulfilled. That single orange and black van with Transportomatic written on it thirteen years ago had now multiplied to sixteen, but bigger and better. Sixteen trucks of mine were speeding up and down motorways nationwide delivering fragile goods at a level of service second to none.

We were the best, and my reward was all around me: a big house in parkland; two cars; a gorgeous wife and family; holidays in Switzerland, Austria, the Canary Islands; prestige and recognition... We could buy anything we wanted – a dream come true.

On the surface, everything was there. In 1972 I'd had the vision of the picture on the completed jigsaw puzzle and, over the years, I had fitted it together: piece by piece, starting with the easy framework round the edges, and gradually filling in the more complicated and sophisticated parts, as the business got more and more specialised.

I remember my wife liked doing jigsaw puzzles when I first met her – BIG jigsaw puzzles. When we moved into our rented bed-sit, our floor was largely taken up with a 6 x 4 ft. piece of board on which was a 5,000-piece jigsaw in the process of being completed. When we weren't doing it, we pushed it under the bed because it was so large. It took us months and months to do, in our spare time. As we got nearer and nearer to completion, we got more and more excited. We would anticipate the day it would be finished, watching the picture build up as we laboured over that board, week after week. The day came. It was the end of a marathon; we only had a few more pieces left. The last piece we had in the box was finally put into place. Now we could get off our knees, straighten our aching backs, stand up and view the masterpiece from a distance. We could look back over those weeks and months, crawling around on our hands and knees with our eyes close to the board searching for pieces of sky, grass, flowers, snow, trees and buildings and say 'That's it, it's complete – we've finished!' It looked good; in fact, it looked magnificent!

But 'wait a minute,' we said, 'isn't that a piece of sky missing towards the top right-hand corner?' And 'Look at the old cart, there's a piece missing that makes up the wheel! Oh no!! We must have lost a piece or two along the way!'

The trouble is, you don't know you're a piece short until you've finished – or think you've finished. The reward for all that labour crawling around on our hands and knees was not complete. Although we could admire the picture in all its splendour, there was still a piece or two missing, and it tainted the completeness. In fact, it was not complete at all. We might as well have lost twenty pieces than one or two. The achievement soon gives way to disappointment. Although you could hardly notice, it wasn't the same without them.

As I admired my material rewards all around me for my past labours in the business, magnificent as they were, there was something missing. I thought I had got all the pieces together, and fitted them in to make the picture which fulfilled my vision in 1972; but there was still a piece missing which was not in my possession. Like that jigsaw piece, maybe there was something I had missed or lost on the way. It was almost as if, while I had been reaching and striving for that goal in front of me, what was important had slipped away. If that was the case then, like a missing jigsaw piece, all I had to do was find it and fit it in. It annoyed me, just like the annoyance of a missing jigsaw piece.

It was from that point that, subconsciously, I believe I started to ask ultimate questions about life, and its meaning and purpose. What else do you do when you appear to have covered all angles from all directions, then you find you haven't and can't fathom what it is or where you've missed something that appears to be missing? When I say 'ultimate questions', I mean the sort of questions that make us uncomfortable because we really don't like to ask them at all, so we don't openly do so. We shut them up in our mind and ask inwardly. Only one person hears those questions – the person of Jesus Christ.

1987

I became a Christian.

1988

Land purchased for £15,000 in 1984, sold for £40,000.

1988

An additional three-bedroom terraced house was purchased for £35,000 cash. Four students occupy the house, giving an annual income of approx. £3,000-£5,000. Any surplus was put into the business bank account.

1988

A four-bedroom 17th century cottage bought for £135,000 with a bridging loan from the bank.

1989

The five-bedroom, two-bathroom house, purchased for £90,000 in 1985 sold for £200,000. The £135,000 bridging loan plus £15,000 interest repaid to the bank. The £30,000 mortgage on the sold house redeemed and reissued against the cottage property. £70,000 put into the business bank account.

1989

The terraced rental house sold for £38,000. All this money goes into the business bank account.

1990

All the surplus money from the three property sales – totalling £113,000 – put into the business bank account is now all gone.

I seriously face the prospect that all my previous hard work and dedication resulting in all the material and financial reward I ever wanted, has now been lost – and that my dream is dying.

Chapter 7: Is God in control? I'm losing it.

18 September 1990
Tuesday night

Lord, thank You for my wife. She felt the need to go and see our eldest daughter's teacher at school. Taking an R.E. lesson, he was reading the Bible from Genesis, while at the same time saying it was a load of rubbish and he didn't believe it. He then proceeded to give his own personal opinion of how the world was created, and this to young impressionable children who really take note of what their teacher says – very dodgy. She went in to see him this morning and asked how he can be qualified to take an R.E. lesson when he doesn't believe in the Bible.

He believes we are all here by chance. So did I! As little as four years ago, I would have whole-heartedly agreed with him. How the Holy Spirit changes our attitude and thinking. 'Do not conform yourselves to the pattern of this world but transform yourselves by a complete change of your mind', says Rom. 12: 2. That's what happened to me and it's still happening – sanctification, I think it's called; taking off the old, putting on the new.

Thank You, Lord, that today I received some money to pay for the fuel, and enough to pay the three phone bills as well. Today I received a demand from the VAT for £18,000. Basically, it's 'pay or have goods removed and sold to pay for the amount due'. As I said the other day, 'If God is in control, why worry?' I should be at peace, but I'm not: I am worried, sometimes panicking. I can't pay, of course, so theoretically the goods go, but in my heart I know it won't come to that. I know we'll be saved. How, I do not know; without a miracle, the situation looks hopeless – so I believe in miracles!

The bank's financial planners are coming in to work tomorrow to commence their plan of action to 'rescue' us. It's cost me £500 so far and will cost another £800 for the next four weeks. I've no idea what they are going to do. The only person who is going to rescue us in the end is the Lord Jesus, Whose plan of action is already in place. It costs me nothing, but it cost Him His life. The latter is by far the better deal, so I'll go for that one. The bank can have the other; that's the sort of plan they'll go for.

21 September 1990
Friday night

Demands from the taxman again. We owe £18,000 to the VAT and now another £18,000 for PAYE/NIC. We believe, as they have already indicated, that we can come to an arrangement with the tax collector for the PAYE/NIC arrears. I have already spoken to the big boss who is, so far, responding to the stop-gap we need.

The VAT is a different kettle of fish. We owe them £18,000 for two VAT periods plus 30%, the maximum surcharge. I spoke to the person responsible at the VAT enforcement office – after writing a letter weeks ago, with no response – and he says, 'It is not the Customs and Excise policy to make arrangements to pay. The next step is distraint on your goods and then procedure to bankruptcy if payment is not made'. No mercy there then – even if it means shutting the business down and putting fifteen people on the dole.

Last night I had a message to ring a friend, who is a member of our church and a close brother in Christ, re-born a year or so before me. I didn't get a chance to phone him back, as my wife and I went to a Christian seminar at Stoke-on-Trent about 'Marriage Under Pressure'; not that *our* marriage is under pressure, but is was good and challenging. The seminar I need is 'Business under Pressure'. Anyway, I digress. Our financial planner, Steve, paid us his second four-hour visit today, and we both agreed, in our quest to buy time from our creditors, that the VAT demand for immediate payment was a priority and rather worrying, to say the least. What would be the point of the bank and the tax collector giving us time if the VAT were not willing to do the same? Either one of them could bankrupt the business, so all three had to play ball at the same time. How do we get out of this one? Enter God.

Something prompted me to return my friend's call from last night right away. He is a bailiff and works for the VAT. Lots of bailiffs work for the VAT, but praise God that a brother in Christ was given *my* debt to handle. He said he had a warrant to distraint on goods to the amount of £7,800 to recover the debt (only one VAT period out of the two we owe). The result being that we have a further two weeks to find less than half the amount we thought. You could have knocked our financial planner friend down with a feather: no amount of financial wizardry could have come up with that one, but God did. The VAT shows no mercy, but God does.

28 September 1990
Friday night

We've been praying about a sixteen-tonne truck for some time; now, we need another. Three months ago, I said to Transfleet (a truck rental company) that we'd buy the one they had for sale, but we were unable to get finance on it. Our financial track record for the last two years is awful, and the bank will not give us a good credit reference. Transfleet wanted a decision by last Tuesday because, if we didn't want it, they would send it for auction next week. I told them there was no way we could have it because we couldn't raise the finance, but suggested that maybe we could hire it for a few weeks until we could get some money released – which would be quite likely after our financial planner friends had finished their report for the bank. However, this arrangement would mean we would pay more for it: the hire charges plus the purchase price once we had the money. Transfleet ummed and ahed a bit, but said they would see what they could do. They rang this morning to say we could hire the motor for four weeks at £350 per week – the going rate – and then buy it. The amazing thing is that they will *knock the hire charges off the purchase price*, so we won't pay any more at all.

Transfleet are one of the biggest truck rental companies in the country, so how did I manage to do a deal like that with them? Easy – the Lord worked, there's no other explanation. The bank even let me have the money for the four weeks' hire charge, all £1,400 of it.

29 September 1990
Saturday evening

Some friends came 'round for tea today.

The big idea was an evangelistic tea where I come straight out with 'We've asked you 'round to tell you about Jesus Christ!', but in reality it wasn't quite as straightforward and forthright as that. It took me about half an hour to get 'round to mentioning Christianity, let alone Jesus, but eventually He was mentioned and a few things were said about what the Lord had done for us, and how He has worked in our lives. But alas, I didn't get bold enough to say a prayer with them, which is what – I believe – sows the seed that falls on fertile ground. Never mind, it was better than nothing – we were all relaxed about it. I pray, Lord, You won't let them go and we'll have another opportunity; sorry for the 50% performance.

The only 100% performances I do in my mind. I imagine one-to-one encounters with my employees where they respond with enthusiastic curiosity, wanting to know more; where the conversion is almost immediate in response to my convincing words of wisdom – the Holy Spirit flows into them, changing them overnight. They come to church and testify how they came to know the power of Christ – how different they now are, and how their whole attitude and outlook on life has changed, shaking off the old and putting on the new.

But alas, in reality it's non-existent. Oh, to be filled with the Holy Spirit enough to be a natural at it, to talk about Jesus openly as passing comments when the opportunity arose; to constantly relate everyday experiences of life in the Spirit. But no, the boldness has yet to come, the barrier has yet to fall; but one day, Lord, it will, won't it? I want it to, so I pray, Lord, that You speed that day along, if it be Your will. In Jesus' name I ask. Amen.

30 September 1990
Sunday evening

The £3,000 grant offer we got ages ago towards the cost of the house roof repairs stipulated that we had to start the work by tomorrow, 1 October.

How things change. Of course we haven't got the money now – neither are we likely to for quite some time – so we've probably lost it. Never mind, that's a thing the Lord is teaching us; how to let go quicker of material things and ideas, and not get bothered. We didn't want to move from our previous house initially because it seemed like a material step backwards, we didn't want to sell the car for the same reason, or make Jeff redundant, or lose drivers and wagons – they all seemed like steps backwards.

But all these so-called 'prestige' things in the material world, worship of material things, are a form of idolatry. When we become Christians it's all part of getting rid of the old and putting on the new. A material thing goes, a spiritual thing takes its place. Dependence on these possessions is replaced by dependence on God; death to the material, life to the Spirit.

5 October 1990

Friday evening

A funny week it's been; funny peculiar, not funny ha-ha.

I can't make my mind up whether we are genuinely busy at work, or whether it just seems that way because we are short staffed and the relief drivers are not always available. If we're busy, then I thank the Lord for an answered prayer. If we're not busy, then I still thank the Lord for an answered prayer.

That may sound double Dutch, but the Lord does not always answer a prayer with the prayer request granted in the affirmative. The Lord always answers my prayers, but if it is not the answer I am looking for, I tend to think He hasn't answered. He has answered, but His answer has been in the negative and that's often not what I want to hear. If I pray for more work for Transportomatic and get it, I praise the Lord for an answered prayer. If I pray for more work and *don't* get it, that is an answered prayer also and I should praise the Lord. I must not say, 'Oh the Lord isn't answering my prayers'. He has answered, but because it's not the answer I want, I tend not to recognise it as an answered prayer or I ignore it. God is in control, He knows what He is doing, He knows things we don't – like the future. He holds the future in His hands and everything works together for good (Rom. 8: 28). Eventually, nothing bad comes from God to His children, so if we pray for more work and don't get it, then that is God's will – that is His answer. He always hears us when we pray in faith, when we are sincere, so we *will* have an answer – God does not ignore prayers. Thank God that He is communicating with us, that Christians are unique in having this communication with the Creator God. Thank God He hasn't 'Sent us to Coventry'. Be pleased that He is communicating, even if it isn't what we want to hear. God knows best. He knows something we don't, so accept that His answer is the right one – He's never wrong.

9 October 1990
Tuesday night

Mr Hoburn, our eldest daughter's school teacher, came to church on Sunday and for lunch after. We talked to Him about our faith. This is the teacher mentioned in the entry on 18 September, when my wife had a word with him about his R.E. lessons. He's surrounded by Baptists where he lives, but feels he cannot join the Christian faith, although he envies our 'friendship and community spirit', as he calls it.

I know what he means – I felt that way before I became a Christian. It's the feeling that no way would you make the grade, no way are you good enough, no way can you conform to living a good life overnight. There are lots of barriers, particularly to an aware, intelligent person like Mr Hoburn, who probably has to know a lot about everything, being a teacher of all subjects. The jump from everything being based on facts, figures, scientific knowledge, past experience, and your own achievements or failures, with no one but you responsible for it, to going over to believing in something else as a basis for everything is too wide a gap to attempt in one go. Like I felt at the time, you have to know a lot more and, if you're doing all right, you don't see a reason to change (why fix it if it isn't broken?). It's a gradual getting alongside that person and gaining his confidence and, with the Holy Spirit, eventually convincing him that he really has nothing to lose through a commitment to Christ, but at the same time instilling in that person that it is important to be sure and sincere.

Sunday night I took some brochures that one of our Church Wardens had obtained from an exhibition 'round to our previous vicar's son. His mum and dad invited me in for a cup of coffee. We got talking about what God was doing in our lives and in our respective jobs. Anyhow, by the end of the evening I had a £1,000 cheque in my pocket from them to help in the business – an 'indefinite, interest-free loan', as they put it.

I've probably said this before – that I've read books where, after praying (or even not after praying), God has provided money to people in times of need, and that I never imagined then that it would happen to me. But the plain, simple truth is that since the end of July, God has provided a total of £6,000. The story of the first £5,000 goes like this:

It was 27 July; I was in the office, doing a normal day's work, when one of our church members came to see me (he is retired and, on the surface, a very British stiff-upperlip type, often greets you with a salute, back straight, chest out and feet together like an army Captain). He sat down opposite me and handed me a piece of paper with one line typed on it, which said, 'An interest free loan of £5,000 to be re-paid/renegotiated after twelve months'. What can you say to someone who hands you this? 'Thank you' seems far too much of an understatement. I was just speechless. He said, 'Think about it and let me know' – and left.

I went to see the vicar as I was a bit worried that if I accepted, it would disappear on to the list of all the other debts which might not be paid back. Shortly before this, we were at one stage resigning ourselves to packing the business in – but the Lord keeps it going somehow. The vicar said I must accept it. This is what we have been praying for; it was an answered prayer. We had prayed many times for Transportomatic and the debt situation, and lots of others from the church family had been praying also – it was all part of an answered prayer. If we refused the offer it would have been rejecting God's intervention and we would have demonstrated that we did not believe in answered prayer.

So we accepted. My wife was quite apprehensive about the whole thing; this was new to us. We'd read about it in Christian books, such as David Waite's book where God provided money when he didn't think it was right to go on the dole, but we never thought it would happen to us. It took a bit of taking in – the wonderful provision of God in such a practical way.

I opened a separate account at another bank and deposited the money on 3 August 1990. We used it for payment of the smaller business debts, the suppliers who were really hounding us. And now, last Sunday, another £1,000 – praise God. That will go towards paying the VAT on the latest distress warrant, which is due tomorrow. I'm about £1,400 short at the moment, but I'm sure the Lord will make sure we get it somehow.

That's one thing I've experienced with the Lords provision – it's last minute as far as finance is concerned: just in time, on the nail, not before. It's a person with a lot of faith who waits patiently and calmly for the Lord to act on financial matters. I get very anxious and twitchy, but I pray I'm getting better at waiting for His intervention. It's realising that He hasn't got a clock ticking away like us. The only point for God to act before needed, would be to ease *our* anxiety and take the pressure off us, but that would be no test of faith. He teaches, guides and tests in this way, and we, as a result, will grow in character, faith and trust, and come to know Him better.

15 October 1990
Monday night

I've been to the church PCC meeting tonight. Again, there were about twenty people of widely diverse backgrounds, all at different stages of their spiritual journey. To get anyone to agree on anything and become of one accord is very rare, and tonight was no exception. How unique these meetings are. I can quite see why some nontraditional church-goers take the 'micky'. It does not take twenty people to decide what has to be decided. Five or less could do the same job in less than half the time and more efficiently. Many times the only decision that is made is to leave it till the next meeting. After spending fifteen to twenty minutes on a subject, still nothing is decided. I thought meetings were to decide things, set things in motion, the process of taking an idea, making it workable and putting it into practice. Too much thought, discussion, postponement, and 'wait and see' leads to discouragement and frustration for me.

24 October 1990
Wednesday night

I'm in a strange bed for the second night running.

28 October 1990
Sunday afternoon

That's as far as I got on the last entry.

I was in a strange bed because we've had a few days in Deganwy, North Wales, courtesy of the vicar, who has a little terraced cottage there. It was a good exercise for me again on being able to leave the business without getting anxious about what happens in my absence. I was anxious; there is no doubt about it. I wasn't able to completely relax, as I phoned in twice a day to answer questions and sort problems, but the family had a good time. Before I went, I thought to myself to think and pray about the report that the financial planners put in about restructuring the business, and to ask myself the big question of whether I should go ahead or wind up. I did plenty of thinking but hardly any praying.

29 October 1990
Monday night

It's the first day back at work after four days off, and big decisions have to be made.

Doubt is bombarding us again about the future of Transportomatic and even the house here where we live. So much so, I went and got a leaflet for a cheaper house down the road just in case.

All these doubts and deeds without consulting the Lord – going off in our own strength on a wing and no prayer. So tonight, after a sing-song with a Christian friend with a lovely voice, we prayed for the Lord's guidance and protection. We prayed for signs to direct, for the Lord to guide and, above all, for increased faith. If there was no doubt, there wouldn't be a problem. There again, we all fall short of the example of Christ – we're only human.

What has brought all this on is the report for the bank from the financial planners. It basically says that the business is in a financial mess because of me, my inability to manage, to make correct decisions, my inability to react quickly enough when we lost all that work in the summer of 1988, and to grasp the full gravity of the situation.

So here I am, owing more than I'm owed, three summonses in my possession – for which no money is available – and the time limit run out. The bailiff is chasing the VAT arrears, I've failed to pay the Inland Revenue for the last three weeks as arranged, and I'm threatened with summonses for capital gains tax and tax on income from lettings, with no hope of paying any of them. Our suppliers are chasing arrears on bills daily; an electricity disconnection notice is in for the business, and still an overdraft of £85,000.

I could go on and on with the bad news. It's easy to dwell on, and make it the pastime many people do. Good news is not news anymore. It has to be bad news to make the headlines, so I should thank the Lord for the good news of the love of Jesus Christ.

I know He's in all this and teaching me a lesson that will be a great testimony to Him in days to come, which is why all this is being written down. We all should have an account of God dealing with His people: Jesus dealing with His loved ones. I have not yet grasped the full abundance of God's grace and mercy and His love for me. I know this because I still carry a heavy burden regarding the business. I still cannot give it all to Jesus and trust Him completely, so I suffer, I worry despite the promises of God to the contrary. It's my own fault, Lord – please forgive me.

2 November 1990
Friday night

The only thing I want when I'm really hassled at work is peace. Not peace and quiet, but peace of mind. If you have peace of mind about anything, you can handle it, no problem. So how can I have peace of mind with an insolvent business, multiple debts of tens of thousands, the prospect of losing my house, constant hounding from suppliers, three summonses with time run out to pay or defend the case (not having the money is no defence), and a visit or phone call from the bailiff long overdue? How can I have peace of mind when I don't know if I can pay for the next fuel delivery or if the money for the next payday is going to be in the bank?

I'll tell you how you can have peace of mind under these circumstances – through Jesus Christ. The person of Jesus Christ, revealed through His Holy Spirit, comes and gives that peace, and says that, despite all this, everything is going to be OK. I can't explain how it happens, but it does. But I know why it happens – because Jesus loves me. He suffers *with* me as He suffered *for* me on that cross. He knows what it's like to be hassled because He also was hassled on this earth, and no matter how much any of us suffer, no matter how bad or awful it is, Jesus suffered more, so He knows what it's like and shares in our suffering. We will never suffer more than Jesus, because He suffered to death. There's nothing worse than death, particularly a slow lingering death. He wasn't shot in the head or heart at point blank range and never felt anything. It was a slow agony compounded by a spear in His side, to produce yet more pain from the weight of His body pulling on the nails in his hands.

But He knows that after suffering and death, peace comes, because He was raised. When Jesus appeared to his disciples after the resurrection, He said, 'Peace be with you' (John 20: 19). That peace which the world cannot give: it's literally out of this world, although we are in the world. Jesus, fill me with Your Holy Spirit and give me Your peace. Amen.

8 November 1990
Thursday night

It's been a bad afternoon at work today. Something we didn't do on the computer payroll last week meant I had to go through the wages all over again after doing it once. I got really wound up and angry. I remember the Scripture ´Do not be angry all day, do not let your anger lead you into sin' (Eph. 4: 26). But I just could not control my mental state – I was on the verge of doing damage to the nearest piece of furniture. I went into the loo and really had a go at the Lord. 'Where is this peace through Jesus Christ?' I yelled. 'Where is this freedom?' I screeched. 'I'm a prisoner in this office, I'm in bondage and chains – what use is Jesus Christ when I'm so wound up?' I nearly snapped! I was in tears at the frustration and torment of it all.

Then I had just a flash thought that maybe I *could* do something. I marched into the main office and pointed and motioned. I ordered in a loud, commanding voice for Deception, Depression and Confusion to get out of the office. At one stage I literally bellowed for all evil spirits and demons to leave my office and even went and opened the outside door to let them out. I went in every room commanding, 'In the name of Jesus Christ I order you out of this office'. I even went in the loo to get an evil spirit who was hiding down the toilet and shot him off in no uncertain terms. If anybody had come in they would have surely thought I'd flipped my lid.

I really did not know if it would do any good, but it did. From that moment I re-did the wages without any hitch and got to the bank just before 3.30pm. Coincidences? No. God's power? Really using God's authority and power? Maybe, or maybe not. I just felt better for getting it off my chest. I must not see demons around every corner – I must see Jesus around every corner – then I probably would not have got into that situation in the first place.

I've been reading a book by Chris Kline called *A Brilliant Deception*. She has realised the results of praising the Lord in difficult and bad times. The results being that things begin to happen. She thanked the Lord for the bad times that came her way, and God started to work in her life. I suppose it's an acknowledgement that *everything* is under the authority and power of God, instead of the logical thinking of 'the good things belong to God and the bad things belong to the devil'. It's made me realise the bad things belong to God also, for He has authority over everything in heaven and on earth, even the cosmic powers and spiritual rulers in the heavenly realms. So, literally, everything is under God; so thank Him for it, acknowledge it, and He'll then do something about it once we acknowledge He can. So praise Him for the bad times, difficult as it is.

I did my second public performance with 'Question Mark' drama group today, in the assembly at Weston Road High School. The first one was in Stafford Prison on Sunday morning. I've got quite a lot of dates coming up. I'm one seagull out of two, but I've learned both parts so it varies which one I play, Sid or Eddie, and I'm enjoying it, praise the Lord.

The house we went to see down the road, first mentioned on 29 October, has been valued by an estate agent and, as expected, it's overpriced. They said offer £75-80,000. It's up at £88,000. We also went to look at a friend's house, which is bigger, the same style but detached. We were 'warmed' to the first one. The estate agent is giving us a valuation on the bigger one tomorrow. At the end of the day it's what the Lord wants that should matter, not what we want.

Chapter 8: Will somebody sack me?

11 November 1990
Sunday night

A friend of ours, who has been a Company Director in his 125-year-old family firm for ages, has lost his job. He's devastated, of course. It just shows that no matter how solid your security appears, it shouldn't be in business, property, human nature or whatever other secular things. It should be in spiritual things, through Jesus Christ. As the Bible says, 'Put your trust in unseen things' (2 Cor. 4: 18). Our friend is a Christian, so he'll be fine.

I wish someone would sack *me*, but there is no one *to* sack me, I'm the boss. I have no partner, no co-directors (I'm not a Limited Company, anyway), no one to sack me. I can't just leave, like anyone else, give seven days' notice. Neither can I sell up – I'd have to pay someone to take it off my hands, I can't even give it away for free. If I was a normal employee with all this hassle I would have been long gone, resigned ages ago. As Chris Kline says in that book I'm reading, *A Brilliant Deception*, if God doesn't say 'Yes' or 'No', don't do anything – just carry on. So that's what I'll do, Lord, just carry on. But Lord, there's a limit to just how far we can go with 'carrying on'. The business continues to lose money, debts continue to mount up and bills continue to be unpaid; we can't 'carry on' indefinitely. I suppose You'll intervene at the very last minute, won't You? After I've nearly had a nervous breakdown. Now that would be an easy answer, wouldn't it? Have a mental breakdown and rest in peace sedated in a psychiatric ward. What a state I must be in for that to sound strangely attractive. Well, Lord, I'll *try* and praise You for all this.

On the other hand, the anticipation of not knowing what's going to happen can be, in a funny kind of way, exciting and challenging. I must try to instil the confidence of God in me. He lives in me so it should be there – it is there. I used it to cleanse the office last Thursday and it was certainly effective; the sort of confidence that faith in Christ brings, but it's which

143

way to direct that confidence and power: either towards letting go of the business and starting again, or towards building it up and making it pay once again.

The influence and respect that having your own business commands, I believe, gives me much more credibility when talking about Jesus. People knowing I have a well known business and employees do not label me as a 'Religious Nut', 'Jesus Freak', or 'Fanatic', or is this just my misguided opinion of what people think? This stems from my own experience of being on the receiving end of the good news from our next-door neighbours at the time, before I became a Christian. With me being in business (although not as successful as them), I admired them and looked up to them, so when they started to talk about Jesus, I 'took note'. I think I would have brushed it to one side as 'irrelevant' if I'd heard it from 'Joe Bloggs' down the street. With someone you admire and respect, for whatever reason, you listen and think, 'If they believe it, then maybe there's something in it'. With anyone else it would have been 'forget it, it's not for me!' and certainly if I'd have heard it from a speaker on a soap box in the Market Square: they would have definitely gone down in my book as a 'religious nut'. I believe God calls specific Christians to tell other specific non-Christians the good news on a one-to-one basis. He matches the teller of the good news to the person He wants to hear it, knowing they will only respond to them, and He goes to great lengths over long periods to eventually guide them to each other. Could it be that the only reason we were moved next door to George and Cindy was for them to tell us the good news of Jesus Christ, and that once this was done, we were moved on, next to the church?

I've just read in the Bible where Pilot sent Jesus to Herod, and Herod asked Him many questions, but Jesus did not answer (Mark 15: 3-5). That's like me. I'm asking Jesus all these questions and He's not answering. So Herod sent Him back to Pilot and He was sent to be crucified. Probably that's what the Lord's telling me: not to get crucified. I want all these answers and signs in our prayers, when I really should just shut up and see what He has *already* done for me – *died on the cross*. Is that not a sign enough?

13 November 1990
Tuesday night

Funny, whenever I write the date – 13 – I always think of how, before I was
a Christian, there was something about the number thirteen, especially if
it fell on a Friday. Thank the Lord that Christianity freed me from all
that superstition. Fate doesn't exist in a Christian life; instead, it's God's
purpose. It's reassuring that I'm in God's hands and I don't leave things to
'fate' anymore. This is one of the old things that Jesus set me free from,
praise Him.

Praise the Lord today for more answered prayer. We've had three enquiries
today from new customers, enquiries that have brought immediate fruit.
And another answered prayer: we've been praying for a profit and, praise
the Lord, in October we got one, a good one, £4,190 to be exact – which,
if repeated monthly, would be £50,000 profit over a year. We now pray
that it's consistent. We can do it with Your help through praying. Thank
You, Jesus.

The last four mornings in school assemblies I've been acting a seagull.
It's a short sketch with another seagull, about taking that first step to
committing yourself. After the sketch, another member of the group
gives a simple message (dressed normally, of course – you can't give
a serious Christian message dressed like a seagull). We're not allowed
to give the 'straight down the line' message of salvation, but it does put
some Christian content into the schools, which is sadly lacking these days.
Before becoming a Christian no one would have ever got me to dress up
as a seagull – yellow tights, too. Despite all my moaning and groaning
about my job lately, without it I would not be able to take time off to do
these dramas.

1 December 1990
Saturday night

I see in Sunday 11 November's entry that I state I'm asking all these
questions and Jesus isn't answering. Well, maybe He is answering but

I'm not listening. I don't often listen to Him or, if I've heard answers in my mind, I've put it down to my 'conscience' – it's my conscience telling me. I often have question and answer sessions in my mind and have never relied on them before, but now Christ is in me, maybe I should be taking more notice. If Christ is in me, He is probably in my mind more than anywhere else. Again I quote Rom. 12: 2, 'Do not conform to the patterns of this world any longer but transform yourself by a renewing of your mind, then you will know the will of God, what is pleasing and perfect to Him'. If my mind is being renewed, maybe it's time to start listening to it. God may be speaking to me, but I'm just not listening or I'm passing it off as my conscience as I did when I wasn't a Christian. I have read in the Bible and books about that 'still, small voice of whisper', (1 Kings 19: 11-13). I do hear a still, small voice if I actually bother to listen, and I can have a conversation with this voice. Is this what conversing two ways with God is, that gentle voice in my mind that I can question and get answers? Is it reliable, is it Jesus or is it not? I suppose if it's not Jesus it's the devil, the deceiver, the liar. But the Holy Spirit lives in me, so it's more than likely Jesus. 1 John 4: 2–3 says, 'By this you know the Spirit of God: every spirit that confesses that Jesus Christ has come in the flesh is of God, and every spirit which does not confess Jesus, is not of God, this is the spirit of the anti-Christ of which you heard that it was coming, and now is in the world already' (RSV). So how do you test if a voice in your head is from God or the anti-Christ? Ask if it confesses Jesus came in the flesh. I'll have to try that.

2 December 1990

Sunday night

Last week we were advised by our financial planners at work to sell the house and not buy another until we know how much money we would have left over, as there probably would not be enough to buy another one at today's prices. I honestly knew when they were spelling it out to me that, from their point of view, it was the only thing to do; but is it the right thing from God's point of view? I can't come to terms with it. The other alternatives were:

1. Get a very large re-mortgage on the house, which would pay the overdraft off, and be cheaper. This would mean what is called 'self certification' as far as my income is concerned. My present income is not high enough to get the size mortgage I would need, so I would have to put down a figure on the self certification form that was false. In other words, I would have to lie. It's tempting, but I won't do it. It would not be obedient to God. I'm sure He'll honour my decision.

2. Carry on as we are and hope we get back into regular profits very quickly: enough to turn the business 'round very dramatically and enough to pay our arrears off to the taxman (PAYE and VAT). We owe about £25,000 to the Inland Revenue and about £19,000 to the VAT. If they wanted their money now there is no way we could pay it. We are just praying for time, but the problem is that, as time goes on, we get deeper into debt.

So they say the best option is to sell the house and wind the business up. I just cannot come to terms with it – I will not accept that! Is it me being completely stubborn and failing to face reality, or is it that if I hang on the business will turn 'round without any major consequences?

I just don't know, Lord, I just *don't know.* Oh, help me, Lord. Nineteen years of my working life for nothing? Nineteen years for it to just fizzle out? I cannot come to terms with it. I cannot believe that after all this time it will just fade away and leave me and my family with nothing. What good is the experience of it all going to be, I ask? I don't, at this moment, feel anything like doing the same sort of job – so what good is nineteen years' experience of running a transport business going to do me, especially when I've run it into the ground? On reflection, it's the same old story: 'I should have sold up and got out when the going was good'. Easily said on hindsight, but, at the time, you sincerely believe the sky's the limit and you'll keep going up, and up, and up.

3 December 1990
Monday night

Tonight we prayed to the Lord that we wouldn't have to sell the house. We've had advice from financial controllers, planners and bank managers, but we haven't heard what God has to say about it; so we pray and listen to what He thinks before taking any action. Amen.

The drama sketch went well this morning. It's three Santa Clauses. 'Santa One' (me) is very grumpy and complaining, extremely cynical about all the Christmas razzmatazz and commercialisation. 'Santa Two' is all dreamy eyed and loves it. 'Santa Three' is a Christian who gets 'round to telling Santa One about the real meaning of Christmas. There's no talk after it, the message is in the sketch. I mustn't forget that being involved in this is an answered prayer from as long ago as 29 March.

4 December 1990

Tuesday night

I've had a letter from the bank today. The gist of it was 'Your financial planners say that the liquidity of the business is getting worse, and that amounts owed to preferential creditors are going up. How are you going to pay them? What are you going to do? They say there is no point in carrying on, and we, the bank, agree. Can you let us know what your next course of action will be?'

Well, Lord, what is my next course of action? Jesus, give me the confidence to carry on and see it through. Guide me through these stormy seas, Lord; if you don't, I'm in danger of crashing on the rocks and sinking. Lord, I'm desperate for guidance and wisdom. I pray my faith isn't blind faith, just carrying on when it really is pointless. Open my eyes, Lord, to what I must do. Am I being stubborn and arrogant, refusing to give in and cut my losses, or is it real faith in the future, knowing the business is going to be saved? Oh, Lord, whatever it is, be with me. In Jesus' name I ask. Amen.

6 December 1990

Thursday night

Today is a day to remember as being the first day in my nineteen years of trading history that the bank refused to let me have the wages, the result of which was – of course – nobody got paid. The reason was that a cheque from one of our customers did not arrive in the post today, although it was posted first class last night; so I pray Lord that I do get it, or at least other monies, tomorrow morning to cover the wages (thank the Lord the manager allows us to draw against cheques without having to wait three days for them to clear). Thank You, Lord, that You *did* prepare me for this. I thought that in this situation I would panic, but I didn't. I went back to the office, told Leena what had happened – she didn't bat an eyelid – and left a message with Paul to tell the rest who were due wages that they'd get paid in the morning. Praise You, Lord, I really feel You are with me in this.

Yesterday I phoned Motor Transport, the weekly trade paper, and put an advert in to sell; I also was speaking to Eddie, who has a transport business in Colwyn Bay (we use them for our North Wales deliveries). I asked him, as a passing comment, really, if he wanted to buy my business. Surprise, surprise – he said he was very interested and even seemed keen to consider some sort of merger, which would keep me in a job! He said he'd come and see me about it next week. That's boosted me up quite a bit! He'll probably be turned right off when he sees the accounts and how much in debt we are, but that would be my problem, my liability to sort out.

The fact is we do have a good business. Good work, which could make money under the right circumstances – with the right management – particularly if it could be integrated into another Company's existing work.

Jacuzzi rang today. They want to get cracking, sign the contract and get the stock up from Maidstone in early January, so praise the Lord for that.

I try to think positive. We read tonight in house group to take in the good things and count it all joy in the Lord, and not dwell on the bad things and worry (Jas. 1: 2-3). So Lord, help me to do this – I *want* to do this, to see the positive side of things. This is part of the answer for our bank manager when he asked what our next move is. Our next move of putting the business up for sale or merger may be a negative act on the surface, but at least it's thinking positive. If it's not God's will He'll block it. It's a step out in faith for me and I'm sure God will honour it.

It's funny how the imagination runs wild and how one's mind latches on to an encouraging situation. Eddie only expressed *interest* in a sale or merger, but already I picture myself working alongside him – organising wagons – moving up to Colwyn Bay to make a fresh start; the children starting a new school, finding a fresh new church to go to and everything working out fine in the end. I must admit when we were on holiday in Deganwy, which is near Eddie's business, I thought to myself, 'I could easily move up here'. It's nice: near the sea and Welsh mountains, Llandudno seems a good shopping centre and there seems to be plenty to do. Well, who knows? Maybe it's not all imagination. They say the grass is always greener in someone else's garden, but if you lived there you'd have to cut and weed it. Amen.

12 December 1990
Wednesday night

Eddie, from Colwyn Bay, hasn't been in touch yet. Things get more urgent, time is running out. The taxman from PAYE/NIC came 'round last week. I wasn't in the office, but he helped himself to the wage records and added up what we owe him. Today, in the post, we had a demand for £26,000 within seven days. We have absolutely no hope of paying.

I get a horrible initial twinge when I open post like that, but that's as far as it goes. Somehow, although on the surface it appears impossible to pay, deep down I feel something will be sorted out. What, I don't know – trust the Lord to work another miracle?

I was speaking this morning to a friend from church about my recent negative attitude towards work and business (not unjustified under the circumstances). But as the Lord promises, 'Everything works together for the good of those who love Him' (Rom. 8: 28). So in all this, God is working somewhere, somehow. I ask for guidance, direction and signs (I'm desperate for them), but nothing comes, so I think God is not there. But if God does not see a different direction, then the guidance must be to stay as I am and work it through, so I just carry on and trust the Lord. That's probably all He is saying – 'Trust Me'. No great revelation, no signs and wonders; just a simple 'Trust Me'.

I am now collecting County Court Judgements (CCJs) – three so far, with about three more pending. I can't pay, so they'll just have to sit on my desk. I have such a long list of people to pay and nothing to pay them with. Letters have gone out to factoring companies enquiring about their services. At any given time the business is owed about £70,000 from our customers, and it gets harder every day to get our money in. A letter went out earlier this week to various bad payers reminding them of our thirty day payment terms. So Lord, another of our problems is getting money in.

I wonder if I'll be able to draw the wages this week. Please, Lord, I pray the bank will let me draw the wages tomorrow. In Jesus' name. Amen.

13 December 1990

Thursday night

I've been on my own at work today, but the Lord's been with me – no problem with the wages today, praise Him. Two breakdowns on the same truck, but I coped well, thank You, Lord.

Tonight in house group we were praying for Transportomatic, and studying peace, that much sought-after state of mind which eludes even the best Christians at some time or another – me most of the time. But as it says in Rom. 5: 1-5, 'Boast about your troubles, for troubles bring endurance and endurance brings God's approval which in turn brings hope' Much easier said than done, but I keep practicing. We have to practice to try and become better.

I must say, on reading previous pages of this journal, one would think I was totally saturated with business problems to the exclusion of all other things, but no, this is a false impression. I do enjoy myself and have time for other activities.

26 December 1990
Wednesday night

I've just watched the film *Poltergeist 2* on TV (what seasonal viewing!).
The people who make these films get some of it right. Yes, there are evil
spirits that manifest themselves in whatever form they choose. They do
wreak havoc in our lives, but the filmmakers always get the solution
wrong. In *Poltergeist 2*, it was some Indian warrior with special powers
(wrong) and the love between a family (partly right). The only solution is,
of course, Jesus Christ. But was the whole thing fiction? They come very
close – from the evil point of view – and very close to the real spiritual
battle that goes on. But who's fighting whom they don't quite get. It's
always evil against good or the other way around. Even the devil – on
the bad side – they get right, but they're wrong on the good side – Jesus.
In *The Omen* the solution was daggers, not Jesus. In *The Exorcist* it was
an exorcist, but was Jesus' name mentioned? No. In *Dracula* it's a cross
(near) and stakes through the heart (miles out). In the recent TV series
The Green Man, an Anglican priest got rid of an evil spirit, but was Jesus
mentioned? No. I suppose if it was, it would almost change the situation
from fiction to reality, and we can't have that, can we? It's only a story,
only entertainment, imagination on the screen... but how close they get to
the real spiritual battle.

When I watch these films and the good guy comes along I often think, 'It
should be Jesus'. But that, from the filmmakers' point of view, would kill
the film off as a money spinner. It would bring 'religion' into it and be a
'bore', and the public would think it totally ridiculous. Strange how they
will believe the most outrageous made up solutions, but throw the real
answer out as even more outrageous. 1 Cor. 2: 14 says 'The man without
the Spirit does not accept the things that come from the Spirit of God,
for they are foolishness to him and he cannot understand them, because
they are spiritually discerned'. Before I was a Christian I would have
dismissed biblical truths as ridiculous and foolish, but, praise the Lord,
'Then you will know the truth, and the truth will set you free' (John 8: 32).

Christmas hasn't been as bad as I thought. I don't like Christmas Day –
never have, except when I was a child. Since I've become a Christian it

hasn't improved much. Before I was a Christian, the predictability of it all got me. Now the predictability of it all still gets me, plus the extravagance and over-consumption of food and drink, considering half the world is hungry and thirsty. And where does it say in the Bible that Jesus was born on 25 December, 1,990 years ago, anyway? It annoys me to see everyone going crazy at Christmas, not really knowing why. OK, they know they're celebrating the birth of Jesus Christ (those that believe the nativity is not a fairy tale), but when I celebrate the birth of one of my daughters, I don't just spend her birthday with her, I spend the other 364 days of the year with her, too. If I go to anyone's birthday party, I know them personally; I've usually known them for quite a long time and know quite a lot about them, otherwise I wouldn't have been invited. People who do not know Jesus or anything about Him are almost gate-crashing the party! So many people just tag along with the presents, the turkey, the parties, the pubbing and the holiday. Do they really know what it's all for? Do they ever question why they are celebrating, what is the reason? And do we ever tell them?

How easy it was for me, as an unbeliever, to say the 'Christ' in the word Christmas when pronouncing it 'Crist' (as in 'crisps'). But how difficult it was to say and pronounce 'Christ' properly and prefix it with Jesus when saying it other than as swear words. The power of the name – it does something to everyone when spoken in its proper context and pronunciation. How easy for the unbeliever to say 'Jesus Christ', 'Jesus Wept', 'Christ Almighty' or just 'Jesus' when cursing or as an exclamation of surprise or gravity of a situation. The devil loves that and won't let the mind think twice about what's been said. But as a non-Christian, when used in the right context, it's often intensely embarrassing to say or touches a nerve and can be inhibiting. Again, The power of the name: 'At the name of Jesus, every knee shall bow' (Phil. 2: 10).

30 December 1990
Sunday night

Maybe my puzzlement at how God speaks to people in that 'still, small voice' has been too obvious to realise. The other night, when settling down to sleep, I just said to God in my head, 'Why is it that I don't get any signs and wonders, and flutters of the Holy Spirit anymore?' The answer in my head came from a still, small voice that said, 'As one matures as a Christian, great anointing and spectacular signs are not so abundant, as we grow and learn to live the Christian life in faith and trust alone'.

Wow!

As I grow, I gather more and more Scriptures into my memory to draw on. I get a history as a Christian with all the past experiences to draw on, whereas a young or newly converted Christian will not have so many of these. So, in the latter case, practical signs and experiences are sent by God to let us know in no uncertain terms that it's Him, that He's alive and loves us. From then on, as we grow as Christians, He puts us to work on other people. He works *through* us as well as *on* us. Whereas, initially, the emphasis is on God revealing Himself to us, as we grow, He wants us to reveal Him to other people, and I believe fresh and further anointing comes through doing that. If we don't get off our backsides then we cannot expect blessings and revelations from Him. We cannot expect happenings if we just sit and wait. We have the foundation of the knowledge that God died for us, was raised, is alive and reveals Himself to us through His word and Holy Spirit living in us. We build on that. These are our work tools. If we don't use these tools, then nothing gets built. As we sang in church today, 'There's a city to build'.

Anyway, I was saying I find it difficult to hear God speaking to me in my head. From that experience the other night I believe the simple answer is I just haven't been listening. All I did was ask a question in my mind and then wait for an answer, and it came – that still, small voice. Also, I've been that bothered about *who* speaks to me in my mind (Jesus or the devil) that, thinking I couldn't discern who it was, didn't take notice of *any* answers, just in case it was the enemy. But with a little thought and prayer, discernment comes – I mean, the devil isn't going to give an answer like the one I had, is he? So it's Jesus – God! If you ask Jesus a question *He's* going to answer. The same as if I ask my wife a question, she answers, not someone else, because I'm not directing the question to someone else.

1 January 1991
Tuesday night, 1.30am

The entry on Thursday 6 December says Eddie at Colwyn Bay has shown interest in buying or a merger with us. Well, since then, things have moved on. He came to see me last Saturday and I've been to see him today. We've talked about lots of things and, praise the Lord, he seems willing to join forces and put up money for our pressing debts to the Inland Revenue and VAT. I am extremely encouraged.

Travelling there, on approaching Colwyn Bay – to the left of the A55 westbound – is a hill. Behind this hill was a break in the black clouds, where very long and distinct sunrays were shining through. You could not actually see the sun, just the golden rays streaming through. The brightness put the hill in front into silhouette. Was this the Lord telling me that behind the black cloud in my life was a light, a light shining through, and that what I was doing – the journey I was making to Colwyn Bay – was the beginning of that light? Also, on the way back, when it was dark, I saw an equally beautiful sight. There was a full, very bright moon; the sort of brightness that, if you switched your headlights off, would make the way ahead still easily seen. Again to the left of the A55, but coming eastbound, you can see the sea. The beautiful sight was the light of the moon reflecting on the water, as far as the horizon. Again, was God telling me there was a light on my horizon? Was He reassuring me that, on the dark seas of my business, there is now a light shining?

6 January 1991
Sunday night

I'm not sure what it is, but I've been quite anti-church this weekend or, more precisely, anti-traditional Anglican Church.

This morning, in the service, the rigid structure and tradition of it all got to me, plus the old hymns we seem to dig up from the ark. It's such a pity when there are such good new songs around with much more relevant tunes and words.

Maybe it boils down to me not being right with God. Not enough prayer, lack of discipline and obedience, unrepented sin, criticisms, petty gripes and getting things totally out of perspective results in not being right with God. Not much falls into place then.

Then after the service, this little 'angel' called Sheila came up to me, obviously sensing something was up; so I unloaded it all on to her – which was a big help – and we ended up laughing, partly due to the fact she'd lost her voice and I couldn't stop saying 'pardon' to most things she said. She just came over and gave me a big hug – God's agent. It was really Him giving me a big hug and saying, 'Look, I still love you'. Thank You, Lord.

Chapter 9: Not prepared for answered prayer.

7 January 1991
Monday night

The Jacuzzi contract, which we have been praying about for the last year, is coming to fruition at the end of this week. Another answered prayer; thank You, Lord.

9 January 1991
Wednesday night

I feel as if I'm regaining my relationship with the Lord after losing it a bit after the last week or so. It's only through prayer that it's come back.

It's my own fault if my relationship with the Lord turns sour. He stays the same, longing for me to be right with Him through Jesus. Now my wife and I have started nightly praying together, after a few days lapse. His Spirit becomes more powerful. We've had a prayer meeting at church tonight, too.

Last weekend I blamed the church, which was wrong because my relationship is personal between Jesus and myself. My relationship is with Jesus first and the church, second. I believe some people's relationship with Jesus is ruined because they put church traditions, rules and customs first or in place of Jesus. My relationship was ruined because of my frustration with this situation and annoyance at seeing this. Some dote on it; I loathe it: another 'brilliant deception' by the enemy that I fell for. But prayer broke it and opened my eyes to what was really going on. An example of why we should praise the Lord in the bad times, because He's teaching us something, something we don't know until we're back to God and reflect on the situation. That's why we must have faith that 'everything works together for good for those who love Him' (Rom. 8: 28), even when we can't see it at the time.

19th January 1991
Late evening

In this particular instance, an answered prayer is hard work.

On 10 January I signed the contract to exclusively warehouse and distribute Jacuzzi products throughout the UK. We first started praying about this on 20 January 1990, nearly twelve months ago. By 'we' I mean the church as well. The Lord has triumphed. He's given little Transportomatic, with only twelve wagons, a contract with a Hanson Corporation subsidiary that was previously operated by a major UK carrier with hundreds of wagons. At present, the stock is being transferred from Maidstone in Kent to our new warehouse, which the Lord directed us to at Seighford (after we ignored His initial prompt), which is tailor-made for the contract (see entry 22 April 1990). This means that, over a period of two weeks, I have to receive about twenty forty-feet articulated lorry loads of Jacuzzi baths and accessories, sort them, label and stack them – and all this after finishing my usual work, four miles away, at our main base. Commissioning this new warehouse has meant two nights last week not getting to bed until 3am, but the Lord's been with me all the way. What I imagined would be a daunting task has not been so bad. Each stage has seemed quite frightening and big, but we've worked it through (the only thing suffering being my sleep, which I can catch up on).

I now pray, Lord, that this new contract will start to make us some money and we can move on to the other new thing.

At the end of this month we'll be taking on deliveries to B&Q stores for a company called Bowman Webber, which we have been praying about for some time now. I also pray for boldness and motivation to reapproach Showerlux at Coventry for their work, which we lost in the summer of 1988.

The other big recent news is the 'Gulf War', as it is known. Iraq has not withdrawn from their occupation of Kuwait by the deadline of 15 January, so allied forces of many countries are attacking Iraq – only from the air, so far. Everything – according to governments on 'our side' – is going very well and it should be a short war, weeks at the minimum, months at the maximum. Iraq has attacked Israel with missiles falling on Tel Aviv and

Haifa, but so far Israel is leaving it up to the allied forces to respond on their behalf. The Bible lands in turmoil.

3 March 1991
Sunday night

The last entry prays for work to be in from Bowman Webber by the end of January. Nothing has happened – probably not the Lord's timing yet.

Also in the last entry I prayed for boldness to approach Showerlux UK Ltd to requote for their work. Well, they have approached us. We've already quoted, about ten days ago, so I must phone them to get some reaction. I pray, Lord, that, if it be Your will, they react positively. In Jesus' name I ask. Amen.

The Gulf War mentioned in the last entry is over. Today a ceasefire has been signed and all United Nations conditions met. We won, but I suppose twenty-eight nations fighting one nation would produce that result. It's all over now. Despite numerous attacks on them from Iraq, thank God Israel didn't enter the war.

I'm having a bad time with my health. The last two weeks have seen me quite ill, but not vomiting or bedridden. It started with my whole body aching and feeling totally exhausted for two days, then my nose running and a headache, then coughing, and all through it all I was so weak. Even when I went to bed at 8pm and had a good 12hours sleep, I was still weak all day. The result is, apart from being a 'wet rag' to everyone, I've got so far behind at work it's become a real burden to me to get up-todate, to the extent that I am resenting the time my Christian activities are taking up, when instead I could be at work, catching up. All the mornings this week are taken up with the 'Question Mark' drama group in the infants and junior schools. I should really have gone to work today, but church and preparing for the evening praise service tonight took the time. This week there are supposed to be church meetings on Monday, Wednesday and Thursday evening, so I've only got five afternoons and two evenings to do my work. I've been telling my wife I feel like resigning from every

Christian activity I'm involved in, but then I would probably not be disciplined enough to use the extra time for working anyway, so I just lift it all up to You, Lord.

I don't want to go to Spring Harvest, Lord – I'm already weeks behind at work. It's such a hassle to get everything prepared before I go away when I'm up-to-date, never mind when I'm behind! I need a proper holiday, a 'peace and quiet' holiday, away from it all. Spring Harvest is too much work and discipline. Even if you opt out of the activities, it's usually far too cold to relax and do other things, although Pwllheli probably won't be as cold as Skegness. I don't feel I'm good at Christian activities lately, anyway. I don't feel I'm a good house group leader or a good worship leader. I no longer get time to prepare and pray, it's always a last minute rush and, of course, if you don't prepare and pray, it doesn't go so well.

9 March 1991
Saturday night

I was convinced we would make a profit in January. I stopped at work this evening to get the figures out and, low and behold, we've made a huge loss! Out of a good January turnover of £30,000 we've managed to make a net loss of £10,000. Our 'assets' are now to the tune of *minus* £91,000 – our capital account is *minus* £46,000 and our net *loss* to date this year after ten months is £37,000. We owe the PAYE/NIC (Inland Revenue) £37,000 and the VAT £24,000 – all from figures as at the end of January.

My usual despair came over me on seeing those bottom lines on the printouts, but tonight the Lord has told me to have faith. When I came to bed and opened my Bible it was Hebrews 11 'By Faith': 'Now faith is being sure of what we hope for and certain of what we do not see' (verse 1, NIV). Well, Lord, I do not see a profit but hope for one. Rom. 5: 1-5 again includes, 'Trouble brings endurance and endurance brings God's approval and God's approval brings hope'. Lord, we're in trouble, but somehow we've endured, and I now have hope, so maybe You're approving.

10 March 1991
Sunday night

There were lots of people in church this morning for Mothering Sunday.

Thank You, Lord, that I am catching up at work. I hope You don't mind me working on Sundays, but I can get a lot done at weekends when it's quiet, because the phone isn't ringing.

Whenever we pray we always pray for more work at Transportomatic. We also pray to start making a consistent profit. Anyone can get more work – its profitable work we need, Lord, at a good rate – quality work.

I pray that the quote we gave to Showerlux will be accepted. I also pray that Bowman Webber hasn't forgotten about us. Maybe the time is too soon. Amen.

12 March 1991
Tuesday night

If we don't make a profit in February we'll be incapable of making a profit ever. I'd say (without checking the figures) that last month we've had the best turnover for about three years; we should have the figures tomorrow.

Praise the Lord we've paid the VAT that was asked for three or four weeks back, all £17,000 of it. The Lord doesn't let us down – the money is found from somewhere. Why I get anxious about it, I do not know; He always provides, in the end. I suppose it will take time for me to really trust Him and have consistent confidence. The more He 'comes up with the goods' over the years, the more my faith will grow. It's a pity the Lord has to prove it to me for me to gain confidence, and that I can't have faith and trust from the start. I suppose it's like any relationship; the longer you know someone, the more you trust them and, after all, I haven't known the Lord for four years yet, which is nothing when there's all eternity to go.

A Mercedes car again would be really nice, Lord. We had a visitor at work today with a 250D H reg., very nice. I'm a bit down in the dumps, Lord,

I need a boost and a nice car would do the trick – or a consistently good profit or a 'real' holiday. When I say a real holiday I mean one where I can forget about work and don't have to ring in, and one that will be worth all the hassle of sorting everything out and preparing for my absence before I go. I've tried it twice before, the Lleyn Peninsula, North Wales, last August and Deganwy last October... and it's not a relaxing time. Half of me is on holiday and the other half's at work. I'm really not bothered about going to Spring Harvest this year because of that. It's not on, so what I've suggested to my wife is that I go Saturday to Tuesday when we're on holiday at work, then come back home and fetch them back the following Saturday. Our good friend Naomi wants to go, so she could be there with my wife and the girls when I wasn't. We've prayed about it so, Lord, we'll see what happens.

I've just about caught up at work after my illness and the time taken out to do 'Question Mark'. Thank You, Lord, that one of the leaders discerned that something was concerning me and gave me a break from performances last Thursday and Friday, plus I worked Saturday and Sunday. Amen.

14 March 1991

Thursday night

My wife's gone to a 'Christian do' at Tunstall Town Hall tonight, called 'Where the Rubber Hits the Road' with Martyn Joseph and the evangelist John Smith from New Zealand (whom I saw at Spring Harvest in 1989). He's the one who told the story about the power station:

Visitors were being shown round a power station where megawatts of power were being generated for sending out to the homes, industry and towns of the nation. At the end of the tour one of the visitors asked the guide, 'Where are all the power lines to carry the power into the towns and cities, which should radiate from the power station?' The tour guide replied, 'Oh, it takes so much power to run this place that we have to use it all ourselves. All the excess energy we produce goes straight back into the power station because it takes so much to run it'.

Of course he wasn't really talking about a power station; he was talking about the established church. It takes so much to administer, that none of the workers have the time or energy to take the product to the customers – to take the Gospel to the people. A good analogy, I thought.

We got February's figures out today and, praise the Lord, we made a very good profit. It's just as well, in view of what I said at the beginning of the entry from Tuesday 12. Sustaining it month after month is what we need now, Lord. I pray we can do it again this month, in spite of the bank's interest coming out on 20 March. In Jesus' name I ask. Amen.

On reflection, I am beginning to realise that the reason why I have had problems with the business since I've known the Lord is that I may have been thinking too small.

'My God is so big, so strong and so mighty, there's nothing that He cannot do', so the song goes and Eph. 3: 20 says, 'Now to Him who is able to do immeasurably more than we ask or imagine according to His power that is at work within us' (NIV). It also says on the pen I am writing with 'The Lord is my strength' (Ps. 18: 1). Up until a few months ago, I had been running the business as if I didn't know the Lord's power. It is only since I've been thinking big that I have realised the powerhouse that is inside me from Christ, which is entirely at my disposal.

20 March 1991
Wednesday night

It's good and bad news at work today (thank God there's *always* the good news of Jesus Christ).

The bad news is that the big Jacuzzi cheque due in the post since Monday has still not arrived. Until that goes in the bank, there is no money. Bank charges, which are usually over £4,000, have come out today which will take us way over our overdraft limit, meaning no wages either, pending receipt of that cheque. Please, Lord, make it be in tomorrow's post. Amen.

The good news (or should I say the 'God' news) is an answered prayer. We have been praying that Bowman Webber, who approached us ages ago to deliver their mirrors to B&Q stores, would not forget us, as the scheduled commencement of the work is way overdue. Today we had a letter from them to say their products were still on trial in various stores. These trials should finish by early summer so they want discussions on distribution to reopen, praise the Lord.

I made the 7.30am Wednesday church prayer meeting today for the second week running. There is now double the amount going than there used to be, four now instead of two; small, but nevertheless it's 100% increase.

24 March 1991

Sunday night

A praise march 'round the streets after morning church; breakfast followed by a report from various people about a new project for homeless pregnant young ladies yesterday morning at a local church; 'Sing and Sup' last night at our church (our new monthly evening event, 'Sup' meaning supper, not supping pints); I had the children all day yesterday as my wife was at a craft fair, so I couldn't sort the delivery notes at work, meaning I had to do it early this morning and this afternoon – church again this evening! Sometimes I wonder about all these Christian activities; in fact, I wonder about them a lot. I'm not sure *what* I wonder. It's a question of the right balance, of dividing time between work, family, and church activities. I suppose everyone else has the same problem.

I never do any DIY or gardening these days, and yet there's more to do here than anywhere we've lived before. I'm still not sure if I even like living here, there's such a lot of work to do on the house. It needs painting, inside and out, there are major cracks in the east gable end wall upstairs, the roof needs doing, all the ground level at the back of the house needs lowering by six inches because it's above the damp course, the gardens need redoing because they're a lot of work to keep tidy in their present state, the garage and shed have major leaks in the roof. There is definitely a practical case for not doing as many Christian activities. Can You help me at all here, Lord? In Jesus' name I ask. Amen.

29 March 1991
Friday night

It's the eve of going to Spring Harvest. We're off to Pwllheli tomorrow, the new Spring Harvest site. I'm not excited, but quite bubbly about having four days off work – that's what's put me in a good mood. Most things at work have been wrapped up until I return on Wednesday, praise the Lord. Since Christmas, work hasn't been the hassle it used to be. It's getting easier. The Lord is working on a sure but slow change in attitude.

Our two youngest daughters have been unusually 'niggly' tonight when going to bed: probably the enemy having a go at us, as we're about to embark on a Christian activity involving them. Lord Jesus, I claim our family for You; to get ready, journey to, have a fruitful four days and a safe journey back. I rebuke in Jesus' name any attempts to delay, disrupt or sabotage our time by the evil one and ask for Your protection. In Jesus' name. Amen.

4 April 1991
Thursday night

I came back from Spring Harvest on Tuesday night. My wife stayed, as Naomi went up on the train on Tuesday to take my place. They all return tomorrow, so at present I'm on my own – a rare occasion.

Spring Harvest was good, despite my being there only three and a half days of it. I didn't go to as many activities as possible, just the mornings and evenings, leaving the afternoons free.

I despair a lot at Spring Harvest, for I know that our church is one of those that the theme and speakers at the event are attempting to stir and shake into action, and it just emphasises what a daunting task it seems. Basically, they say all that needs to be done is get more of the existing regular church-goers – who are already physically active in the church – to be filled with the Holy Spirit so they become *spiritually* active. The Spirit will then lead and motivate and we will get Jesus in the centre and maybe the rituals, ceremonies and tradition that holds us back will not be so much of a priority. Simple in theory, yet difficult in practice; remember, we're dealing with *people*. Amen.

8 April 1991
Monday night

The prayer and praise service (the first Sunday evening in the month) is very informal and gives the opportunity for anyone to stand up at the front and say whatever they like. Last night it was thought a good idea for people who had been to Spring Harvest to say a few words. My wife did so, and then I went up. You quite often read in the book of Revelation the words 'And the Spirit took control of me' – that's probably what happened to me.

I have never known how to put into words – how to get across to the congregation – that we all need to be filled with the Holy Spirit and that a Spirit-filled church is a growing church; that we need to change (which will be painful and there will be casualties); that we need to come together and centre on Jesus; that yes, the building is important, but Jesus is more important – even more important than the Bishop who is visiting us next week, with everyone 'rushing around' in preparation. But last night the Lord gave me the words to wrap that all up in an orderly loving way that surprised everybody, not least me.

It encouraged me to hear at Spring Harvest that John Wesley got banned from the churches for being too controversial and revolutionary, yet today he is heralded as one of the Lord's champions in the history of Christianity; so to be bold and controversial for Jesus is not such a bad thing. Jesus was a revolutionary when He was on this earth, so we are in the best company.

11 April 1991
Thursday night

We don't have to go to Spring Harvest to feel that power and presence of the Holy Spirit just once a year; He's not only in numbers, whoopees, seminars or powerful speakers. Most of all, Jesus is in the hearts of those individuals in the local church who carry His dismay at our apathy and 'comfortableness'.

Oh Lord, make us uncomfortable and shake us into action. You're alive, so why is the Church dead? Is it because people haven't felt the living God in their hearts, because they haven't experienced the person of Jesus touching them? The living God is not in them, so they're not alive; and if the people aren't alive, the Church isn't alive, because the Church is the people. So why aren't the people alive? We preach the Gospel, we preach the teachings of Jesus and the Apostles, we preach the person of Jesus and the need to be filled with the Holy Spirit, and the living word of God flows in the sermons. The fact is that live words will not be alive to a dead person (1 Cor. 1: 18). So why aren't people filled with the Holy Spirit when they are asked time after time? Because the Church never tells them *how*. No one prays with them to be filled and no one explains *who* the Holy Spirit is. There's a void between the word given and the application of that word, no one is telling how to apply it. We are assuming that people can understand the word and apply it all by themselves. What about the people who hear the word, want to be filled with the Holy Spirit, but are too afraid to ask how they go about it for fear of ridicule, or are just too shy or embarrassed? Eph. 5: 18 says, 'Be filled with the Holy Spirit'. It's a command, not an option. Read Philip and the Ethiopian official, Acts 8: 26-39. Philip explained the good news of Jesus to him, but didn't leave it there. He baptised him and the official was filled with the Holy Spirit and went on his way rejoicing.

14 April 1991
Sunday night

The Bishop of Lichfield gave the sermon at church today. It was a good message. Praise God Amy came. She said the last part of the talk was so relevant to her it was just like they were talking one-to-one.

Amy was a regular member of our church, married and living in the parish. She was an active Christian and, while prison visiting, befriended a prisoner whom, when he was released, she 'ran off' with. On 7 April she turned up destitute at our house enroute from Cornwall to Blackpool. We went over to the church to pray, which turned out to be a very hallowed occasion for her and was amazing to witness. It was a very personal re-encounter with God following her repentance at what she had done.

I went with Amy to see the vicar this afternoon. She wants to come back to our church to worship and her and her boyfriend also want to return to Stafford to now live apart – she wanted the OK from the vicar. The vicar says he can't stop anyone worshipping in the church, but to come back on a permanent basis would require a public account of herself that she was following up her repentance with action, i.e. changing her ways. He also said that it would have to be sanctioned by the Elders and prayed about. After the service tonight they had an impromptu meeting to talk about it. Since then, Amy has been to see her husband (not a Christian) and he says he will agree to a divorce.

I find it quite exciting to anticipate how God is going to work in this and how it will turn out.

22 April 1991
Monday night

Concerning Amy and her boyfriend again: The vicar has been to see Amy's husband and has come to the conclusion that the relationship is dead, which means that, biblically speaking, there is no right way out of the situation. Whichever way Amy goes, it's the lesser or greater of various evils. Our previous Minister said that the biblical obedience would be to return to her husband and try and make a go of it, but when there's nothing there to rekindle and when one partner is not a Christian, what do you do? It's much easier said than done to go back to square one and start again. So how will the Lord sort this one out, assuming Amy will allow Him to guide her?

I believe that 'blanket' forgiveness is the logical thing to do. No judgements, sanctioning from leaders, public apologies and such like. The Prodigal Son returned without having to give an account of himself. No questions;

just an instant acceptance back into the family, plus a feast and rejoicing. And here Amy is – the prodigal daughter! The church is reacting like the brother, not the father (Luke 15: 24-32). Jesus preached forgiveness, the Bishop preached forgiveness, 'No matter what we have done'. A Bible teacher visiting our fellowship yesterday and Saturday preached forgiveness, so what's the problem with Amy, why are we not *practising* forgiveness? 'Almighty God, who forgives all who truly repent'; we say it every week in church, what's the problem?

I've been quite demoralised – and slightly annoyed – at this 'now just wait a minute!' attitude. Still, probably it's me. I know, from my witnessing Amy's repentance in the church and the resultant dramatic encounter with God, that the Lord Jesus forgave her, so I find it difficult to accept even the slightest hesitation from the church to do the same. Maybe we needed the vicar or an Elder there to witness it.

A Bible teacher at the church on Saturday morning last weekend did 'Man on the Run', Jonah chapter 1. Jonah gets busy doing other things to avoid the calling of the Lord, goes the opposite way, runs away – just like me, I thought. I told him after his talk that I was a 'man on the run'; too busy with my business, using the reason that I have to stay at work to work my way out of the financial mess I'm in, that I'm tied to it. The answer he gave me was so positive and instant: 'Stay where you are in business. If you left being a failure we would not accept you at Bible college, neither would anyone else. It's easy to fall back on Christian service after being a failure at everything else and is an extremely bad witness, a witness that would not be accepted by any prospective Christian employers'.

Is this another confirmation that I am in the right place, Lord, and not going to fail? How am I going to get out of this financial mess? I have not paid *any* PAYE/NIC for 1990/91 tax year. This amounts to approximately £45,000. Where do I get that sort of money without selling the house? We accumulate more summonses for arrears every week. I'm now beginning to lose count and cannot pay *any* of them – deeper and deeper we go. We aren't having a very busy April, either. What an awful witness. It frightens me, and that fear is very difficult to drive out. So, Lord, fill me with Your Holy Spirit, give me confidence in You, show me how to get out of this mess. It seems an impossible task and gets worse as time goes on. I had a letter ages ago from the Inland Revenue saying they were going to issue bankruptcy proceedings against me. It's that threat that frightens me, Lord. It hovers over me like a dark cloud and follows me around. There seems no way of getting rid of it. Please help me, Lord Jesus. In Your name I ask. Amen.

24 April 1991
Wednesday night

Today we won our case at Reading County Court against a client who accused Transportomatic of seriously damaging some double glazed doors we were delivering for them. Really it's just been their excuse for not paying us. The defendant applied at the last minute to dismiss the case and didn't turn up for the trial today, so we won by default. The judge ordered our client to pay all the costs, which would be between £8,000 and £10,000, but our solicitor reckons they may not have enough money, as their accounts read they're insolvent. So do ours, for that matter, but we won, praise the Lord. He works in very weird and wonderful ways. Who would have thought it would turn out like this? He looks after me, there is no doubt, but how He is going to sort this £45,000 I owe the tax collector, I do not know! They're hovering just waiting to pounce. It's only a matter of time and well overdue already. Please help me, Lord. In Jesus' name. Amen.

27 April 1991
Saturday lunchtime

It's a lovely sunny day today. My wife has gone to a drama and dance workshop near Stoke with a few others from the church, so I'm looking after the children.

Despite the beauty of the day I wonder if it is how God intended it to be. The answer is, of course, it's not. Despite the beauty of the day there is pollution in the air. I'm sure the sky isn't as blue as it used to be because there is such a lot of muck up there between from where I look and outer space. Sometimes there's a haze instead of a clear sky and I think, 'That's not right!' What lousy stewards of the Earth we have become because of our greed and selfish ends.

I've just read Isa. 41: 1. 'God says be silent and listen to me you distant lands; get ready to present your case in court, you will have your chance to speak, let us come together and decide who is right.' Although mankind will have a chance to present their case for what we have done, I don't think there will be much deciding to work out who is right.

28 April 1991
Sunday night

Last night, after coming in from work, I watched a film from the 'Banned' series on Channel Four: programmes that have previously been banned. This was a two and a quarter hour documentary about how man abuses animals; again, a catalogue of lousy stewardship of the creation. Dog fights, bull fights, private abuse, factory farming, whaling and animal experimentation for so-called 'progress' in the commercial and medical world funded by government and business. It was a sorry witness to what ends we will go to satisfy out greed and the so-called 'needs of the customer'. I almost felt like becoming an immediate vegetarian. I'm not an animal *lover;* I respect animals and believe in their right to an existence that God originally intended, but that's as far as it goes.

I went to another church tonight to support a first 'informal' service prompted by people who'd been to Spring Harvest who, like me, probably felt the need to start to break out of a 500-year-old mould. The Lord is to be praised for sowing the seeds in someone's heart to try and bring about change. The first fruits of the Holy Spirit may be small, but God knows what that church needs and He will inspire accordingly. To many people in that church it could have been that first bold step forward, to many people it would have been a step backwards. Tradition is a hard thing to break. The Pharisees and Jewish leaders in Jesus' time would have none of it, rooted as it was in hundreds of years of Old Testament Scripture. Just like the established church today – rooted in tradition that doesn't bear a lot of relevance to today's world. Jesus' word to us is the same word He gave to the Jewish leaders. His teachings are full of revolutionary ideas which, in many churches, are still revolutionary today. 'Love one another', 'love your neighbour (and enemies)', 'be born again', 'give up everything and follow Me'. Complete and unconditional forgiveness – even 'Evangelism' is a word not to be used in some churches.

It's just as if we're still nailing Jesus to the cross. We don't want Him off it. If He comes off it and comes among us, it'll rock the boat too much. 'We're very comfortable, thank You, Jesus, as long as You stay nailed to the cross.'

But we've got news for you! Jesus is not on the cross and the burial tomb is empty. HE'S ALIVE. Too many churches still have a DEAD Jesus; as Rheinehart Bonke asked at Spring Harvest – 'Is your Jesus a dead Jesus?'

30 April 1991
Tuesday night

We can praise the Lord yet again tonight. Our chief salesman, J. Christ, seems to have pulled off another major business deal. We start delivering for Showerlux again tomorrow – a major account which we lost over two years ago, then worth between £8,000 and £12,000 per month, is back with us. I'm not sure how the Lord does this. All I know is that this has fallen into our lap with very little effort on our part from the selling and marketing point of view. We have had no major sales push, neither have we been persistent with Showerlux to get the work back. Everything has been at their request; firstly for us to quote, then the customer returned goods work, now we've got the deliveries.

So what have we done right? I'll tell you what we've done right – we've prayed. Our effort hasn't been in the business world, our effort has been in the spiritual world. We've prayed a long time for more work, specifically mentioning this company's name, particularly when we had any dialogue with them. Other people have been praying also – prayer works! God works for, and with us, through prayer. 'Seek first the Kingdom of God and it shall be given' (Mat 6: 33. Luke 12: 31). 'Fix your attention on things that are unseen' (2 Cor. 4: 18. Heb. 12: 2). I put this major business breakthrough down to prayer, as I put the breakthrough when we signed the contract and started working for Jacuzzi down to prayer. I put the finding of the right warehouse for Jacuzzi – and the new warehouse we will shortly move into – down to prayer. All we've done is pray and it's all come together.

To all you sceptics who say it would all be coming together anyway, I don't think so. How does one explain why we are still in business? We have been insolvent now for three years, but we are still trading. We have not been able to pay any PAYE/NIC for *twelve months* and now owe £45,000 – yet they have not, as yet, foreclosed. The Lord is intervening here without a doubt. He's obviously not saying 'don't pay', we know we will have to pay (how, I don't know, but I'm sure the Lord will pull something out of His heavenly bag). He must be stalling; He must be delaying until we can afford to start paying. In the meantime, He's sending lots more work our way. If it be His will, we shall soon be starting the B&Q mirror work, and His timing is perfect; in three weeks' time we shall be moving and have the extra space to do it. It's all part of God's plan, which is worked out in getting to know Him more through prayer and action. What a wonderful God He is, praise Him.

1 May 1991

Wednesday night

The reality of getting the Showerlux work back is slowly dawning. It's like the last major answered prayer for work, when we started the Jacuzzi contract. Putting this answered prayer into practice is going to be a hard and anxious time, Lord. Please stay with me and keep my spirits up. Tomorrow there are 275 units to collect and we have no room at our present premises, so Morgan James is going to let us put goods into the new warehouse, although it's not yet finished. The sooner we can move, the better.

I estimate we will need at least two more wagons to do this extra work. We're collecting a hire wagon in the morning as an interim measure, and we need an extra driver ASAP, possibly two. We can't start delivering

Showerlux in earnest till next week, as we are fully committed on delivering existing work this week, which means there will be a backlog to clear. Coupled with Monday being a bank holiday, leaving only four working days next week to deliver, it will be one of 'those' weeks. Please, Lord, help me through it. Give me stamina and motivation. Keep me self-controlled and calm. Give me wisdom and good judgement and fill me with Your Holy Spirit. Keep me from being pressurised and anxious, and keep my efficiency level high. Help Leena and all the staff too, Lord. In Jesus' name I ask. Amen.

17 May 1991
Friday night, 2.05am

The strain of answered prayer continues. I wrote in the last entry, 'putting this answered prayer into practice is going to be a hard and anxious time'. It's not so much the hard and anxious time, Lord, but the long hours. I'm up at 5am some days, working till gone midnight, then up at 5am again. Last night I managed about seven hours' sleep, which was good. The night before it was three and, last week, one night, it was down to two and a half. I'm OK, Lord, as long as I can catch up a few nights later. I asked for help and You haven't let me down. Thank You.

The anxious time is about trying to keep on top of things and keep customers satisfied. My office work is suffering. My desk looks like a bomb's hit it, post not opened for three days (except cheques), we have one motor on hire, one on contract for a week from another local haulier, an owner-driver on subcontract, and another one starting on Monday. We have taken three new employees on, are desperate to acquire two more motors, and have got behind with deliveries because we are moving to much larger premises.

The first night's loading operation from the new warehouse was last night. It's organised – and sometimes disorganised – chaos and, on top of this (ironically, because we're so busy), we've had a Bankruptcy Enforcement Notice for arrears of PAYE/NIC for £32,000 which I haven't had time to do anything about. Anything can happen, Lord! Please keep all my creditors holding on until we get money in from all this work. In Jesus' name I ask. Amen.

19 May 1991
Sunday night, 12.30am

Another late one and up at 6am this morning to work again.

Things are still terribly hectic at work. As from last Wednesday, we started loading wagons from the new warehouse at Seighford. There is a backlog of goods due to the move and, despite it being twice the size, is choc-a-bloc and goods are still pouring in, particularly from Showerlux, who offloaded all their output onto us on 1 May with only 24 hours' notice.

I sometimes wonder if we're coping. I'm constantly concerned to get the Showerlux deliveries out within the four-day deadline quoted – it's a struggle. We really need more motors and drivers, despite taking three on last Monday. It's exactly what we need with moving, but it's a lot of hard work and long hours. The Lord's being very good, He's a good manager. He knows that nothing less than the work we've got will pay for these new premises and, although physically and mentally I'm stretched, I know He will not stretch me to breaking point. When I get near to that point, such as a week last Friday, I only have the Lord to cry out to and He answers; not immediately, but He answers.

Concerning that Friday, I was in tears three times through sheer pressure and exasperation. I fear that a nervous breakdown would have happened if I did not have the help of God. In these situations, even the unbeliever cries out, 'God, help me – please'.

My wife is being very good about hardly seeing me these last two weeks. I get in at night after she's gone to bed and I'm up again before she wakes up; and of course it's the same with the children. A most unsatisfactory family situation, accepted only because we all know it's temporary.

Lord, help me to cope with it all, and to put my innovations to make it easier into practice. In Jesus' name I ask. Amen.

20 May 1991
Monday night, 2.10am

Lord, when is this going to end? I was up at 5.20am yesterday and in to bed at 2.10am the next day.

Lord, I can't carry on like this. I need a competent person to do some of my work. My family is so understanding, but they hardly ever see me. I missed church on Sunday – working. I missed the church swimming party on Saturday evening – working. When I go to a social event, such as the 'Question Mark' meeting on Friday night, I'm nearly falling asleep. All it is at the moment is work and sleep, work and sleep. Oh Lord, I wouldn't mind if we were coping, but I'm finding it very difficult to believe I *can* cope. If we were getting the deliveries out on time I would be less anxious, but we're getting behind. We need to catch up quickly or we'll be getting complaints about long deliveries. Oh help me, Lord! In Jesus' name I ask. Amen.

21 May 1991
Tuesday night

Thank You, Lord, that tonight I was home by 9.45pm. The key is to start route planning earlier and, with such a backlog of goods in the warehouse, there's no reason why I shouldn't.

We've had a few things go wrong with some of the wagons today and yesterday. Lord, I pray they won't break down anymore. We don't need this at this mega busy time. Amen.

23 May 1991
Thursday night, 12.2am

Another extremely exasperating day! Just general problems brought on by me overbooking tomorrow and not enough wagons for the runs to be done, but it's turned out all right in the end. We're not keeping up with Showerlux

Lord. I pray next week we can get more wagons in, even with two drivers being on holiday, so we can clear the backlog. In Jesus' name. Amen.

3 June 1991
Monday night

At last, the 1.30-2.30am finishes have stopped. Tonight it was 11pm, which is good, but even midnight and a bit after is better than it was. We are slowly getting sorted out, but still moving stuff from our old premises, although only office equipment now. Lord, we need a person in the office to help us. We just cannot cope with all the paperwork on a long-term basis. Send someone who is good, Lord. In Jesus' name. Amen.

8 June 1991
Saturday night

The church walkers are back today after doing 190 miles coast to coast – St. Bees to Robin Hood's Bay in about two weeks, I think. My dad was support and back-up man. I thought he might come back converted. He will certainly have a lot to think about. Thank the Lord that one of the walkers would not be inhibited to be open about the person of Jesus to my dad. To think one can walk through all that beautiful countryside and still believe it all came from an explosion or whatever other scientific theory was supposed to have happened X million years ago... I did it for forty years, who am I to say that?

9 June 1991
Sunday night

Thank the Lord things are at last settling down at work. When looking back, it has been a big job accomplished, apart from a few loose ends and, again, despite my doubts, the Lord has been there all the way. We have caught up with deliveries; we are just about coping. It goes to show, if you are really serious about what you are asking in prayer, be prepared to receive the answer in a serious way. We have been praying for more work, and the Lord has answered with perfect timing, but it comes with a lot of effort to work the answered prayer through.

It's not easy. I've been at my wits' end at times, particularly when it involved long hours and not much sleep. The body gets run down and one's resistance is low – resistance to everything, including the devil. When your defences are down, he'll strike. We blame many things for our cracks being prised open by Satan's attack when often, as in my case over the last few weeks, all that is required to fight the situation is a good 8 hours' sleep – the wonderful, restoring power of sleep. We can 'over spiritualise' solutions to the times we get under attack – just get a good night's sleep.

12 June 1991

Wednesday night, 12.45am

My wife and I were saying last night that being in the established, traditional Anglican Church 'set up' is like being in an institution and she is beginning to feel institutionalised. It's like being part of the National Health Service or a nationalised company, part of a big union instead of being free. Yes, it's like being part of an institution: rules and regulations, meetings and committees, subcommittees, standing committees, councils and representatives. If you don't keep your eyes fixed on Jesus you become part of the institution, not part of the Kingdom of God. Another subtle trick of the evil one: 'we haven't got time for Jesus; we're too involved in the church!'

13 June 1991

Thursday night

The number thirteen again, as if it's almost built-in, that it's a number that is symbolic of the change from secular to Christian. Once it was unlucky; now it's just a number, but the memory lingers on.

It's still long hours at work. I've not had to get up really early this week so far, but intend to get up at 5am today (it's now 12.40am) to do some work that I haven't yet got 'round to. I can go to bed early on Fridays, as it's the last proper working day of the week and no runs to do in the evening.

Thank You, Lord, for the answered prayer last Monday morning, when the meeting with the bank manager went OK. Nothing drastic happened. He wants figures, but that's no problem. Thank You, Lord, that although he wealds a lot of power over us, You have the power over him; that although he may be pulling Transportomatic's strings, You're pulling his – the ultimate authority stops at You. Amen.

14 June 1991
Friday night

What an awful day. At the end of the day we had one of the drivers' wage packets stolen. There were only four people in the office at the time that could have done it.

I've eliminated three, which leaves the guilty one, but how do I approach the situation? Lord, You deal with it! All I'm bothered about is that one of our drivers has not received his £216.61 wages tonight.

19 June 1991
Wednesday night, 2.10am

Well, praise the Lord! In April and May we made a profit; £10,000 in April and, despite some big bills and a larger than normal payroll, we made £5,000 in May. My spirits are lifted, Lord. Somehow, when you're making money, things don't seem such a chore. I wouldn't say that working till 2am yesterday and 1.30am today just to get the figures out was worth it, but it wasn't the totally demoralising event it usually is when that profit and loss sheet runs off and all the figures are minus. Thank You, Lord Jesus, it's down to answered prayer. Amen.

23 June 1991

Sunday night, 12.40am

The start of another answered prayer today.

For about nine months we have prayed for the Bowman Webber enquiry – for us to distribute their mirror products to B&Q stores nationwide – to come to fruition. Today we had our first delivery of mirrors into the warehouse.

The blessings continue: since January we have had three major contracts awarded us as a result of prayer. On 15 January we started Jacuzzi; on 1 May, Showerlux; and today, 23 June, Bowman Webber. The expected combined annual income from these three customers alone is half a million pounds. Our sales turnover for May shot up to a massive £48,000, the most we have ever done in nineteen years' trading.

We are still greatly in arrears, though. We need massive profits, Lord ,to pay our debts. The total up-to-date debt owed to the Inland Revenue is now a huge £56,000. We haven't paid any tax and NIC since the end of March 1990 – we owe more than one year's contributions, Lord. Please show us the way out. We haven't paid any pension contributions for ages, either. All this money has been deducted from employees' wages, and it's not on to have not passed it on to the taxman and pension scheme, but – because we have been making heavy losses – we simply have not had the money. Wages and fuel obviously come first, to keep the business running. So please, Lord, help us.

We had a letter from the legal office of the Inland Revenue last week, saying that because we have not responded to their Bankruptcy Enforcement Notice they are now passing the matter to the High Court for bankruptcy proceedings to take place. I didn't respond to their first communication because I had no money to pay them. We still haven't, until all the money for this new work comes on stream, and a lot of that will have to be for working capital. We are in a situation where, on the one hand, we can hardly cope with the work and, on the other, we have no money and can't pay our debts. We are still insolvent. Our net assets from the end of May's balance sheet show a deficit of £69,000. Can we really trade out of this hole? Is the Lord Jesus really going to lead us out of this mess? Well, Lord, You're our only hope – other than someone coming along with about £70,000 to invest.

26 June 1991
Tuesday night

We could investigate the possibility of forming a worker's co-operative where everyone, in return for a capital investment, would have a share of the profits. That way we could easily raise the capital needed to pay the Inland Revenue. Eighteen people, say at £3,000 each – that's £54,000 – plus the rest from me and that would be enough. Most of our employees are home owners; well, not most, but at least half, so they shouldn't have any problem in raising a few thousand pounds each – but I think that's all a bit pie in the sky, Lord. The amount of legal work required to get it all properly signed up, plus the fact it is highly unlikely we would get everyone to agree at meetings about policy, etc. – it would be like a PCC meeting! No, stick as I am; being faithful that, somehow, the Lord will get us out of this situation. God knows much more than me about it, so I'll try and leave it to Him.

Lord Jesus, help me to be open to Your will and to trust in You more without asking the reason why and wanting to know how. Amen.

29 June 1991
Saturday night, 12.27am

Concerning people who know their Bible back to front, people who have favourite passages, people who represent the Church in one way or another... they may be on a committee, an elder, lay reader, very well versed in church matters – procedures, liturgy, chants, creeds etc. – but, despite all this head knowledge, they do not seem to know a person very well: the person of Jesus.

I mention this because, on the way home from work tonight, I was just thinking of how many people in business get on, not because of *what* they know, but because of who they know. That over-used phrase in all walks of life is 'it's not what you know, it's who you know'. How true that is in our walk with God.

1 July 1991
Monday night

An evening at work when, from about 8pm onwards, all I wanted to do was come home; but I have to stay and do the work. Just when you think you've finished, there's something else you haven't done and you have to stop a bit longer: the sort of evening when you wish you had a job with reasonable hours and less responsibility.

I long for a holiday, Lord; hills and green fields with a sea shore and just the family in the sunshine. But while I'm running this business on my own, it will never be.

2 July 1991
Tuesday morning, 9am

There is no doubt that in the last few months the business has turned dramatically. We have been praying for extra work and we have got it in a big way. Our turnover in May rocketed to an all-time high and, although we have moved to premises three times the size of our previous depot, the warehouse is full and we are now ordering racking to expand upwards. However, more work in the quantity the Lord has blessed us with does have its problems. We need more wagons. Two are on hire at present, but that's expensive. We need to purchase or lease, but the last three years' accounts are terrible, so we cannot get finance. We need more working capital to finance the extra personnel and labour involved in implementing the expansion, but the bank won't increase our overdraft. With being so 'hands on' in the running of the business, one cannot see solutions from a distance that someone from outside looking in could see. This is where the Lord steps in. As He oversees the business, He can guide and direct, but, Lord, it's so hard to hear Your voice in the midst of all the hussle and bustle of the daily rat race. I am also physically and mentally drained a lot of the time, when rational and logical thinking don't come easy. Again, Lord, help me to be open to Your guidance and direction. In Jesus' name I ask. Amen.

Chapter 10: Beside the self-destruct button.

5 July 1991
Friday night, 1.30am

1.30am into bed, Lord, and I was up at 4.30am. Please, Lord, give me an easy day at work after a decent sleep. In Jesus' name I ask. Amen.

11 July 1991
Thursday night, 12.45am

And so it goes on; after midnight again, although tonight I was home about 10.15pm. I hardly ever see the children. I came home for tea on Wednesday just to see everybody, but when I'm at home, I'm not doing my work, so that puts me behind, meaning I'm later coming home at night after I go back after tea. It's a constant struggle to get time with my wife, the girls and the garden. Again, the lawn hasn't been cut for two weeks because I haven't been able to fit it in. The hedge cuttings from two weeks ago are still not cleared up outside. The weeds are about three feet high. The things wrong with the house go unmaintained, such as the back door needs a new handle system and damp is appearing in the lounge at eye level, which means the rainwater guttering must be faulty... and so it goes on.

I'm beginning to realise what hope is because, at the moment, I hope for such a lot. I hope for a holiday, but it's not possible. I hope for more time, but it's unlikely. Hope is something we haven't realised yet, but one day we will. I know one day I'll have a holiday; one day I will have more time; and one day I will not be tied to the business. One day I will be free from it, for I know one day the Lord Jesus Christ will release me. As a Christian, I have more hope because there is a lot of hope in Jesus Christ. He can make things possible that would not be possible if I didn't know Him, for all things are possible through Jesus Christ (Mark 9: 23, 10: 27). So I put up with my present burdens, knowing that what I hope for will one day be mine. He is working in, and through, everything. Although He may seem far away, He's not – He's right with me.

Without Him, it is a false hope and a deception of the evil one, for which many of us fall. The false hope of money, of winning the pools, of owning property, even of running a business – for they all bring their problems. When hoping, we only see the good points; again a deception of the devil – he makes *everything* attractive.

Bait is attractive until you bite. Then the hook is stuck and you're hauled into the devil's net for him to put you in and out of the water as he pleases.

No, I'd sooner swim against the flow – it's harder, but the right direction. It takes longer to get to the head of the river and it's harder work, but it's where the water of life springs which never dries up. So we swim in the knowledge that one day we will get there against the flow, the opposite direction to those who 'go with the flow', down stream, with the emphasis on the 'down'. It's down hill all the way and you don't even have to know how to swim – you just get carried along with the flow which, eventually, ends at the sea. So you're all at sea with millions of others, lost in a sea, tossed up and down and not knowing which way the wind is going to blow you next. So I go for the hard way – the Jesus way.

12 July 1991
Friday night, 11.45pm

I've actually managed to cut most of the lawn tonight. It's Friday, the only weeknight I can come home early.

Money problems, it's all money problems. If it wasn't for money problems, I'd be fine. Remember the Bankruptcy Enforcement Notice against us at the beginning of May – which I've done nothing about – and on 6 June a letter to say that, as nothing had been heard from us, they were putting the matter into the hands of the High Court for commencement of proceedings? Well, I've still done nothing about it, Lord, nothing at all. It's almost as if I'm willing them to come and shut the business down. Then at least I'd have time with the family, the pressure would be lifted – or would it?

The problems with the customers would be enormous. Suddenly the carrier they depend on to deliver their goods would not be there. All their goods would be in our warehouse, they would have to fetch them out. Our suppliers would not get their money and they would be after *me*.

Sometimes I think I'm being a fool thinking I can trade out of this hole. The money we owe the PAYE/NIC must be at least £60,000 now; in other words: the £60,000 I've taken off my employees, I've kept. I haven't handed it over to its rightful owner. How awful that is, considering I'm a Christian. It's fraud, it's dishonest and deceitful, and is now probably impossible to pay without selling the house and business; in fact even that wouldn't realise enough money to pay debts anywhere near what I owe. In addition to the aforementioned, I still have an £85,000 overdraft, owe £14,000 on the Business Development Loan, about £20,000 to the VAT and £24,000 to my Dad. The figures show it's totally out of hand and just a hopeless situation.

I often ask myself, 'Is putting my faith in Jesus Christ to save the business foolish? Faith in Jesus Christ saves the person who has the faith, it doesn't save that person's business'. Or does it? We shall find out. I believe the answered prayers of all this extra work will not be so the business just goes bust. There is a bigger purpose behind it. It's not just to make me money either – that is a long time away. What purpose has God in all this? Will it one day be an attractive proposition for someone to invest in the business the amount we owe, or am I just going down the wrong road altogether, totally out of touch with the Lord's will and on the road to disaster?

Thank the Lord people are praying for me. I am personally too confused, mentally and physically exhausted, to see His clear will. Amen.

21 July 1991
Sunday night, 12.50am

Work reduced me to tears today – not for the first time, but one of the few times when man's weakness without the Lord was demonstrated in front of my wife and the children. It doesn't take a lot to get me in a temper at work at the moment. I have a short fuse so I quickly explode. It's getting to me without a doubt, all this work! I'm almost at the stage where I'm trying to pray my way out of answered prayers because of the extreme burden and pressure it has brought upon me.

But when I look back over the last few weeks I realise we have stopped praying on a regular basis, so the strength of the Lord, which is released through prayer, has been gradually draining out of me. I feel absolutely drained, physically, and especially mentally. One gets to the stage when one doesn't want to pray. I have been at that stage today when I have nearly been convinced that I have lost the battle and it's time to give in – and in spiritual warfare, that's serious. It virtually means that I have surrendered to the devil and I'm ready to go over to his side to stop him hassling me. I've felt I've literally been slipping back into the old self, into the secular world and back to the devil himself. I've been swearing at setbacks at work and reacting with temper tantrums and unpleasantness to other people. I've been blunt, rude and snapped at people. I bang around at work in a huff, making life generally uneasy for everyone, and then jump in to my car at the end of the day with a 'Peace with God' or a 'Thank God for Jesus' sticker in the back window.

What a let down to the Lord I am. How difficult it is to keep rising back up, time and again, setback after setback. I really feel that next time I will just lie down and take the knocks – that taking the beating is less hassle than fighting back; just lie down, take it all and give up the fight. Admit defeat and stop fighting, just for peace and quiet.

The devil nearly had me today. I very nearly fell for the lie. He very nearly convinced me that the lie was in fact the truth, and that being a Christian was the lie. Here I am again – the nearly man. How subtle he is – 'Come and join me and have the quiet life'. But at 11.30pm we decided to pray – the weapons were picked up and aimed. The slide back was checked and we went on the advance, somewhat reluctantly and sheepishly. But the devil has no protection at all, so even the feeblest prayer will have some effect.

Today I nearly went over the edge. Thank You, Lord, that Your lifeline was thrown out to me. I didn't even reach out for it; You placed it in my hand. Amen.

22 July 1991
Monday night

Thank You, Lord, that today hasn't been a bad day at all. I was home at 9.30pm and the children weren't asleep.

26 July 1991
Friday night, 1.15am

I don't know whether I'm doing right, Lord. I'm spending money on extra wagons when I should be spending it on paying my debts. But without more wagons we cannot earn the money to pay them – Catch 22. It's costing us a fortune to hire motors; we must get rid of them as soon as possible. I suppose I'm expecting our creditors to hang on just a little while longer and that the huge debt and Bankruptcy Enforcement Notice will take a long time to reach the High Court. I am assuming I will have right up to the hearing date to pay it off.

I'm sure I get confused with 'Trusting in the Lord' and 'Burying my head in the sand'.

28 July 1991
Sunday night, 2am

It definitely makes a difference to pray. We started praying together again on a fairly regular basis last Sunday, and I've had a better week; not a utopian week, probably no fewer things have gone wrong, but the ability to cope with them comes easier. I say 'fairly regular' because my work pattern often unavoidably clashes with my wife's, but today we knew it would, so we prayed *before* I went to work. Sometimes, when you pray about things that concern you (like today it was to get the delivery notes and runs sorted quickly), it definitely is easier – I just seemed to get a lot done. I only expected to get the notes sorted into delivery areas, but I also did five runs, so thank You, Lord.

When I'm at work at odd hours, when it's quiet with no phone ringing and an empty office, I do get time to reflect on situations. Tonight I sat in the warehouse, having a break with a cup of coffee, and thought how vast the new warehouse is compared to twelve months ago. Then we were struggling away with 2,000 sq. ft., a back street yard and a damp downstairs of an old house as offices. Now we have 12,000 sq. ft. of brand new warehousing, purpose-built offices, parking for thirty trucks and we're thinking of taking on an extra 2,400 sq. ft. I sat down and thought, 'It's vast' and I thank the Lord that it's all due to Him answering our prayers. Amen.

6 August 1991
Tuesday night, 1.05am

To not fill this journal in may seem to suggest that the Lord doesn't figure too much in my life at the moment. Well, that's wrong. If you went by my attendance at church and church meetings, one might even say I've lost interest. Well, nothing could be further from the truth. Jesus works everyday in my life, constantly buzzing away in my head. I rarely stop thinking about Jesus and Christianity in general.

8 August 1991
Thursday night, 11.55pm

A beautiful day today, sunny with a breeze, praise the Lord. Although it was nice to see my Christian bailiff friend visit us at work today, what he brought with him was a bit of a blow – a VAT distress warrant for £17,000 plus. That means that, at the end of this month, instead of being able to clear some of our PAYE/NIC debt, it will be the VAT, and the rest will pile up. I was hoping to get a big chunk sliced off the PAYE, but not now.

Something is happening to my temperament in times of uncertainty at work. It's only in the last few weeks. I always used to panic a bit on pay days when I wasn't sure if we had enough money in the bank to pay the wages and I got extremely annoyed at the bank's stubbornness to not allow us to go a *little* over our limit to draw the full amount. It used to be most exasperating to have to phone customers who owed us money and insist I collect a cheque to get in the bank that day so we didn't go that little bit over. It often became a race against time, involving up to two and a half to three hours out of the office going round Stoke and charging back to catch the bank before they shut. But now I'm quite calm about it all. Although the situation is still the same, I am at peace and of the reasoning that, if the money is not there, then we can't pay out. But the money *has* been there recently, praise the Lord. It's just *been there*. Last week we knew we didn't have enough, so my wife drew £300 out of her building society, I got £650 out of our main bank, and we had, almost to the penny, the rest in the other bank. Now, I had no way of knowing in advance how much was in either of those banks, or how much the wage bill would be until the payroll had been calculated – I didn't know which cheques had been cleared and which hadn't. The Lord works like that! He knows, which is why we should trust Him. And all this was done in a calm, orderly manner. We were, for a change, trusting in the Lord, and of course He provided. The same happened today, just enough in the bank for the employees who were back tonight, praise God. Amen.

19 August 1991
Monday night, 12.30am

Today President Gorbachev, of Russia, was deposed by right wing hardliners who didn't agree on his liberal and reformist policies. We prayed tonight for justice to prevail and only good come out of it.

On Sunday, in the morning thanksgiving service, my wife and I stood up to say what a difference being a Christian made to our family life.

25 August 1991
Sunday night

The last entry mentions a coup in Russia, Gorbachev under house arrest. It didn't last long. The will of the people won the day, the coup collapsed and the leader shot himself. Boris Yeltsin and Gorbachev are back in power. The Communist Party has been banned and will be disbanded.

I've turned down two requests to get involved in the Lord's work today: once to go on an evangelism training weekend and once to start leading a house group again. This presents a conscience challenge to me.

26 August 1991
Monday night

'This is the day that the Lord has made', and everything went wrong.

The alarm this morning was set for 6am so I could get up early to go to work, be back for late morning and this afternoon and evening. I had it all planned to cut the hedge and front lawn. I didn't hear the alarm, for starters. It was 10am before I got up, so there were four hours lost, which put me in a foul mood, particularly when my shaver didn't work properly. I was on a short fuse to start with, and as the day went on, it got shorter.

I finally ended up at work at 11.30am. I particularly wanted to get in early this morning, knowing that in the afternoon the office would be roasting with the sun through the windows and on the roof, so it was very hot. I was so hyper and exasperated I broke down and wept, crying that God would release me from this burden of a business, this millstone round my neck which takes so much time to operate – bank holiday Monday and I still have to work. When am I ever going to get a single day when I can forget about work? I'm ready to throw the towel in, once again. I've had my second breakdown into tears in two weeks, so why do I go on?

Because it's such a huge thing to finish with. I have such a responsibility to other people that it would be totally selfish to just give in. Lord, give me mountains of strength to boost me up, with mountains in reserve. In Jesus' name I ask. Amen.

28 August 1991
Wednesday morning, 9am

I was woken this morning at 7.15am by a phone call from a driver who had broken down, which, in itself, is a normal occurrence from time to time in a transport business. But this time it really hit me what an awkward and unsociable business I'm in. What other job would you be disturbed from sleep at such odd hours? I get calls at 3am in the morning sometimes. This is such a stupid business I'm in – I had a real moan this morning.

It's really hitting me lately; how I loathe it all. It hit me this bank holiday weekend when I had to work yet again. There's no let up. I have to work day in, day out without a single day off. There must be easier ways of making a living. I'm a slave to it now: it rules my life – I'm behind bars like a prisoner, cannot escape, cannot get away.

The thing is, I know the Lord Jesus can release me, but I haven't got the guts to hand it all over to Him. I hand bits and bobs over daily. Things that are problematical we pray about and He sorts it out. But to say 'Here Lord, You take *the lot* off my shoulders' – well, I'm not brave enough.

I fear for my employees and customers, but, really, I fear for myself. People tell me I provide a living for my employees who use the money they earn at Transportomatic to provide for their wives, feed and clothe their children and pay their mortgages. In turn this gives them self-esteem, a sense of belonging, financial security and peace of mind, and they're right. I *do* feel responsible for this and it gives me a sense of duty very much to carry on, but at times like these, even that gets lost in the desperation to be released. God cares as much about my employees and customers as I do, so He'll look after them. We prayed about Jeff's situation when we made him redundant last summer and he was looked after. But to put twenty people and a business turning over in excess of half a million in jeopardy by putting it up for sale is a different kettle of fish; what would I do, where would we live – the future would be totally unknown. But maybe I'm wrong; God is big enough to take anything on.

This is where I fall. I know this is what the Lord wants me to do. He *wants* me to put my total future in His hands; total trust in Him. But I say again, I haven't got the guts to do it. I want to know beforehand what I'm going to be doing, but the Lord says, 'No, put your trust in me *first, then* I'll show you what you'll be doing'.

It's like my commitment to the Lord four years ago. I wanted to know *before* I committed myself what was going to happen, which is why I took so long. But in the end, you just commit yourself with no conditions attached. You cannot attach strings or conditions when you trust in the Lord or it wouldn't be total trust.

So I know what I'm supposed to be doing, Lord. I'm supposed to be trusting You totally and selling up, but I won't because I daren't. But I know You're working on me and we are now very close to the time when You'll either give me no choice or You'll bring me to the point where I'm strong enough in faith to do it.

I said this morning, 'That's it, I've had enough, I'm selling, I don't care what happens as long as I get rid of it!', and all my wife could say was, 'Have I remembered the rolls for the picnic?' Maybe I'm taking this whole thing far too seriously. It's taken me over so much I no longer have a sense of humour.

Oh Lord Jesus, I pray this is the start of something new and exciting, but it's also very frightening, so I don't want to go through with it. But to stay where I am is just making me bad tempered, grumpy and totally fed up. Either way seems very difficult, and I'm looking for an easy option, but I don't suppose there is one, is there? What a life this is. Amen.

3 September 1991

Tuesday night

The weekend was awful. At the time it was awful, but since then the Lord has done something in my life. I'm not sure what, but something – I feel different.

My wife had a craft fair on Saturday, so I looked after the children. They don't take a lot of looking after, as mostly they play together quite happily, and this is what they were doing on Saturday morning when I was sitting in the kitchen (the playroom is above the kitchen and has its own separate staircase).

Suddenly our youngest let out a cry and came running downstairs saying that our eldest, who was at the top of the stairs, had smacked her. Well, I hit the roof. I yelled at her in a temper, growling at her to get in her bedroom 'NOW and bloody quickly'. I was half uncontrolled and, alas, gave her a push as she passed me on the stairs. She didn't fall, but hit the door at the bottom with a fair force and awkwardly. But in her panic to get away from me losing complete control, she continued to run to her bedroom, obviously in shock at the explosiveness of my outburst – I had undoubtedly 'lost my rag' with her.

The realisation of what I had done did not take long. This wasn't the real me. I had temporarily exploded, being on a very short fuse anyway, and immediately was filled with remorse at what I had done. There is no excuse for yelling in an uncontrolled way. Thank the Lord I hadn't inflicted a deliberate physical blow, but the push was enough for her to sense what was inside me and fill her with fear.

Prompted by the grieved Spirit of God the situation became quickly defused and I was filled with guilt. I quickly went upstairs to say sorry and talk it over. I began by saying that she shouldn't smack for such a small reason and tried to explain that I was on a very short fuse due to the pressure at work, which is why I lost my temper with her. What she said in reply shook me and made me realise that she has feelings, too.

She said that she loses her temper quickly as well, which is why she smacked Laura. How could I have been so blind, so ignorant to think that I was the only one with feelings; that only I was allowed to lose my temper and no one else. What right had I alone to try and justify what I had done? Her reason for smacking our youngest was just as valid; in fact, it was the same reason I had given for losing my temper with her! I sat down on the bed with her on my knee and began to weep. I was begging for forgiveness, but of course there was no need to beg, she had already forgiven me, she had already said, 'It's OK, I forgive you'.

What a lesson we adults can learn from our children about repentance and forgiveness. I knew her barrier towards me had come down without any hesitation, but again, we adults don't release ourselves from the effects so quickly. It was quite a while before I was totally at ease with her again. For the rest of the day I kept wanting to go up to her to just check she really had forgiven me and to reassure her I really was sorry. I wanted to hear, once again, that she had forgiven me; but of course she had, right from the start. With adults, barriers linger, but children are so resilient and soon put things behind them and start afresh, almost immediately, sometimes.

Since then, there is no doubt that we are closer. I sense her concern for me. She hugs me more now, I get a bigger welcome when I come home and a more willing kiss when I go out, and more requests for a hug. What seem like splitting moments at the time often turn out to be blessings in the end. That promise of God, once again. 'Everything works together for good to those that love Him' (Rom. 8: 28).

4 September 1991

Wednesday night

Sunday was fairly uneventful until the evening.

Because the vicar is away on holiday, a Church Army prison chaplain took our evening praise service. I didn't attend church on Sunday morning due to work, but I had to go Sunday evening because I was leading the worship. I hadn't been right all weekend, either mentally (work pressure) or physically (a sore throat, then aches and lethargy). However, I arrived at church Sunday evening feeling better and quite ready to give my contribution; no usual nerves, but wishing I hadn't volunteered for the job.

Prayer time came led by our visiting minister, where an open invitation was given for anyone to thank the Lord for anything in particular. I found myself praying out loud thanking the Lord for just 'being there' – but at the same time I felt so far from Him. I think it must have been a confused plea on my behalf for the Lord to reveal Himself a little more to me.

There was stony silence after I'd finished, interrupted only by the minister inviting me up to the front. He said that ever since he entered the church he sensed a heavy burden being carried by someone, and the Lord pointed His finger, through him, at me. He started praying for me, laying his hands on me, and I started to weep – I just wept. While he was praying in front of everyone else, I just wept – I seem to be always weeping, lately. When he'd finished he gave me a big hug, then I just went and sat down.

I didn't feel anything after or later in the evening, but I knew spiritually something must have happened. I thought maybe I'd be walking on air the following Monday morning and maybe fly to work, but no.

However, I did have a very strange, vivid dream that evening:

My wife was leaving me and the children: it was her or the business, which was the gist of the reason. She was younger, the age she was when we were courting. It was a very detailed and vivid dream that could be remembered for quite a long time after waking up. I don't know what it was supposed to tell me, if anything. Maybe it was a warning from Jesus of things to come if I carry on as I am. Anyway, as at Monday morning, apart from that dream, nothing was different.

5 September 1991
Thursday night, 10.15pm

Continuing from the last entry saying 'As at Monday morning I didn't seem to feel any effects from Sunday evening' – on reflection, there *has* been an effect.

Something has happened, of which the most significant is that I've been home the last four evenings relatively early. Twice the children have still been up. Now this may seem a totally unspiritual and irrelevant thing to happen as a result of the Lord lifting a burden off me, but when I tell you that the long evenings and getting in so late that my wife and the children have been fast asleep was really getting me down, you can see that actually coming home early is a great burden lifted. It's difficult to work out how this has come about. We are not *quite* as busy as we normally are due to many firms coming back off holiday this week – so I am not *quite* as busy in the evenings – but by no means has the work slacked off enough to get me home at times like 8.50pm tonight, 10pm last night, 9.15pm the night before and a similar time on Monday. Maybe I've started route-planning a little earlier, but it hasn't been a conscious effort. Anyway, these early nights home have 'unburdened' me. Praise the Lord. Amen.

Chapter 11: Brilliant, yet disastrous.

10 November 1991
Sunday night

A two-month gap in entries – mainly because I've been engrossed in two books. One called *Spiritual Warfare for Every Christian* by Dean Sherman (every page leaps out and grabs you), and now I'm reading Billy Graham's *Angels, God's Secret Agents.*

One of many things that come out of both books is, I believe, that nothing happens here in the natural, physical world involving human beings without something happening in the spiritual world first. If we think that strife and wars are becoming more acute, intense and numerous here on earth, then it's much worse between good and evil in the heavenly realms, the battle above: for earthly happenings are a mere spin-off of spiritual happenings. This is one of the reasons why prayer can be so effective in interrupting or changing events here on earth, because they originated in the spiritual world. Prayer immediately releases God's agents, the angels, into battle on our behalf in the heavenly realms. It's the spiritual world that changes people's minds. It's the bad spirits that put evil thoughts of war, conniving, insurrection, perversion and all the rest into people's minds; and the good spirits – God's agents – who counteract them, and visa versa. With enough Christians praying – or persistent prayer from the few – the evil spirits are eventually defeated and the victory is won through Jesus. The first line of the Graham Kendrick song *For This Purpose* says, 'For this purpose Christ was revealed, to destroy all the works of the evil one'.

But we must not stand smugly by in the knowledge that victory is ours in the end, no matter what. We are to counteract Satan's attempts to keep people to his side. We must do our utmost to win as many as possible for Christ. God can only work on this earth through His people. We are God's agents here in the physical world and are commissioned to infiltrate the enemy's territory and win it back for Jesus as His bride for that last marriage ceremony between Him and His people. Our fighting weapons are as described in Ephesians 6, prayer and action release these weapons.

Prayer and action are the triggers on the guns to fire the bullets and missiles of God. Without these, the triggers cannot be pulled to release the weapons. The guns will remain cocked, ready and waiting, but useless without prayer first, then action.

So what has the Lord been doing in our lives these past two months? As usual, He's been active. So what have I been doing in the Lord's life these past two months? As usual, I've been pretty inactive – but that's the measure of God's grace. He loves us so much that, although we probably don't do much for Him, He's still very active doing lots of things for us.

I don't have time anymore for house groups or Wednesday morning 7.30 prayer meetings. The first Saturday in the month, Dawn Patrol meeting, I miss. I no longer have time for 'Question Mark' drama group – I don't even make both Sunday services.

But the Lord doesn't count our failures and the number of times we let Him down or fail to appear. He doesn't need to count the cost because He paid the price for our failures in full. They were taken by Him and nailed to the cross – they cost Him His life. Despite our failures He still pours out His blessings, because He loves us so much.

So, what has He done for the business these last two months? Well, despite our balance sheet being the worst it's ever been (hopelessly insolvent), in the past two months we've managed to:

1. Pay £29,000 of PAYE/NIC arrears.

2. Buy three more vehicles for cash (we still cannot get finance)

3. Increase our workload so that last month, October, we nearly topped a £60,000 sales turnover, more than double what it was twelve months ago. We now have fifteen vehicles (we only had ten last May) and another on the way.

4. Keep me sane through all this.

5. Last but not least, we are making consistent profits. Our six-month figures as at 30 September show a net profit of £18,000 – and that's after depreciation of over £6,000.

This has not been achieved through good management, a hard sell, or luck. It has been achieved through prayer. We have been praying for over two years for a profit, and the Lord has answered. Amen.

15 November 1991
Friday night, 10.15pm

Not a good week at work – is any week a good one? We endure, we struggle through. The daily hassle hardens me off. People phoning in all the time: when are we going to pay this or that invoice? Everything well overdue. Transportomatic phoning out all the time: when are such and such clients going to pay us? Well overdue. All so we can pay the people chasing us, so they can pay the people chasing them and down the line it goes, the money merry-go-round turns ever faster, 'round and 'round in circles, everyone chasing each other. It's like Eccles. 2: 11, 17: 'Chasing the wind, it's all useless'. The writer says in Chapter 1: 13b, 'It is an unhappy business that God has given to the sons of men to be busy with'.

My hope lies in faith, the unseen things, for the seen things are only temporary. Money comes, money goes; people are employed, people leave; work comes in, work falls off. We fool ourselves that we are in control, that we can decide our own destiny. The only thing that is certain is that we die, that's a dead cert!

At work I see no material hope without God's intervention. I have been talking about the financial situation at work today. The Lord has blessed the business greatly. The story of how He showed us where to relocate has been told and since moving in May the work has poured in. The comparative position now in November is:

	April	October
Sales	£30,000	£60,000
Workforce	15	22
Warehouse space	2,000 sq. ft.	14,400 sq. ft.
Vehicles	10	15

How can an insolvent business achieve this in full open view of financial institutions and government revenue departments who appear to fight against us? I don't know. I'm as mystified as anyone how we stand still, let alone expand.

It was a huge business risk to move to much larger premises – particularly under such poor trading conditions at the time – and the fact we moved before we had the work. But the step in faith was honoured by the Lord.

We are coping, but only with His help. He supplies our needs daily, particularly in financial terms; the VAT due always gets into a distraint situation where we have to pay by a short deadline. The sums requested are always large, but somehow the deadlines are met and the burden of debt is lifted. We pray (not as often as we should), but we always pray in desperate situations, don't we? We ask the Lord to get us out of the mess, which sometimes looks impossible, but He does it – not till the last minute, but He does it. (God doesn't have a clock ticking away or a calendar – He's in eternity.)

Somehow, out of cash flow alone, in the last six weeks we have managed to pay the taxman £29,000 and buy five extra trucks, totalling £27,000. Although these are achievements worked in partnership with the Lord, they have created a considerable problem, which is very worrying to me and other people at work who are involved, but I don't suppose it will be much of a problem to the Lord if we trust and follow His guidance.

Many times I wonder what the Lord is up to, not seeing the purpose of it or an immediate end result. I'm in that situation totally at the moment, both at work and at home.

1. WORK:

I have a current debt of approx. £50,000 in PAYE/NIC arrears for the whole of 1990/91 tax year. As previously mentioned, the fact I have paid £29,000 to the Inland Revenue and £27,000 for additional vehicles has left the business desperately short of cash. I struggle to pay the wages every week. I haven't paid any pension contributions to the contracted out scheme for the same period. I have been on a 30% VAT surcharge for about two years and, with our turnover rocketing, the VAT due has gone up pro rata. The last quarter it was £19,000. I haven't been able to pay, so I will be charged another £5,700 (30%) for nothing (just for failing to pay). I already owe £14,000 in surcharges on top of that, so that's a total of £38,700.

In the meantime, as I go on trading, yet more VAT and PAYE/NIC is accruing – it goes on and on. How on earth am I going to pay these amounts? I still have the Bankruptcy Enforcement Notice hanging over me, but since last May, when I was first notified, I've heard nothing except that the case has gone to the High Court (the Lord's definitely working on that one). The situation is seemingly hopeless. Our overdraft is £81,000, which is now being forced down by the bank, who is reducing our facility by £1,000 per month (very helpful). There are County Court writs and judgements against us flying around everywhere, which we cannot pay, although some have been settled. Yet we still trade vigorously, are extremely busy and are, at last, making a profit. He's definitely in all this somewhere, praise Him.

2. HOME:

I've been toying around with the idea of selling the house. Mainly because now I'm so busy at work I just haven't got time for the maintenance and many other little jobs that an old house demands. The garden is also too big for a person with very little time. In the summer it was difficult to find time to cut the lawn, never mind all the other jobs. We have about half an acre here, and it's too much. The potential here is enormous for someone with lots of time.

There are two major problems at work. As mentioned before, these are the extremely tight financial conditions imposed by the bank and the long hours. Could it be that if this house is sold, we are to move to a cheaper property and pay the overdraft or tax arrears with what's left over? That would release a considerable burden off me. Maybe that will be the case. Probably the Lord knows the taxman is going to pounce with an ultimatum to pay up or be bankrupted – after all, there is a Bankruptcy Order out for me and it can't be delayed for ever. But we've sold property before, and the money raised just fell down the black hole of increasing debt.

On the one hand, this is the excitement of it all when you're a Christian: what's the Lord got in mind for you? What is the next stage of His grand plan? He loves us so much that it will be nothing bad, so it's exciting, like a mystery tour; not knowing what's around the corner or what the next destination is.

We have also been prompted to go for outline planning permission to build a detached house at the bottom of the garden. That should sell the house much quicker.

16 November 1991
Saturday afternoon, 2.25pm

We have put our house up for sale. The asking price is £175,000 and someone is coming to view it at 2.30pm. I pray, Lord, that, if it be Your will, she'll buy it. In Jesus' name I ask. Amen.

16 November 1991
Saturday night, 9.40pm

An early night. It's been our youngest daughter's birthday today; bowling this morning, roller skating this afternoon, no sit-down party with food and games – she's seven. Thank You, Lord, that You've brought all our children safely to the beginning of this day. They are now seven, eight and a half, and eleven. Praise You.

25 November 1991

Monday night

At work today I did an end-of-month cleardown, and again we have made a net profit in October of £4,722, praise the Lord. We have now made a consistent profit for about six months: an answered prayer.

I didn't make church at all on Sunday. Although I'm working long hours, I usually get to at least one of the services, but not yesterday. Having said that, the services are hardly worth busting a gut for, at the moment! I'm really cheesed off with the boredom of them. The continuous repetition of Creeds, Glorias, the Lord's prayer and communion pre-amble; none of it from the heart, all read as a script from books. After a while their meaning diminishes, even when I try to say it with renewed freshness, trying to make it personal to myself and Jesus. We both feel we are becoming institutionalised into a sort of 'religious rut', which we shall not be able to get out of. We don't want to become religious; we want to follow Jesus Christ. We are thinking it may be time for a change of church as well as a change of house. Yesterday's service was a thanksgiving for the release of Terry Waite. My wife says it was far too solemn for what the title suggested, which has not helped her relationship with 'the church'. Still, I say it's your relationship with Jesus that counts. It's late, I'm going to sleep.

29 December 1991

Sunday night

I'm writing this journal from a strange bed in a rented property at a place called Inverness, Florida, USA; 3,600 miles away from where I usually write. A business friend has a property here. All that praying about having a 'proper' holiday with peace and quiet and not having to phone in to work has finally been answered.

Today we went to Main Street Baptist Church and have met some new friends. This morning was a normal service, and this evening we went to a 'Faith Supper'. On Tuesday we have been invited to a New Year's Eve party at a private house about ten miles away. I pray, Lord, I'll have lots more time to fill this in. We have a lot of catching up to do about what the Lord is doing in our lives – He's moving us along pretty fast at the moment. Amen.

31 December 1991
Tuesday night

We're still in Inverness, Florida.

Do you know we came here without knowing the address of where we were staying? We had everything except the most important thing. The only way we got it was by phoning the owner in England and asking. The flight was long – two flights, really. Manchester to Atlanta, Atlanta to Orlando; from leaving Stafford at 9am Friday to arriving here at 4am Saturday (10am British time). We got lost trying to get here from Orlando airport and it wasn't until my wife said a prayer that we found the right way. It was quite frightening; strange country, an automatic car I'd never driven before – and on the other side of the road – dark and foggy... very dodgy. We got lost again yesterday coming back from Sea World. Again we didn't get on the right road until we prayed. Tonight we went to a New Year's Eve party. This time we prayed before we set off and found it no problem – straight there. There's a message in that story – pray to start with to avoid getting lost – pray as the first resort, not the last.

There are lots of churches here mixed in with the cafés, shops, and petrol stations on the main roads. Thank the Lord that here churches have a much higher profile. They are openly advertised on the billboards, on TV, on big lit-up signs over their buildings and on big boards advertising 'what's on' when you enter the towns and cities. Christianity is much more open. It was a really good sermon on Sunday.

14 January 1992
Tuesday morning, 9.30am

We're back in Stafford. We arrived back about 12.15pm Saturday 11 January with the central heating pump not working; a bit of a shock, from temperatures of 75 degrees in Florida to 32 degrees here.

Last night, the Lord, in no uncertain terms, made quite clear to me the heavy burden of debt we have at Tranportomatic. I was extremely uncomfortable about it to the point of near panic. We still have mounting debts: PAYE/NIC/VAT and summonses and judgements against us not cleared. We have a writ from the High Court to pay £33,000 plus, or have our goods removed to pay it. I have written back to them asking for a 'Stay of Execution' stating I cannot pay until the house is sold, but it may be too late for that, as I have had various opportunities in the past to contact them, but didn't.

Am I really going to be bankrupted? In one way it would be a relief. The business would go and I would have lots of time with the family for a change. But would we have anywhere to live, would our furniture be taken away from under our noses and would we be evicted from our house? These thoughts, and more, play havoc in my mind and brought me close to panic about 3.30am last night in bed.

Oh, Lord Jesus, please look after us and help us to weather this storm. I pray that somehow we can pay this £33,000 to the Inland Revenue. In Romans it says we must pay our taxes (Rom. 13: 5-7). In Jesus' name I ask. Amen.

16 January 1992
Thursday morning, 11am

Yesterday morning I was fed up and despondent.

We were having a cup of tea at the breakfast table. My wife said we ought to pray, (we don't often feel like praying in these circumstances, but we should). So we prayed for the Lord to lift our spirits and remind us of the hope in Christ. When we'd finished, the post had come and, praise the Lord, one of the letters was to say we had obtained planning approval for a house to be built at the bottom of the garden. An answered prayer; we had been praying for that.

I now pray, Lord, that this approval will enable us to sell this house quickly, if it be Your will.

17 January 1992
Friday night, 1.35am

Still worried about this £33,000? Well, we now have an extra £32,000 to worry about. A VAT bailiff, my Christian friend, rang today to say he has a VAT demand for £32,000.

We can't pay it; it's hopeless. We now have demands for £65,000 from tax departments, who will, if we don't pay, just seize and force-sell all our assets. We don't stand a chance. It'll take a miracle to get out of this one. There is just no way we can pay this unless both the house and the business can be sold in the next two weeks. I don't believe even the Lord can do that. The good news of the planning soon vanished on hearing this drastic news. I've been so despondent today after hearing it.

I can't win! J.F. Clough versus the Establishment. If it's not a battle against the VAT and the Inland Revenue, it's against the bank or our suppliers. I'm just ripped off from all ways. If I can't pay the VAT, they slap a 30% surcharge on my next payment. If I can't pay my taxes, they charge me interest on what's overdue. If I can't pay the *original* amounts, how on earth do they expect me to pay interest and surcharges as well? The bank charge me 5.5% over the base rate for the overdraft – another rip-off – £1,000 arrangement fee just to *arrange* the overdraft, £10 now for a bankers draft, £3 for a counter cheque... how do they justify these charges? I'm now being fined a £600 lump sum, then £100 per month for not getting my annual PAYE return in. I'm levied £800-£1,000 per year by the RTITB (Road Transport Industry Training Board) for nothing. There is just obstacle after obstacle when you're in business. The only incentive I get is to wrap it all up and call it a day.

On the other side of the coin, 'profit' is a dirty word when you're doing well. Success only makes people envious and jealous, and once people see you've got money, they'll just try and rip you off a little bit more. I feel like a criminal. I genuinely cannot pay these demands because we've had an extremely bad time in the business! I'm being punished like a criminal!

All I've been doing is making sure we keep trading, as the only way I genuinely believed we'd get out of our financial difficulty was to trade out of it. It is beginning to appear we will not trade out of it; the costs are too high to use cash flow money to service them. We need a quick capital injection, Lord, not repayable; instead, the investor can get a share of the business in return. Can You arrange that, Lord, please, or are we to just let it go and not do anything until it's all over?

These are times when doubt can really get a hold, when the clearness and sureness seen when away on holiday becomes fogged up and starts fading due to the worries of deep involvement in a troubled business.

I know how the Israelites felt now when travelling from Egypt to the promised land: totally fed up, believing they'd never get there and that You had forgotten them – despite the pillar of cloud and fire, manna and water from the rock (Exod. 13: 21, 16: 31-32, 17: 6).

Lord, I am quite willing to forsake everything if You'd only give me another chance in a promised land – a new start. I'm 44, young enough to start again, the children are young enough to cope with the change, and my wife loves me enough to just follow. I'm quite willing to start again with nothing in a promised land. But, like the Israelites, I cannot start again in the land where I've been a slave, where I've toiled and worked all hours and still been beaten. Can You give me a new land, flowing with milk and honey, to pioneer a new start? No matter how humble the beginnings, I am willing to work hard to build again, this time for You. Most of what I've done at Transportomatic in the last twenty years has been without You, so it would not be a bad thing to shake off. There must be a lot of previous sin in Transportomatic, so we could bury it in the name of Christ, off with the old and on with the new. Amen.

18 January 1992
Saturday lunchtime

I finally got to trying to get some sleep after the last entry (Thursday night) at about 2.30 in the morning. I was at peace, but couldn't get to sleep and, at about 3.15am, I felt a strong prompting to put the bedside light on and open my Bible. It was as if the Lord Jesus was telling me we hadn't finished together; there was something more He wanted to say. So I put the light on and reached down on the floor by my bed and picked up my small NIV Bible. It literally fell open at Matthew's Gospel, chapter 26. It did so because, for some reason, the right hand page – page 1009 – had been crumpled up. I must have read that page on a previous occasion and shut the book without realising the page wasn't flat. My eye went to verse 36 onwards. In the Garden of Gethsemane, Jesus was praying for the Father to take the cup of suffering away from Him (verse 39 and 42). We all know that cup of suffering was *not* taken away from Jesus, He had to suffer and die for our sake (a few minutes later, Judas came along with other people who were armed, betrayed Him, and took Him away).

But for me it's different. Because Jesus took the cup of suffering, I don't have to; the cup of suffering it looks as if I am going to have to drink because of these huge debts. Jesus was saying to me that I don't have to suffer, for He suffered in my place. He also brought to me on that night the story of the Israelites being taken out of slavery in Egypt, being led through the desert for forty years and finally reaching the promised land, the land of Canaan, which is now called Israel. The story is likened to me being in slavery to the business at the moment. I cannot leave, but to be finally freed from it I have gone through, and will go through, a time of wilderness and trouble like the Israelites experienced – and like them, I must keep going. That for me, the manna from heaven and water from the rock will keep coming to sustain my journey and that, at the end of it, there will be a promised land.

20 January 1992
Monday morning, 9.30am

Yesterday the morning family service was packed; a lot of people there. The theme was 'Following Jesus'.

Apparently, the vicar has been praying with one house group for the gifts of the Spirit. If he's praying with people who have not been baptised with the Holy Spirit, then he's wasting his time. If you're not already filled with the Spirit, how can you receive a gift from it? The gift is from the

Spirit inside a person, not from the person alone; the Spirit comes first, then the gifts, not the other way round. I suppose the Spirit and the gift can come simultaneously, but definitely not a gift before the Spirit.

21 January 1992
Tuesday night

The time is coming very near when the Lord is going to break me free from this heavy yolk of a business, release me from the captivity that work is. He chases me until I give in. For about three years now He has chased me. I believe, more than ever now, that it is the Lord's will for me to be free from Transportomatic. He is leading me up to it. He will keep chasing me until it goes. He says that I am His and must not cling on to the worthless value that my work is.

Where I go to or what I do from here, I know not. The Lord will show me, but not until I am rid of my burden will He reveal it. I believe He wants an unconditional commitment. It is not to be 'yes, I will follow Lord *if*' or 'tell me what You want me to do and then *I'll* tell You if I'll do it'.

The fear of what people will say after or what will happen is disappearing, because the fear there is in staying where I am is getting greater.

Another demand has come in the post today. This time for current PAYE/NIC, totalling £24,000. I have seven days to pay – not a hope. I now have three demands, that run out very soon, totalling £89,000 (VAT £33,000, PAYE/NIC and capital gains arrears £32,000, and this latest one of £24,000). It looks more and more hopeless by the day. Delays in acting will only mount more debts: I must do something. How easy it is just to carry on into oblivion.

If the holiday has done anything it has made me realise reality – that there really are other things to do of which I am quite capable – that there really is an escape. That people do actually do other things other than own and run a transport business. I feel more confident in starting something different than I do about carrying on with something I've done for the last twenty years. A holiday has brought home to me that I can break out, and I'm getting excited about it, but I have a very hard time ahead of me.

I feel like Jesus before they came and took Him away. I feel I'm going to be questioned and interrogated and 'invaded' by awesome powers like the bank, the Inland Revenue, bailiffs and prosecutors. Oh Lord, if only it were possible to remove this daunting prospect from me. I know I have to go through with it like You did; You must have felt awful, Lord! You knew You were going to suffer mental and physical pain and die. All I'm going to go through with is mental anguish and humiliation. How I pray, Lord, that there will be enough money left over to start again. What a crashing disappointment it will be if, after twenty years of working in my own business, I'm left with nothing. Father, I pray You'll walk with me all the way and close. I'm still holding on to Isaiah 43:

> I have called you by name, you are mine.
>
> When you pass through deep waters I will be with you,
>
> your troubles will not overwhelm you.
>
> When you pass through the fire you will not be burned,
>
> the hard trials that come will not hurt you.
>
> For I Am the Lord your God, the Holy One of Israel
>
> Who saves you
>
> Amen.

30 January 1992

Thursday morning, 9.45am

Today the Inland Revenue turned up to collect £24,000. There is no way I can pay, so we signed the usual distraint notice. We have got five working days to pay. No way, Lord – perhaps You have got something up Your sleeve. I always continue to pray for this debt situation but, Lord, a 'big crunch' is going to come very, very soon. If I can't sort an arrangement out with the Inland Revenue we are already in a 'big crunch'. If motors are removed by bailiffs, then the business will fold; we cannot operate with fewer vehicles than we already have.

I pray You will be with me today, Lord. We have no spare money in the bank. My wife has not been paid wages for two weeks (she works for Transportomatic, too), neither has she had any housekeeping this week. The bank would not let me have any money yesterday; I keep borrowing off her for petrol for the car. We therefore have no money to pay the wages today, unless there's some in the mail when I get to work. So I pray, Lord, You'll give me peace and security in Christ. We have little or no security in money, so we lean on You, Lord. We have to be backed up to the financial wall though before we *do* lean on You, don't we? Sorry, Lord. Help me to lean on You *all* the time, not just in times of crisis. In Jesus' name I ask. Amen.

8 February 1992
Saturday,12 noon

I opened my RSV Bible tonight and it was in the Gospel of John, chapter 14. The first words I read were, 'I will not leave you desolate, I will come to you' (verse 18). Verses 27 says, 'Peace I leave with you, My peace I give to you, not as the world gives do I give to you. Let not your hearts be troubled, neither let them be afraid'.

11 May 1992
Monday night, 11.20pm

A three-month gap in filling this in!

There have been times of desolation, times of great blessing, times of frustration and oppression, but the Lord has stayed with us.

2 June 1992
Tuesday night, 11.45pm

I really feel moved to write – to write about the bombshell the VAT man brought me today. Transportomatic have had a Statutory Demand for

£60,000 of arrears and surcharges. Lord, we have plans that we've lifted up to You, but we didn't account for this. Although we knew we owed a lot of VAT, we didn't think this would come so quick and so large. All I can say, Lord, is hear my cry for help. We cannot pay this, Lord, no way – so what do we do? In Jesus' name I ask. Amen.

18 June 1992

Thursday night, 12.30am

Again I write to You, Lord, when I'm in dire trouble. Like the last entry, we hadn't planned for this, an even bigger bombshell.

Unknown to me, although the notice must have landed on my desk, I should have appeared in court on 10 June to answer a petition for bankruptcy (not the same as a Bankruptcy Enforcement Notice, which we still haven't heard about). I didn't appear, so an order was made on that day that I was bankrupt. I had a call from the receivers in Stoke-on-Trent today confirming this, saying I couldn't do anything about it. All I could do if I acted *very quickly* was apply to the court to have the bankruptcy order lifted, but I'd have to get the money that I owed in cash or banker's draft, which was about £8,000. Two firms have petitioned to wind us up, Neachells Hall Garage – who supply us with truck parts – and B.T. Rolatruc – who lease us a fork lift truck. I have to appear in Stoke-on-Trent court at 1.50pm tomorrow 19 June (today, really, it's now 12.30am) with the money I owe, explain why I didn't do anything about all the reminders and warnings, and beg for the court to lift the bankruptcy order (plus there are lots of figures and information they need).

I have a meeting with a solicitor at 9.30 in the morning. I may be short on raising the money. I am frightened, although I'm calming down a bit now after prayers for us, by us and other people. My wife has phoned one or two people and they are praying. Oh Lord, I'm desperate to get this over with. It's going into the unknown I don't like; all this is new to me. Please, stay with me, help me, please. In Jesus' name. Amen.

19 June 1992
Friday night

Today has just been a 'whirlwind'. I don't know how it was done, but I am no longer bankrupt. The bank manager let me have £8,000 no problem, the solicitor was brilliant (and so he should have been – he cost me £500 for the day). All I can say is thank You, Jesus. Amen.

22 July 1992
Wednesday night, 10.35pm

I am to speak at a Stafford Council of Churches meeting in September to do with Mission to Stafford next year. What do I talk about? Well, I suppose I just tell my story. In order to tell my story, I have to continue to write events in this journal as they happen. 'As they happen' are the operative three words to catch the detail and truth of the moment. I often think, 'Well there's nothing to write about'.

We tend to think God is doing nothing if there's nothing spectacular going on as a result of His divine intervention, or that there is nothing to pray about unless we have a deep tragedy or fraught situation in our midst or a major crisis on our hands or in the world. Nothing could be further from the truth. God is beavering away all the time and waiting in the wings in eager anticipation of getting involved with His people, but we never give Him a part to play. 'The world is a stage', someone famous said, 'each of us has a part to play'. We are involved in the world, whether we like it or not. But God does not get involved in *your* world unless He is asked. He loves us so much that He will not force Himself upon us. He has to be asked, and because we don't ask enough, we don't see Him getting involved enough. So if He appears to be fairly dormant, it's because we aren't asking Him to play a part in our lives. The Scriptures say He is 'The Author and Perfector of our faith' (Heb. 12: 2). He wrote the script intending for Him to play the leading role, but we keep on changing the script, altering it around to suit ourselves and writing Him out; and then we wonder why it's such a flop. We've written greed and selfishness in, and what was supposed to be a good production with a cast of millions, has been turned into a tragedy when we look at starvation and oppression, and a farce when we examine ourselves and the crazy values we hold. If only we'd get back to the original script: the Bible, God the original Author, and Jesus as the leading man.

12 August 1992
Wednesday night, 10.40pm

An early night, with motivation enough to write in this journal.

I am on painkillers for a strained muscle at the top of my leg. It's very painful otherwise, and severely restricts my movements. Before I went to the doctor this morning, my wife had to dress me, as I could hardly move.

Last week we had a tragedy. One of our longest serving driver's son was killed in a road accident, aged only seventeen.

Steve Dimmock said to me in the office, 'Doesn't something like this shake your faith?', meaning, 'why does God allow this to happen?'

Sceptics, most of the time, do not believe in God – or if they do, it's not to the extent that it affects their lives or that He is a God of intervention. But when tragedies like this occur, God is mentioned in words such as 'why did God allow it to happen?' or 'don't you start to have doubts in a God that allows this?'

It's ironic that when something of a tragic nature occurs that bothers them, and can't be reasoned with – as in the case of a seventeen year old boy losing his life – then suddenly, not only do they believe ('why does God allow...'), but they are blaming God for not intervening ('...this to happen'). Suddenly there *is* a God.

16 August 1992
Sunday night, 11.55pm

I didn't make church tonight, Lord – working again.

What has transpired at work in the last three months is proving to be a major answered prayer and has, so far, been fulfilled to the letter.

Since we have got really busy at work (over twelve months ago), we have been praying for a helper because, for me, the hours were long. My wife and the children didn't see much of me for long periods (although I only work four miles away, it might as well have been four hundred) and, at times, it was very difficult to cope. We prayed for a helper, as can be seen in previous journal entries. I thought the Lord would put into our minds one of the current long-serving drivers, but no.

About three months ago, Steve Dimmock who had driven for us before, phoned to see if we had a vacancy in the office or warehouse, as he wanted to come 'off the road' and have more regular hours (my good friend Jeff, whom we had to make redundant, was re-employed as the Jacuzzi contract manager; he was a friend of Steve Dimmock and told him of the possibility of a job here). Anyway, he came to see me on Saturday morning and it became clear as we talked that here was our answered prayer. As we chatted, the thought evolved in both our minds that he was capable of making the change from the operational side, of which he had fifteen years' experience as a driver, to the administrative side. So we set him on, quite convinced that this was an intervention from God.

As his first few days went by, the feeling grew that this was it. Katie, in the office, left quite shortly after Steve started. She had a go at him for telling her what to do, saying she 'only took orders from me', but it got out of hand and she stormed out, dramatic at the time, no doubt (I was out). Katie was an exemplary employee, efficient, businesslike, and knew the transport industry well – she will be greatly missed. Nevertheless, it may have been the Lord's doing, maybe she was in the way of an answered prayer; if so, the Lord will look after her. It opened the way for Steve to do her job, which is enabling him to master the administration of the accounts, payroll, etc. – an essential part of learning the business.

The Lord works in mysterious ways. He can change circumstances to a position that one would not have thought possible six months ago – another victory through regular praying. Lord, we continue to pray that you will bless this situation. Give Steve wisdom and knowledge, the ability to pick things up quickly, sound judgement and decision-making and the anointing of Your Holy Spirit upon him. In Jesus' name. Amen.

1 September 1992
Tuesday morning, 11am

This is very much a waiting game. Waiting on the Lord is not easy. It is a great temptation to go off on our own because of impatience, ego or restlessness, when in fact the Lord is saying, 'Be still, leave it to Me'. We have to realise that once we lift our plans to the Lord, the timing of when those plans happen are in His hands, not ours. If we have faith and believe the Lord can do great things in our lives, they will happen all right, but only when He says so. It could be tomorrow, it could be in ten years.

I will never forget the time we prayed fervently for a new warehouse. We found ourselves, due to the Lord's direction through those prayers, looking at some units that hadn't been built, just steel girders lying on the ground, nothing had been started. 'This is no good,' we thought, 'it would take far too long to get the units built and ready for use'. We got impatient, rejected them, and went off in another direction in our own strength. We continued to pray and looked at two other sites with warehouses already built and ready for immediate occupation, even coming close to taking one on. This fell through at the last minute and we wasted an awful lot of time talking and negotiating about the other, which came to nothing. So long, in fact, that the original warehouse the Lord directed us to was built and nearly finished, and that's where we are now.

If only we had believed that the first site was the one and just waited for the warehouse to be built, it would have saved us a lot of time, trouble, anxiety and money. Two things happened here: one, we prayed; and two, our prayer was answered. But we introduced an unnecessary third happening that put 'the spanner in the works'; we didn't believe our answered prayer and act on it! What we should have done was rest in the knowledge of our answered prayer and just waited. Fortunately, if we keep praying as we did, the Lord leads us back to the point just before we started to go wrong and we can pick up again and follow His direction; just one more measure of His great love and concern for us. And then He leads us on. Listen to this for coinciding of extra work, availability of warehousing and the relocation of the business:

We started renting the first warehouse that was finished on 12 January 1991: perfect timing to start the dedicated Jacuzzi Contract. On 1 April 1991, we were offered a large contract with Showerlux UK Ltd, carrying shower screens and enclosures. At that time we could not warehouse all the delivery stock at our old premises, but the new warehouses had just been secured, that is, the loading doors had just been installed – so we were able to use them for overspill. On 18 May 1991 all the goods were transferred from the old premises. On 28 May 1991 the offices were moved, establishing us in our entirety at the new premises. On 1 June 1991 we started a new contract with Bowman Webber distributing mirrors to DIY stores. Come September that year, we took an extra 2,400 sq. ft. to accommodate the extra volume of work, taking our total square footage to 14,400. In early 1992, Jacuzzi UK Ltd rented a further 2,400 sq. ft., making a total of 16,800 sq. ft. under our control. This is of a magnitude that, twelve months previously, would have frightened me; I could not have comprehended the business on such a comparatively large scale in such a short space of time. Yet through trusting in the Lord (most of the time) and praying for more business, coupled with hard work in partnership with Christ Jesus, this is now the reality. Eph. 3: 20 says, 'Now to Him who is able to do immeasurably more than all we can ask or imagine, according to His power that is at work within us'. Amen.

Transportomatic may grow in size; sales figures may double and even triple, trucks are purchased to handle more work, extra employees are taken on and bank managers are impressed with increased cash flow and losses turned into profits – but behind the scenes, all is not as rosy as the outward appearance.

Debts and payments for extra equipment mount up, and trucks have to be serviced. Money used to purchase goods in cash because you cannot get credit should be going elsewhere to pay VAT and PAYE/NIC – the taxman. It says in Rom. 13: 7, 'Pay your taxes'. The wage bill rockets, a sum which has to be paid in cash every week without fail. It becomes so essential to pay current bills such as fuel, parts, maintenance and truck servicing just to keep the business going, that the old bills cannot be paid.

It was for this reason, with two particular suppliers, that an envelope was given to me personally by a bailiff one day last May. I opened it immediately; it was a petition for bankruptcy.

The title of this sounds menacingly terminal, but, in fact, what it says is that I have to pay those particular bills on the petition within a certain period of time or, if I can't pay, appear in court to explain why or seek a court ruling to pay them off in instalments. The English justice system is very fair concerning creditors, and only extends to drastic terminal action as a very last resort. There are many stages during the procedures where time and opportunity is given to pay, either in full, or by arrangement; and I have to admit that we have had to take full advantage of this leniency many times because of our inability to pay. So this petition for bankruptcy was, in the light of the aforementioned and our continuing permanent financial squeeze, no big deal. I would put the document with one or two County Court summonses we had, and dig it out in about fourteen days, well in time to pay it by the 28 day deadline. So I secretly put it away (you don't share that sort of thing with other employees, so I was the only one that knew about it). But, with the busyness of the office (phones going all the time, my attention constantly required by employees and clients, and the general priority of just the day-to-day running of the business), I forgot all about it.

You can afford to let summonses slip your mind, because on a certain day, whether you're in court or not, all that happens is a judgement is made against you to pay, which is when you can pay your bill if you haven't managed it before – no problem. In the rush of things in the office, I didn't really read the 'small print' on the bankruptcy petition. When you're rushing around all the time, sometimes you are going so fast that there are things you don't see because you pass them by too quickly. The result of this is what happened in the entries on 18 and 19 of last June.

You may be wondering, at this very minute, how come I am in such a mess. How come, after all this extra work, expansion and good gifts from God – which, on the surface, projects such an exceptional business turnaround – I'm in a mess.

The reason is bad management and stewardship of these gifts. If we misuse what is given to us and what resources we have, then the ultimate destiny of that business is destruction; and if you're self employed, like me, self-destruction. A direct parallel with the world:

Originally we were given good gifts, everything we needed for all time. The Godgiven Earth was ours to manage, not own. We are supposed to be the workers in the vineyard of the world, not the owners. We were supposed to tend and look after it carefully and, if that had been the case, it would have supplied all our needs and stayed beautiful. But instead, through greed and selfishness, we have raped it, pillaged it and not shared the fruits among all the people.

This is what I may have done with my business. Despite the many blessings from the Lord, the seed of my mismanagement had already been sown prior to the turnaround. The bad fruit is now being reaped in the form of bad historic debt, and I believe the people who harvest that bad fruit will come soon. There will not be enough time for the bad fruit to rot and the good fruit of a new harvest from that extra work to take its place.

Chapter 12: The end of the chase.

26 September 1992
Saturday, midnight

We (the boss of the corporate advisers we have called in – who specialise in trouble – and myself) had a meeting with the VAT on Tuesday last, 22 September.

They want to make Transportomatic bankrupt because I now owe them over £100,000. I've sent all my returns in, which, added to all their surcharges for non-payment, comes to this huge amount. We are trying to come to an arrangement with them. They sounded as if they might have played ball with us at £20,000 down and £2,000 per month thereafter – that would have taken three years to pay off. We were mistaken. On Friday we had a letter from them stating they would not agree to an arrangement and that a date has been set, 12 October, for a bankruptcy hearing at Stafford Court.

When one actually reads one of these letters, particularly when it refers to you, a sense of fear and slight numbness sets in for about two hours, and a black cloud seems to hang over you for the rest of the day. The thought of my whole life and standard of living just wound up (for the second time in three months), is one of deep prolonged fear. Fear of the unknown, of what's going to happen, fear of the business ceasing to trade, the chopping off of twenty-five people's employment and what they would think and say about me – or even *do* to me. Fear of well-established clients – who rely on me – losing their transport company: the chaos that would follow with the goods in my possession not being able to be delivered because the business had been shut down. The house would have to be force-sold. The problems would be enormous and really don't bear thinking about. I'd lose everything materially, but I would not lose the Lord, Jesus.

That's the difference being a Christian; when all else is gone, He is still there – *no one* can take Jesus away from me.

When the prospect of losing everything and going through a very humiliating and embarrassing time is very definitely possible, I look to Jesus. When there seems no way out of the situation, I look to Jesus. The only person who can get me out of this one is Jesus. 'Turn your eyes upon Jesus', Heb. 12: 2 says, and that's what I'll do. I look to Jesus to sort it out, to give me comfort and confidence in the situation that hangs over me like a hangman's noose poised menacingly above my head or like an axe waiting to fall. There's nothing between the axe and my head but Jesus, the author of all things.

In the book of commerce, finance, and litigation, it's a forgone conclusion that if I don't come up with £101,180.40 I'm a dead duck. But in the book of Jesus, 'Everything is possible for him who believes' (Mark 9: 23), and 'Now to Him who is able to do immeasurably more than all we ask or imagine' (Eph. 3: 20, again). The worker of miracles will work, for a miracle I need, Lord. I can only trust and pray that Your will be done, not mine.

I think lots of traumatic thoughts, 'the worst scenario' as Steve, at work, would say. But I take comfort in the words in Isa. 43: 2, as the Lord showed me:

When you pass through deep waters I will be with you.

Your troubles will not overwhelm you.

When you pass through the fire you will no be burned, The hard trials that come will not hurt you. (GNB).

I'm a Christian, and my business is faced with bankruptcy – I have to grasp these promises of God. It's very difficult, sometimes, but this is what He says and this is what He means. I have to grasp the double-edged sword of the word of God and thrust it into the situation, believing this is what He says so this is what He'll do. They are not idle words, but promised powerful help, weapons to fight with in a situation such as this. There is no alternative when I'm backed up to a wall or into a corner but to cry out to the Lord for help, and Lord Jesus, this is what I do now.

I need Your help. I admit I'm the only one to blame for this sorry situation – please, Lord, help me. My enemies close in on me like a pack of hungry wolves ready for the kill. I begin to walk through the valley of the shadow of death (Psalm 23: 4). Satan prowls like a roaring lion (1 Pet 5: 8). I'm probably being a bit melodramatic, Lord, but to me it's almost the be all and end all of everything; in other words, very important. I know You'll meet me on that level, Lord, that You will come into the situation at whatever level is appropriate. You are the God of intervention and I pray You will intervene. In Jesus' name I ask. Amen.

28 September 1992
Monday night, 11.30pm

My corporate advisors phoned today. They have a copy of the letter from the VAT saying they are going for bankruptcy. They are going to take out an 'Interim Order' to stop the VAT closing me down. This is possible by taking out what they call an 'Individual Voluntary Arrangement' to pay my creditors off (everyone I owe money to). An Interim Order will delay any foreclosure pending an appointment of a trustee to handle my business financial affairs. But 75% of the creditors – in proportion to the total money I owe – then have to agree to the arrangement. It is my job to demonstrate to them that they will get more of what I owe them by agreeing to an arrangement than by not agreeing; it's an alternative to bankruptcy. If the 75% do not agree to an arrangement, then the VAT can bankrupt me. The problem is, the VAT will have to agree to the arrangement, as they are the largest creditors.

So where does all this fit in with God's plan for me? You can be sure it fits in perfectly with something He has in store. Maybe this is His way of getting me out of the bondage of Transportomatic and into freedom to do something else. I am not sure where it all fits in, and the Lord won't tell me, He just wants me to trust Him. This is where I'm going to enter the 'deep waters' of Isa. 43: 2 and experience the 'fire' that, although I will walk through it, will not burn me. This is where I have to grasp hold of this promise and apply it to myself over the next few days and weeks.

Steve, my number two at work, is losing sleep over this. I share everything with him, so he knows everything. To him the situation is different. He sees what he calls the injustice of it all; of coming this far on a business turnaround, from loss to profit, from not much work to being snowed under, all the hours and hard work I've put in; and just at the point when we're about to break back into serious money making and be in a position to pay our historic debt, the VAT want to bankrupt us.

From my personal point of view I only see this as a door opening for me to escape the trap the business has got me in. The trouble with four years of striving to get myself out of a hole, with clawing my way back, with working all hours and constantly living on the edge, is that it has taken its toll on my body, both mentally and physically. That body, which is the temple of the Holy Spirit, where Jesus lives in me (1 Cor. 6: 19), gets exhausted and tired to the point where all I want to do is give it a rest, give it the respect it deserves. And after all the diversions from God in the form of stress, pressure and business priorities, it will be nice to just turn around, face Jesus and say 'Here I am, Lord, wholly available'. But this is probably not the Lord's will, so we have to pray. We have to put the Lord's authority over these traumatic times, for this is the sort of situation where, if we are not on our guard, Satan will wreak havoc.

Lord, I pray for Your authority in my mind and body, over everyone involved in these times. Lord Jesus, take control please and let Your will be done. In Jesus' name I pray. Amen.

3 October 1992
Saturday night, 12.45am

Phil – one of the partners from our corporate advisers – and I went to see David, an insolvency practitioner, last Wednesday morning. He has accepted to act on my behalf for an IVA (Individual Voluntary Arrangement), so the wheels are now set in motion in my last fight to keep the business trading. I'm now putting a lot of trust in advisers – corporate advisers, insolvency practitioner and a factoring company. My wife and I signed up with the latter on Friday to factor the limited company, which is the change of trading status we have moved into. Factoring companies release monies you are owed immediately on receipt of the invoices to your customers, considerably increasing cash flow. They chase up these invoices and charge a percentage, and they're expensive. This way we don't have to wait for our clients to pay us.

Transportomatic have had a Limited Company (Transportomatic Ltd) since 14 August 1981, but it has been dormant until now. The plan is to put the current business, John F. Clough trading as Transportomatic, into the Individual Voluntary Arrangement and carry on trading under the company name, Transportomatic Ltd, for which an empty account exists at the bank. I do not know a lot about the legalities of all this, Lord Jesus, so I will try not to put too much trust in the people I'm dealing with, but trust You with it instead – that at the end of the day, You will guide them in their ways. In Jesus' name I pray. Amen.

7 October 1992
Wednesday, midnight

I'm getting very little sleep, so I get up in the morning thinking I'm going to be extremely run down, irritable and tired all day – but I'm not. The Lord is giving me strength. I plod on through a daily heavy workload, particularly this week with Steve on holiday. Today I had to sign and swear an 'affidavit'. I took the Bible in my hand and repeated words after a solicitor.

I suppose to him the Bible was just a tool of the trade. To think in that book is the beginning and the end of the world and everything in between – but to the solicitor it was part of the scenery, just a book! How many people have sworn on that Bible to tell the truth and done no such thing? It's just a book, a formality, part of a procedure. It belittles the word of God and the importance of the Bible.

Every day I get more nervous – I'm going into unknown territory. I'm worried, there is no doubt. My conscience is pricked constantly about the rightness or wrongness of everything. Worrying is a sin, but I'm finding it very difficult not to do it. I'm living so close to the edge, the slightest hiccup will send me over. There are so many things that are uncertain. Oh,

Lord, help me to trust You. Please intercede, hold everything together – things are so volatile. Every circumstance, if it goes wrong, can be a major catastrophe. Help me to leave it to You, Lord. Amen.

10 October 1992
Saturday night, 12.45am

Thank You for an answered prayer. Ever since we've applied for an IVA I've been worried about how to tell the bank. We've moved into a limited company and we'll need to start moving money in and out of the account that has been dormant since 1981. I've thought that, if we suddenly start using it, the bank will be asking questions in an already jittery situation, and I didn't know if the charge on the house as security on the sole trader overdraft could be automatically transferred; so I was worrying about the bank panicking and pulling the plug. My worrying was for nothing.

On Friday at teatime, shortly before the bank closed, I had drawn the balance of the wages and was just about to leave when Alex Jordan, the manager, walked in from outside; we could not avoid each other. 'Hello, John,' he said, 'I hear you've gone limited'. It took me a second to compose myself after the initial surprise that he knew this, but I don't think he noticed. He continued, 'You'll be transferring all your direct debits etc. on to your company account soon, then?' 'Yes, Alex', I said. He continued again, 'Let me have your memorandum, articles of association and certificate of incorporation ASAP, then'. 'I'll come in early next week', I replied, and off he walked.

I couldn't believe it! How did *he* know we'd gone limited? *He* approached *me* and had just suggested everything I had been too worried and frightened about to ask! It just *had* to be the Lord, I thought. As I walked out of the bank I just kept saying to myself, 'Praise the Lord, thank You, Jesus'. It had to be Him – how else could he have known!? How wonderful the Lord is, how mysteriously He works.

On Friday night I told my wife the serious implications about the court hearing on Monday morning. It doesn't sink in at all, just talking about it. I don't think we'll ever know the experience of bankruptcy until it happens, *if* it happens. At 10.15am on Monday morning we will know – the prospect is very frightening.

The people who know about bankruptcy do not help. Accountants, solicitors, corporate advisers, financial planners – they all paint a picture of doom and gloom. They tell me I will have three years of virtual hell while I'm a registered bankrupt, and the period immediately following bankruptcy is worse than death itself (which is why a proportion of bankrupts commit suicide before or after the event). I get frightened just hearing about it, never mind experiencing it.

We pray about it. All we can pray is that the Lord's will be done. If it's the Lord's will that we are made bankrupt, then so be it. Amen.

11 October 1992
Sunday night, 1.15am

Another late night, but I was in from work at 11.15pm. I've been watching the three presidential candidates for the USA on TV, live in a debate. Bill Clinton, Ross Pero, and George Bush – it's their presidential elections next month.

Well, it's now officially Monday morning, 'D' day, as my wife calls it. In a little over nine hours I will know if I am bankrupt or not.

I stayed behind a bit after finishing normal duties at work to get a few things together to support my case this morning – David, the insolvency practitioner, wants me to appear as well as him. Normally he would go on his own, but he wants me there as he feels my particular case may be more difficult than normal. Did You hear that, Lord Jesus? My case is *more difficult than normal.* I lack credibility, so I presume my appearance is to assure them of my commitment and sincerity to pay them off if they accept an Individual Voluntary Arrangement. What a situation I find myself in.

Thank You, Lord, that You prompted me to go and see Morgan James (the person from whom we lease all our warehouse units and offices) and tell him what was happening. He is very understanding. 'No problem,' he said, 'we'll play it whichever way you want to, John!' Another hurdle over, after getting over the bank hurdle last Friday. But the biggest hurdle is this morning. We must get people praying. Remind me, Lord (not that I'll forget), to phone a few people to start praying 10.15am onwards.

I should be getting more nervous as the time draws near, but I'm not. I feel that as long as we are praying and the Lord's will is done, then it'll be OK. I feel my confidence in the Lord more than before, rather than confidence in the Court's decision; in other words, whichever way the decision goes, I am confident the Lord will provide for us.

I've mentioned before that there is an argument in favour of actually going bankrupt. The reason being that bankruptcy would mean home every night for tea, much more time with the family and for Christian activities. More sleep, regular 'awake' hours and generally a lot less hassle to life. OK, we'd be tied to an official receiver and have very little money compared to what we're used to, we'd have to move house to the minimum of comfort for our size family and all our assets would be sold; quite a traumatic time, in fact – but not the end of the world. The wonderful thing about being a Christian is that no one can take your faith away, no one can take Jesus Christ away. So am I ready for this? Rom. 8: 33 says, 'Who will bring any charge against those whom God has chosen? It is God who justifies'. Going on to verses 37- 39, 'No, in all these things we are more than conquerors through Him who loved us. For I am convinced that neither death nor life, neither angels nor demons, neither the present nor the future, nor any powers, neither height nor depth, nor anything else in all creation, will be able to separate us from the love of God that is in Christ Jesus our Lord'.

I'm ready.

Chapter 13: When you pass through the fire you will...

12 October 1992

Monday night, 12.20am

At 10.45 this morning, 12 October 1992, before an Insolvency Practitioner, the VAT's Solicitor and a District Judge, and after over twenty years' trading, I was declared bankrupt. I was taken upstairs to a lady who phoned the Official receiver in Stoke-onTrent. After she had explained the situation to him I had to speak and give him details of my assets, which are no longer mine. He agreed that it would not be in anyone's interests to shut the business down but to keep it trading, so he is going to appoint a trustee who will come and assess the situation. It's a man I've met, from KPMG Peat Marwick.

Off I go again into unknown territory – but the Lord goes before me.

When I started to leave the court building, after the formalities had been completed, still upstairs, the first person I saw was Carol Davids, a Christian friend – she must work there. 'What are you doing here?' she asked with a surprised look on her face. I replied, in a matter-of-fact way, that 'I've just been made bankrupt'. Her mouth just fell open with no sound; she looked stunned – I just walked on, not quite believing that the first person I saw after going bankrupt was a Christian. To me, she was a sign that in the corridors of the legalistic powers of the secular world, the Lord Jesus still rules and was with me. No, they can never take the Lord away from me.

My wife is upset. When I arrived home, the vicar's wife was with her, and she'd been crying (I phoned her from the court with the news).

It's not a good day for the family. Our middle daughter had tummy ache so she didn't go to school. Our eldest was crying because she didn't want to go to school, which upset my wife because, being family, you tend to get upset yourself in sympathy.

So, this morning's 'trauma', as everyone was telling me it would be, was not so bad after all; in fact, straight after, it was quite a relief – a bit of a burden off me. The most important thing is that, at the time, people were praying. I asked for the prayer cover to be for the Lord's will to be done, so whatever decision was made, it would be the Lord's will. One may ask 'The Lord's will for you to go bankrupt?' Well, what seems crazy in our society is not necessarily crazy in the Kingdom of God. 'We know that in all things God works for the good of those who love Him', Rom. 8: 28 yet again, and verse 31 says, 'What shall we say in response to this, if God is for us, who can be against us?' So I believe we will see God working in a mysterious and marvellous way in the next few days and weeks.

This has been, and is, living on the edge with Jesus. It's hard – very hard sometimes, but it's awesome, it's powerful, it's exciting, and you never know what's coming next. But what you do know is that Jesus' promises of 'I will never leave you' (Heb 13:5), 'Nothing can separate us from the love of God' (Rom. 8: 38-39) and 'Do not worry what tomorrow will bring' (Mat. 6: 25, 34), are promises to be grasped – in times like these they come alive.

It's now 1.05am. I'm afraid being awake at this time is the norm this last week or two. It's my eczema, which is bad. I pick and scratch until my skin weeps, then it gets very uncomfortable and sore, so I wipe the weepiness off the sores for a while then put more ointment on, then another part starts to itch. It is then extremely uncomfortable with the bed covers against my skin – and so it goes on. This last week has been regular for not getting to sleep until 2 or 3am. It's mainly my legs and feet – I'm quite a mess. I need a bath. I need a haircut, but never get round to it. I suppose Job in the Bible felt like this, but he was worse, *completely* covered in sores. I think, deep down, it's worry, subconscious worry about the present situation, and that I'm run down because of the strain and lack of sleep. I don't know how my wife sleeps through all my scratching and fidgeting, but she does. I suppose after fifteen years of sleeping together, she's used to it.

So, Lord, I'm bankrupt. My assets no longer belong to me. The wagons, the workshop equipment, the racking, the cages for stacking mirrors, the small forklift truck (the big one is leased), the office equipment, one of the cars, my money, my bank account and the house now belong to the official receiver, who can dispose of them how he wishes. What a predicament. Still, we try and 'Rejoice in our sufferings, for suffering brings perseverance, perseverance brings character, and character brings hope' (Rom. 5: 3-4). So if all else has gone, we still have hope. Hope, faith and charity – the latter may be needed, also. Amen.

13 October 1992
Tuesday night, 12.35am

The receivers have been in work today, listing my assets and going through everything. They say a buyer has to be found very quickly. A deal has to be agreed by Friday or they will close us down.

The fuel cards have been stopped, meaning we cannot buy any fuel away from base.

We have no requirement to do this, but the receivers won't, so my wife has drawn £250 from her account at the Building Society for me to distribute among the drivers to take with them on runs to buy fuel. I am telling the employees as I see them what has happened and what may happen, but for now it's business as usual. How we will pay the wages on Thursday, I am not sure.

The trustees for the receiver are delving into everything. We have done one or two things wrong, mainly through ignorance or because we had no choice, so they may have to be put right by paying back money to them from the limited company.

I cannot see how we can keep the house. The bank overdraft and the business development loan can only be paid off by selling it – there is no other way. If we remortgage the house to pay them off it would have to be in my wife's name, as I am no longer allowed credit of any sort for three years, and there is no way she would be able to afford the much-higher repayments anyway. We must resign ourselves to the worst possible scenario.

I'm tired but I'm not writing this in bed as usual. Once I get undressed I start scratching and picking my eczema, so I though I'd stop up until I was tired enough to go to bed and get straight to sleep. I'm not sleeping till the early hours of the morning anyway, it was 3.30am last night before I finally 'dropped off'. I'm worn out with the mental strain and lack of sleep; I've also got a sore throat. Soon I'll be in the situation when I'll be quite glad if they close us down just to get a good night's sleep, see the family on a regular basis and cut the strain. Lord Jesus, I'm getting to the point where I'm not going to really mind what happens, just to get it over with will be my only desire.

What a lot of shattered plans, though, materially it's all come to nothing. What a waste it seems. I've worked hard for twenty years just to be made bankrupt and end up with nothing. I could write my very own book of Ecclesiastes on how 'it's all useless' and just 'chasing the wind'.

Lord Jesus, help me to set my eyes on the unseen things of this world, not the seen things, then all these material things should grow slowly dim and I should start seeing more of You. Amen.

24 October 1992

Saturday night

What an awful ten days since the last entry, the 'joys of bankruptcy'.

On 13 October (the last entry), the receivers were listing my assets. They didn't even look at the trucks to put a value on them; I just gave them the make, model, year and mileage, and that was it. They have been valued at £43,150 and the equipment, fixtures and fittings, at £2,160. With a bit of 'goodwill' thrown in the total assets will be about £50,000, which will be the asking price for any prospective buyers. Needless to say, they didn't shut us down on the Friday following bankruptcy. They just left us to run the business on our own; apparently they are extremely busy on bankruptcies elsewhere!

It turns out that Morgan James, our landlord and owner of the warehouses we rent, has offered in excess of the asking price, and it looks like on

Monday 26 October he will purchase. He has obviously been worried about another purchaser moving the business or the receivers shutting us down and leaving all his warehouse units empty, where he would stand to lose over £50,000 per year in rent, so he is protecting his own investment by purchasing us.

So, Morgan James gets to own our assets, and the business of Transportomatic carries on. He says the money paid for it can be in the form of a loan to Transportomatic Ltd, with a bit of interest, which can be repaid over the years out of the profits – so that's the business sorted out!

This coming week the trustees will come and look at the house and decide what to do with it. It's not very saleable at the moment. We were having a garage and driveway built? Well, I had to tell the builders what had happened and naturally they suspended work on the site, which leaves us with half the back garden dug out to a depth of two feet, the new garage not cement-rendered or painted, no side door, window or rainwater guttering, and a mountain of soil in the front garden in front of the house.

We have had to abandon two side gates and the boundary fence. Fortunately the driveway from the road to the garage is finished. To get the jobs on the garage finished – excluding the painting, which I can do myself – will cost £2,000. Where do I get that from, Lord?

Lord Jesus, I continue to pray for Your leading in this situation. This is, for the first time in twenty years, an opportunity for me to say I want to get out of Transportomatic and do something else. So guide me, Lord, and Your will be done, not mine. Amen.

25 October 1992
Sunday night, 11.50pm

I'm trying to reflect on the last two weeks since the day I was bankrupted. The overriding thing that comes to mind is Isa. 43: 2. 'When you pass through the fire you will not be burned; the hard trials that come will not hurt you'. Despite walking through the fire of bankruptcy, I do not appear to have been burned, nor do the hard trials I've been through seem to have hurt me. I hear You saying, Lord, 'Well, what did you expect! I do keep my promises, you know'. Sorry, Lord.

Yes, I am a bankrupt – I have nothing material, neither am I likely to have much over the next three years as the receiver will not allow me more than a living wage over and above what I should give to my creditors. The builders have left the site of the new garage, leaving the front and back gardens looking like an archaeological dig, but worse. We have had no money for about ten days, but somehow my wife presents a good meal for the family and guests every time, so the Lord provides. 'He prepares a table before us in the presence of our enemies' (Psalm 23: 5).

The only thing is, my working hours have been so erratic that my awake and sleep pattern has been shot to pieces. That's the main challenge for the immediate future, Lord – to cut my hours and make them to be during the normal part of the working day, not evenings, nights or silly early mornings. Lord, I pray for a plan to be worked out where my hours become normal. Amen.

27 October 1992
Tuesday night, 11.45pm

Jesus says, in Luke 6: 30, 'Give what you have to anyone who asks you for it and when things are taken away from you don't worry about getting them back' (The Living Bible). The Bible fell open at that chapter and verse last night, the one thing preachers say is not advisable to take any notice of (Bibles falling open, that is), but many will admit that words from the Lord have been given to them in this way. I believe these are words for me, highly relevant to my present circumstances. Amen.

30 October 1992
Friday night

An 81-hour week, this last week – the highest so far in the last five weeks. I'm keeping a record – it's a struggle.

Thank God the authority at the end of the day is the Lord's. Thank God that, although we may lose the odd skirmish, the whole battle belongs to Him. He wins in the end, the final analysis and the bottom line is Jesus Christ is Lord.

1 November 1992
Sunday, midnight

In my entry of 11 October, the night before I went bankrupt, I said there was an argument in favour of going bankrupt, such as home for tea every night, seeing more of the family, etc. Well, after actually being bankrupted, that is certainly not the case.

We were talking to some friends who were saying how pleased they were that everything seemed to be working out OK. My wife said that, outwardly, Transportomatic Ltd was the same as before: same vehicles, same employees, I was still in charge, but it wasn't quite right because I was working longer hours, such as last week (I worked 81 hours).

But we mustn't complain. The Lord has really provided through a very confusing and fraught time. I still have a job, we are still in our house – although the receiver has yet to sort that out – we are not now short of money, and we are happy and healthy.

8 November 1992
Sunday night

We have been saying that, not only did the Lord show us the site at Seighford before we moved to tell us to go there for our new offices and warehouse, but he must also have foreseen the present situation, knowing Morgan James would intervene after going bankrupt. We found out another thing this weekend; that Morgan James' solicitor is a Christian and he and Carol Davids, the first person I saw after going bankrupt, got together to pray about what they thought were two separate issues when the sale of the assets was being negotiated. It was not until they talked prior to praying, that they realised their separate subjects were in fact related; the troubles of Transportomatic. Another piece of the jigsaw goes into place. Amen.

Chapter 14: From the edge to the gentle slopes.

23 November 1992
Monday night, 11.20pm

At the time leading up to bankruptcy, I would have though that the actual experience of going through it would have been harder. That isn't to say it's been easy, but what I'm trying to say is that I thought it would be much more traumatic than it has been so far. I ask myself why it has not been the ordeal it's cracked up to be. Why, apart from long hours, it has been almost plain sailing. Why do I actually feel better now than before I went bankrupt.

I believe the answer is that the Lord has been there all the way. If He had not been there it would have been a bad time, a very bad time. If you haven't got Jesus and you lose everything, and you're stuck with the stigma and title of being a bankrupt, then what *is* left? Without Jesus there *isn't* anything left! That is the difference when you're a Christian. When you're a Christian you have Jesus, who is all you need because when you are weak, He is strong and, because He lives in you, you also become strong, (2 Cor. 12: 9).

I will never stop thanking the Lord Jesus for coming into my life when He did. I will never stop thanking Him for His promises, which I have been able to hold on to and take as a gift from Him. Promises like 'I will never leave you', 'As you walk through the fire you will not be burned', 'Cast your cares upon Him' and 'Do not worry about what tomorrow will bring'. No, I cannot quote chapter and verse for these without looking them up. Why? Because they're written on my heart. When the time came, they dropped from my head to my heart. During this period of trouble and strife, they have been inscribed indelibly on my heart. So my trouble and strife isn't! It's joy and peace. The Lord turns our trouble and strife, our disappointment and our broken dreams into renewed hope and excitement.

Yes, some of our dreams have been broken, our plans thwarted, our visions wiped out – but wait a minute! From a worldly point of view, one may make an assumption that bankruptcy means the end of a vision, the end of a dream; but if Jesus is in your world, anything is possible. Jesus is bigger than all of this – much bigger. Bankruptcy is a mere hiccup in the Kingdom of God, the centre of the driving force for the universe. Let us remember how big God is; how He created the world and everything in it, how He opened the Red Sea, how He flooded the world, how He controls the forces of nature, just one of the things that man will never master. Just because I go bankrupt, does this mean that God has given up on me? Does this mean that God has changed His plans for me? Does this mean that I have lost faith? Does this mean that He has abandoned His plan and purpose for us? No, no and no, it doesn't!

29 November 1992

Sunday night, 11.10pm

It's the Lord's Day again. On the seventh day the Lord rested, and so have I. The last three weeks I have worked six days and rested on the seventh. At last my working hours are coming down. Last week was 63 hours (and a quarter), the shortest since I started keeping a record, nine or ten weeks ago.

I continue to feel pretty good in the changing circumstances of my life. One of the main things gone is the business being a burden. I have spoken in the past of being a slave to the business, in bondage, trapped in something I couldn't get out of because of the nature of being a sole proprietor, the heavy burden of debt, and the great responsibility to carry on for the sake of the employees and the customers. I could not just turn 'round and walk away; I felt I had to stay and carry the burden.

The times when I was almost being crushed by the pressure has gone. The Lord found a way to release it. Yes, it was through bankruptcy, but all the Lord is bothered about in my personal relationship with Him – through this part of my life I have realised above all else – is me. I am His child, so as my heavenly Father, He looks after *me*. As a father of my children

I am expected to look after *them*. I am not expected to look after my neighbour's children or the children from the family across the road; they have their own father. I have been so concerned about the employees, the customers and the bank, etc., and what other people would say, when all Jesus has been concerned about is me. All I should have concentrated on was my relationship with Jesus. If *that's* right, then nothing else matters, because Jesus takes care of all the things on my behalf that I'm concerned about. All my other concerns should have been directed to Jesus for Him to take care of, which He only did in the end because I had no other choice than to hand them over. So Jesus literally took care of everything.

Jesus has lifted the burden of pressure and debt and handed it to the receivers. He has lifted the bondage and slavery and made me an employee of Transportomatic Ltd – meaning I can leave whenever I want – and He has taken care of the employees and customers. They all still have their jobs, the customers still have their transport company, with no break in service, and we are using the same wagons and premises. In fact, all that has changed is the ownership and the trading status, from sole trader to limited company – what *was* I panicking about? OK, it looks as though we will have to sell the house to satisfy the debt to the bank, but if the Lord has so far sorted everything else, finding somewhere else for us to live isn't going to be a problem, is it? I'm sure He'll find us a lovely little house somewhere where we'll be very happy.

4 January 1993
Monday night, 10.15pm

That's Christmas and New Year over; we're now in something called Epiphany.

I'm finding it quite difficult to write as much in this journal this New Year, mainly because I haven't got so many problems – financial ones, that is. When I look back I see a lot of my conversations with You, Lord, were about money and business problems. Most of that is now over, so what are we going to talk about? I don't want this journal to turn into just an account of everyday routine happenings like a normal diary, so we'll have to get on a different angle of conversation. Not so many problems? Of course, I wouldn't have it any other way, but a period of mental adjustment is required, I think.

11 February 1993
Thursday night, 11.15pm

Since Christmas I have been – what I would call – 'enjoying the relative freedom of burdens lifted'. I no longer have the hassle of money pressures on a daily basis. There is still the old sole trader overdraft and Business Development Loan to be paid off, which is accruing interest, but that's in the capable hands of the receiver. We have resigned ourselves to God's will on whether we lose or keep the house.

After the Christmas holiday I had an extra week off. When I returned to work I decided to go on a five-day week and we arranged for me to have Sunday and Monday off, which, praise God, is working. Again, it is not a requirement as the receivers own our house, but I am using the time to finish the garden and garage, so if the house does have to be sold, everything will be spick and span and the whole property should command a higher asking price. If God gives us a miracle and we don't lose the house, then everything outside will be finished to enjoy in the spring and summers to come.

My late-night working is over. We have taken a driver off the road to work in the office and warehouse, so I can concentrate on my designated role of running the business. In addition, early mornings have gone due to a lot of my work now being delegated to others.

Four burdens lifted – long hours, early mornings, late nights and financial pressure. The effect on my life has been very pleasant and dramatic: two whole days off – a five-day week (virtually unknown for the last twenty years) and I see a lot more of the family. I am starting to get the family/ business balance more into line and have a better perspective of my priorities. I'm having another week off this next week to carry on with the garden, which has coincided nicely with half-term school holidays. No late nights and very early starts means I'm usually around at breakfast time and give the children a prayer and a goodnight kiss in the evening. My wife and I are actually going up to bed *together* and we get up *together,* praise the Lord.

I am now the new general manager of the new Transportomatic Ltd. My directors are Morgan James and his daughter, who have been very good to me. I am on a starting salary of £25,000 per year, paid weekly in cash, which the receivers have agreed is a 'living wage'. I have my own company Mercedes car, all expenses paid (an answered prayer from 12 March 1991, nearly two years ago and exactly the model I prayed for – a 250D), totally flexible hours and five weeks' annual holiday when I want. The steadiness and consistency of this is making us financially stable. I have arranged for most bills to be spread over direct debit instalments from the bank; the account is in my wife's name as I am not allowed a bank account. Since going bankrupt we have not had the gas or electricity reps round to cut us off, or any final demands for the phone bill.

It has taken a bit of adjusting; I'm used to living on the edge, not on the gentle slopes. After walking through 'the valley of the shadow of death' the Lord Jesus is leading me 'beside the still waters' and 'restoring my soul'. I pray that You will 'guide me in the paths of righteousness' and that 'Your goodness and mercy will follow me all the days of my life' (Psalm 23). Amen.

Chapter 15: 31 October 2007 – fifteen years later.

Looking back, the whole episode of those years seems like another life, a different era – it's over fifteen years ago.

I suppose our lives are broken up into sections – chapters – where we can see the beginning and the end and then, after so many years, it's just a memory because since then other chapters have opened and closed. Life continues and changes, but the Lord still remains steadfast and reliable, a never-ending anchor to hold on to as the waves take us up and down and toss us about on the sea of life.

Back in 1993, by the grace of God, even though the house had been repossessed, we stayed until July 1995 – in the end, the bank turned out to be very gracious. Likewise, the receivers let us keep our furniture, car and clothes.

When the time came to move, under the bank's instructions, although we had nowhere to go, the Lord did not let us down. A friend and former teacher at St. Paul's Infants School, where our girls attended, was moving out of his property in Stafford to temporary look after his sick Mum in Hereford (do you remember the R.E. teacher my wife had a word with about teaching Genesis but not believing it? Mr Hoburn. Well, that's whom I'm talking about). He offered to rent us the property, a three-bedroom bungalow, so we moved in. There was a huge garden and we had lots of Christian neighbours with children the same age as ours – what a blessing.

Meanwhile, I had left Transportomatic. It was not the same as owning the business. I left to drive trucks, not administer them; in a way, back to what I always enjoyed doing. A small family transport business just outside Stafford – the directors knowing me – provided the job immediately. A more than 50% cut in pay, but the Lord Jesus provided all our needs.

In time, the receivers' job was done. The gathering of the debtor's payments owed to the business realised 84p in the £1 to preferential creditors – a good result. Unfortunately, the sundry creditors got nothing, so I lost some of my business friends. After fifteen months in our rented bungalow, Mr Hoburn had to sell, as he needed to purchase a property in Hereford – his Mum needed constant care.

Again, the Lord provided. I noticed a 'For Sale' sign outside an old friend's house. I hadn't associated with him since the late sixties or early seventies, so this was a long shot but, on praying, we had a definite prompt to do something. In the late summer of 96 I knocked on his front door. No one was at home, the place was empty. His brother provided us with his phone number – in California, where he had moved. He agreed to take the house off the market and rent it to us – a miracle! At the end of October we moved in. A lovely Georgian town house, grade-two listed, in a conservation area, a secluded quiet back garden, and yet so close to the town centre – what a gift from God.

During that time in 1996 I was still friends with many of the employees at Transportomatic. Steve Dimmock, one of our answered prayers, was the new general manager, but he'd resigned and his deputy had taken over. The drivers I knew said the business was in 'chaos'. My main thought was, with me being the only breadwinner in the family and only earning about £12,000 per year, we needed to do something financially if we wanted to buy a house. All the girls were expensive teenagers and we didn't want to rent property for the rest of our lives. House prices were static, a buyer's market; wouldn't this be the time for us to buy? We continued to pray for something to happen, knowing that if I could return to Transportomatic as general manager with the salary that would command, we were in with a chance of getting back to owning our own home.

In the summer of 1997 I went to see Morgan James, the managing director. After a little probing, he confirmed the business was losing money and being badly run. The top man was off sick with stress, leaving a leadership vacuum, and he didn't expect him back. Trusting the Lord, I offered myself forward for a return. In July I started back as general manager, agreeing a starting salary of £25,000 with annual rises at the rate of inflation plus 15% of the profits, paid as a yearly bonus (at the time, the latter meant nothing, as there were no profits).

A year later the business was turning a profit, and in September 1998 I was paid my first bonus. The house we were renting still held its charm and character, so we phoned our landlord in California asking him if he wanted to sell. He agreed. Moreover, he agreed to let us have it at the original asking price from two years previously, minus a reduction of £100 per month for every month we'd rented, amounting to £2,400. The stipulation was we had to complete within two weeks – more praying. Thank the Lord that the boss of Transportomatic's auditors was also chairman of a local building society so, with the help of our directors, a quick mortgage was arranged. We put my bonus of £13,000 down as a deposit, a £67,000 mortgage was available because of my well-improved pay, and by the end of October 1998 the house was ours. (Do you remember in the diary entry on 29 November 1992, when I said 'I'm sure the Lord will find us a lovely little house somewhere where we'll be very happy'? Well, this was it and eleven years later, we're still here.) The Lord's timing in everything was perfect. I was 51 and, after six years, we were back with our own home.

I continued at Transportomatic until the end of May 2001. To say my time there was purely a financial exercise to get us back into property would be only partly true. Along the way I enjoyed turning the business 'round, it gave great job satisfaction and fulfilment, and, above all, it gave me back the confidence I had lost following bankruptcy. By the spring of 2001 the task was done. At the time of leaving, the business had turned over £2,048.000 the twelve months preceding. I didn't get to see the profit.

Transportomatic Ltd have now moved to much larger premises, have a fleet of thirty trucks, 42,000 sq. ft. of warehousing and employ fifty-five people, including some who were with us during those traumatic years. Little do the others know that the business is only there, literally, by the grace of God!

By this time my wife had returned to work after a fourteen-year break bringing up the children, so we decided a cut in pay for me was acceptable and I gave that small family transport business just outside Stafford another call. Again there was a job waiting. I finished at Transportomatic Ltd on the Thursday, never to return. On the following Monday I started driving trucks again. It was June 2001; definitely the best time of year to be out and about driving in God's glorious creation.

Secretly I had always wanted to drive an articulated truck, the ultimate in size and weight. I obtained a licence to drive one in the 1980s, but to date had never dared take the plunge. But the Lord knows the desires of our heart and, in August of that year, He presented me with the opportunity. There was just one artic at work, and the driver fell seriously ill. Out of nine drivers I was the only one with the right licence so, in fear and trepidation but trusting the Lord, I took up the boss' offer. I suppose it's a 'man thing', but to me the job satisfaction and fulfilment of driving a fully loaded artic is immense. In Eddie Stobart's biography (he and his wife being evangelical Christians, I've read it twice), when he first started out, he tells of the thrill of the pulling power and size of the machine when loaded with slag from the steelworks to spread on the fields of his local area in North Cumbria. It's the same for me. I was in my element, and good pay, too. With my wife working, we were not far off having an income equal to being general manager at Transportomatic. Life was good; the Lord never ceases to shower blessings on His children.

As human beings, is it that we are never satisfied or that constant drive in us to socalled 'improve our lifestyle'? Despite life being so good, I was still up for this 'improvement'. I had my eye on a newly-built warehouse off Junction 14, on the M6. It was a huge high-bay building with lots of loading bays; surely only a large transport and distribution company would be moving in there. So, with a little prayer directed that way every time I drove past, I kept my eye on it looking for any signs of occupation, or adverts for drivers in the local paper. Sure enough, come Christmas 2005, a big advert appeared in the Stafford Newsletter. I applied.

On 2 February 2006 I started my new job at Culina Logistics Ltd. Running on six axles at forty-four tonnes, it couldn't get any better. Compared to my previous job I had an extra day off, the trucks and trailers were mostly new, it was only ten minutes from home, and I was earning an extra £4,000 per year. By this time we'd also reduced our mortgage to £30,000. In January 2007 my wife changed jobs to a teaching assistant at a local high school; 30 hours a week, good pay, school holidays, and she really liked it. The children were doing well; our eldest in her first job in London since graduating; our middle daughter married with two boys and only living 'round the corner, and the youngest, starting in September, her fourth year at University, having a blue chip company sponsoring her and a job to go to. In April we had celebrated our thirtieth wedding anniversary and my sixtieth birthday at our honeymoon hotel in Llangollen, with thirty friends and family. Financially we had been completely restored and very secure. Could life get any better?

And then I had a heart attack.

It was Thursday, 7 June 2007, my first day off for that working week. The ache was in my left shoulder, which I was convinced was muscle pain, and so that morning I happily came away from the doctor's with a prescription for painkillers. But by 4pm, when my wife returned from work, it had spread to my left arm and neck, and was creeping down my chest. It was not right at all, so I asked her to call an ambulance. From then on, until after it was all over and I had a visitor on the Saturday afternoon, I recall nothing, even though I was apparently conscious and communicating some of the time. I say I recall nothing – except Rom. 8: 28 and Eph. 3: 20, two Scriptures I had hung on to fifteen years previously.

Those two verses were all that was going 'round and 'round in my head when I was flat on my back surrounded by frantic doctors and nurses. For me, they were the comfort of Jesus' assurance I was going to be all right. Rom. 8: 28 – 'For we know that in all things God works for the good of those who love Him who have been called according to His purpose'. Something good is going to come out of this, and Eph 3: 20 – 'Now to Him who is able to do immeasurable more than we ask or imagine according to His power that is at work within us'. Not only is something good going to come out of this, but whatever it is, is going to be more than I can ask for or imagine. To say that, now in October and still off work in cardiac rehabilitation, that I am excited may be exaggerating but, through these Scriptures, Jesus has brought a glimpse of hope and expectation into the future.

Because I couldn't remember anything during my heart attack, my wife and the girls had the entire trauma. Christian friends and my brother and sister were desperately phoned and lots of prayers went up immediately. The clot in my artery would not clear, I went into cardiac arrest twice. My wife was told by the hospital to take a break and go home because she was so upset. At home they phoned her to tell her I wasn't going to make it. In addition to the family, two vicars were quickly on the scene praying (one of whom was our vicar when I committed my life to Jesus twenty years previously). I was rushed by ambulance to Stoke-on-Trent, where they had a specialist cardiac unit – and survived. I am now what the medical profession call 'living with heart failure', and have a stent fitted, which keeps the artery open. I will be on lots of tablets for the rest of my life, but there is hope in God through Jesus; He made me, so He can repair me.

I cannot help thinking of that Scripture in Luke 12: 19-20 about how we build our lives up with possessions and money, accumulating more and more nice things around us. But Jesus says 'You fool, this very night your life will be demanded from you then who will get what you have prepared for yourself'. Then there's Eccles. 9: 11-12, 'The race is not to the swift, or the battle to the strong, nor does food come to the wise, or wealth to the brilliant, or favour to the learned. But time and chance happen to them all. Moreover, no man knows when his hour will come'.

In the diary entry on 28 September 1992 I quote, 'The trouble with four years of trying to get myself out of a hole, with clawing my way back, with working all hours and constantly living on the edge, is that it has taken its toll on my body, both mentally and physically.' Could it be that the events described in my diary have considerably contributed to my heart attack, fifteen years later? The question goes through my mind over and over.

I don't comment anymore about the church not being the best place – in its man made structures, traditions, rules and customs – to help the Holy Spirit lead the people, or moan about the old songs nobody knows. It's certainly not the people, they're wonderful. A prominent church member suggested to me it's because, as a Christian, I've matured. Not so, I think. My opinions have not changed one bit, neither has the church, which has only re-enforced my thinking. Shall we just say I'm 'dormant' or 'waiting'? It's not because I'm 'comfortable'; I haven't been sucked into the evil jaws of apathy and passiveness.

My wife no longer goes to church. I don't blame her, the same old thing week in, week out. She's joined the growing number of Christians whom I've read about; still enthusiastic about Jesus Christ but prefer to be out of the established church structure. It's more interesting for me; I'm in the music group so I stay, but for how long, only the Lord knows.

However, I believe the Lord is preparing, or has already prepared, a new chapter in our lives; that soon it will be up to us as to whether we take up God's invitation to step through that door and once again go into the unknown; but this time a gentle, secure and inviting unknown. I am now approaching my twilight years and believe He will lead us somewhere in tune with this. I no longer keep a spiritual diary – dare I start another one and see what happens this time?

In the Book of Joshua, chapter 24, Joshua gathers everyone together to remind them of, in spite of their hardships and trials, what great things the Lord God had done in their lives – just like ours. And the challenge, the free choice, went out to the people, 'Who are you going to serve?'. Verse 15 says to us all, 'But if serving the Lord seems undesirable to you, then choose for yourselves this day who you will serve... but as for me and my household, we will serve the Lord'.

And the challenge still goes out. We too have that free choice.

Amen

At the end of May 2012, Transportomatic Ltd. was closed down. The reason is not known. They had been trading for forty years.